Comings and Goings: 13,000 Years of Migrations In and Around Rock Art Ranch, Northeastern Arizona, Part 1
(Color Edition)

Edited by
E. Charles Adams
and
Richard C. Lange

Report of Archaeological Survey, Testing, and Excavations
by the
Rock Art Ranch Archaeological Field School,
Arizona State Museum and School of Anthropology,
University of Arizona
2011-2016

August 2023

The Arizona Archaeologist

August 2023 — Number 45

Series Editor: Bill Burkett
azarched@azarchsoc.org

Copyright © 2023 Arizona Archaeological Society

All rights reserved. No part of this publication may be reproduced, stored in retrieval systems, or transmitted in any form or by any means, electronic, mechanical, photocopying, recording, or otherwise, except for the inclusion of brief quotations in a review or scholarly work, without prior written permission from the publisher. For information and permissions on reproduction, please contact azarched@azarchsoc.org.

ISBN (paper): 9798850911836

Published by the Arizona Archaeological Society, Inc.
P.O. Box 9665
Phoenix AZ 85068-9665

www.AzArchSoc.org

Members of the Arizona Archaeological Society, at the time of publication, have the option of receiving a free hardcopy of this volume. Members can also download PDF versions, and when available, Kindle ebook versions of the *Arizona Archaeologist* from the Member-Only area of the Society's website.

COVER: The front cover shows part of a petroglyph a panel at The Steps rock art site, at Chevelon Canyon in northeastern Arizona. Photograph by E. Charles Adams.

Contents

Contents	iii
List of Figures	x
List of Tables	xvi

Part 1

Chapter 1. Background and Introduction *by E. Charles Adams*	1
Contexts Provided by Regional Research	4
Paleoindian through Middle Archaic	4
Late Archaic/Early Agricultural	5
Ceramic Period (600-1400 CE)	10
Hopi Buttes/Little Colorado River	10
Upper Chevelon and Clear Creek Canyons	12
Previous Research Within a 10km Radius of Rock Art Ranch	14
The Rock Art Ranch Archaeological Field School	14
Research Goals	16
Organization of the Volume	18
Chapter 2. The Rock Art Ranch Area: Physical Environment, Geology, and Native Plant Communities	
by Karen R. Adams, Susan J. Smith, and E. Charles Adams	19
Physical Environment	19
Geology of Rock Art Ranch *by E. Charles Adams*	21
Descriptions of the Geologic Formations	22
Coconino Sandstone	22
Holbrook Member, Moenkopi Formation	22
Shinarump Conglomerate	22
Effects on Plant Communities	23
Effects on the Availability of Water	23
Other Resources	23
Modern Plant Studies: Insights into Ancient Plant Communities and Resources	
at Rock Art Ranch *by Karen R. Adams and Susan J. Smith*	24
Introduction	24
Historic Land Use and the Analog Problem	25
Climate Considerations	25
Previous Studies of Modern Plant Communities	26
Composition of Three Plant Communities	27
Grasslands	27
Sand Dunes	27
Washes/Floodplains	29
Hands-On Learning Experiences	30
Closing Thoughts	32
Chapter 3. Chevelon Canyon and "The Steps" Petroglyph Site at Rock Art Ranch	
by Darlene L. Brinkerhoff	39
Introduction	39
Location	40
History	42
Palavayu Anthropomorphic Style and the Petroglyphs at The Steps	44
Human Figures and the Amphitheater	45
Snake Figures	47

Zoomorphs	50
Other Petroglyphs	50
Dating of Petrolyphs	54
Comparing Stylistic Traditions	56
Archaic	56
Basketmaker II	57
Modifications	60
Pueblo Period	60
Historic	61
Conclusions	64
Future Work	66
Chapter 4. Accessing the Audience: An Interpretation of Panel Seven at The Steps *by Mairead K. Doery*	69
Introduction	69
Petroglyphs and the Cultural Landscape	69
Assessing Petroglyph Publicity	70
The Steps and Rock Art Ranch	70
The Herd at The Steps	71
Visibility	71
Accessibility	72
Iconography and Publicity	73
Iconographic Type	73
Anthropomorphic Sex/Gender	77
Modification Frequency	77
Interpreting The Herd	78
Power	78
Tradition	79
Spirituality	80
Conclusions and Future Directions	81
Chapter 5. Archaeological Surveys and Testing in and Around Rock Art Ranch, Northeastern Arizona *by Richard C. Lange, Samantha G. Fladd, and E. Charles Adams*	83
Survey and Field Methods	83
Project Results	85
The Rock Art Ranch Core Area	85
RAR-Core Ceramics Overview	92
Ceramics in RAR-Core	93
RAR-Core Flaked Stone	97
Flaked Stone in RAR-Core	97
RAR-Core Ground Stone	98
Rock Art at RAR	103
Testing at RAR	103
Summary of RAR-Core	107
Surveys and Collections on Aztec Land and Cattle Company Properties	108
AZLAC Sites—Ceramics	108
AZLAC Sites—Flaked Stone	110
Summary of Loci on AZLAC Properties	111
Archaeological Work West of Rock Art Ranch (RAR-West)	111
Surveys West of Chevelon Canyon	111
Ceramics West of Chevelon Canyon	112
Flaked Stone West of Chevelon Canyon	113
Ground Stone from West of Chevelon Canyon	114

Testing at AZ P:2:56(ASM)	114
Summary of Loci West of Chevelon Canyon	120
Sites and Survey in RAR-South and RAR-Southeast	120
Sites—RAR-Southeast and RAR-South	120
RAR-Southeast and RAR-South—Ceramics	121
RAR-Southeast and RAR-South—Flaked Stone	123
Projectile Points and Other Flaked Stone Tools—RAR-South and RAR-Southeast	123
RAR-South and RAR-Southeast—Ground Stone	128
Summary of RAR-Southeast and RAR-South Areas	128
Summary of Site and Scatter Distributions	128
Temporal Trends in the Rock Art Ranch Research Areas	129
Paleoindian and Early/Middle Archaic	129
Late Archaic and Basketmaker II	130
Basketmaker III and Pueblo I	133
Pueblo II	134
Pueblo III	136
Pueblo IV and Historic	137
Discussion and Conclusions	138

Part 2

Chapter 6. Rock Art Ranch Field School Study of the Multi-Kiva Site *by Richard C. Lange*	203
Archaeological Activities at Multi-Kiva Site	204
Surface Collections at AZ P:3:112(ASM)	206
Ceramics from Formal Surface Collections	206
Wares and Types at MK—Overall	206
Wares and Types by Collection Units	207
Flaked Stone from Formal Surface Collections	209
Ground Stone from Surface Collections	209
Soil-Auger Tests	210
Descriptions of Features and Structures	210
Outlying Rocks and Scatters/Features	210
Exploration of the Midden at MK Site	212
S.100	212
S.101	217
S.102	218
Construction and Layout Revealed by Wall Tracing and Plaza Testing	224
S.28	239
S.16	243
S.17	246
S.18 and S.19	250
Ceramics and Chronology	257
Absolute Dates from the MK Site	262
Flaked Stone at Multi-Kiva Site	263
Projectile Points from MK Site Excavations	264
Ground Stone at MK Site	268
Fauna from MK Site *by Kimberly Sheets*	270
Methodology	270
The Assemblage	271
Lagomorphs	271
Rodents	272

Carnivores	272
Artiodactyls	273
Aves	274
Fish, Reptiles, and Amphibians	274
Worked Bone	274
Summary	274
Other Noteworthy Artifacts at MK Site	276
Worked Sherds	276
Worked Stone Ornaments	277
Crystals from RAR-South	282
Marine, Freshwater, and Terrestrial Shell at MK Site	282
Summary of RARFS Work at Multi-Kiva Site	282
Chapter 7. Brandy's Pueblo (AZ P:3:114[ASM]) *by E. Charles Adams and Vincent M. LaMotta*	333
Introduction	333
Area Summaries	333
Exploratory Testing East and Southeast of Main Rubble Mound	333
Horizontal Exposures East of Main Rubble Mound	336
Testing in the Room Block	339
Structure 6	340
Structure 3	340
Structures 7 and 10	343
Summary of Interior Space	343
External Workspace (Ramada and Beyond)	344
Structure 4	344
Conclusions	346
Structure 4-exterior	346
Conclusions	348
Structure 3-exterior	351
Conclusions	354
Midden Area East of Occupation Surfaces	354
Conclusions	357
Structure 8 (North Trench)	357
Conclusions	358
Summary and Conclusions for AZ P:3:114(ASM)	358
AZ P:3:132(ASM)	362
Structure 2	362
Walls and Features	362
Floors and Features	363
Roof	363
Fill	364
Discussion	364
Pottery *by Byron M. Estes and E. Charles Adams*	365
Ceramics by Excavation Area	365
Ceramics Within Structures	365
Ceramics from Outside Spaces	367
Ceramics Associated with Exterior Surfaces	368
Conclusions	368
Ground Stone *by E. Charles Adam*s	370
Summary	371
Flaked Adams Stone *by E. Charles Adams*	372
Projectile Points	373

Summary	375
Faunal Remains *by Kimberly Sheets and E. Charles Adams*	375
Macrobotanical Remains *by E. Charles Adams*	375
Summary and Comparisons	376

Chapter 8. Regional Patterns and Social Relationships in Pueblo III Period Settlement *by Krystal L. Britt*	391
Archaeological Background of the PIII Period	391
PIII Occupation of the RAR Area	394
Ceramic Networks	398
Ceramic Compositional Analysis	402
Methodology	402
Sample	402
LA-ICP-MS Procedures	410
Results of LA=ICP-MS Sampling	412
Petrographic Analysis	416
Discussion: Connections, Interactions, and Boundaries	421

Chapter 9. Place Persistence and Landscape Memory at Rock Art Ranch *by Danielle R. Soza*	425
Introduction	425
Rock Art Ranch	426
The Preceramic US Southwest: 11,500 BCE-600 CE	426
Paleoindian (Terminal Pleistocene to Early Holocene 11,500-8000 BCE)	426
Archaic (Middle Holocene 8000-800 BCE)	427
Basketmaker II (Middle-Late Holocene 800 BCE-600 CE)	428
Preceramic Petroglyph Styles	429
Landscape Archaeology	430
Landscape Memory in Contemporary Indigenous Communities	430
Projectile Points in Ethnohistoric and Contemporary Communities	431
Methodology and Analysis	433
Projectile Point Distribution Through Time	434
Projectile Point Raw Material Types	442
Rock Art Ranch: A Remembered Place	443
Identity and Territoriality	445
Conclusion	446

Chapter 10. Ceramics *by Byron M. Estes*	453
Survey of Rock Art Ranch Area (RAR-Core)	453
Painted and Decorated Wares	453
Tusayan White Ware	454
Little Colorado White Ware	454
Cibola White Ware	454
Tsegi Orange Ware	456
Jeddito Yellow Ware	456
Mogollon BrownWare—Decorated	457
Less Common Painted/Decorated Wares	457
Utility Wares	457
Mogollon Brown Ware	457
Tusayan Gray Ware	458
Alameda Brown Ware	458
Puerco Valley Utility Ware	458
Awatovi Yellow Ware	459

Little Colorado Gray Ware	459
Unidentified Utility Wares	459
Other Surface Collections/Analyses by RARFS	459
Wares and Type Analysis—Other Surface Collections	459
Painted and Decorated Wares	459
Tusayan White Ware	460
Little Colorado White Ware	460
Cibola White Ware	460
Tsegi Orange Ware	460
Mogollon BrownWare—Decorated	461
Other Decorated Wares	461
Utility Wares	461
Mogollon Brown Ware	461
Tusayan Gray Ware	462
Puerco Valley Utility Ware	462
Alameda Brown Ware	462
Little Colorado Gray Ware	463
Other Utility Ware	463
Summary and Comparisons of Surface Collections	463
Excavation and Testing at the Multi-Kiva Site (AZ P:3:112[ASM])	464
Wares and Type Analysis—Multi-Kiva Pueblo	464
Painted and Decorated Ware	464
Little Colorado White Ware	464
Tusayan White Ware	466
Cibola White Ware	466
Mogollon Brown Ware—Decorated	466
Tsegi Orange Ware	467
Less Common Painted/Decorated Wares	467
Utility Wares	467
Mogollon Brown Ware	467
Puerco Valley Utility Ware	467
Tusayan Gray Ware	468
Alameda Brown Ware	468
Little Colorado Gray Ware	468
Unknown Utility Wares	468
Excavation at Brandy's Pueblo (AZ P:3:114[ASM])	468
Wares and Type Analysis—Brandy's Pueblo	469
Painted and Decorated Wares	469
Cibola White Ware	469
Little Colorado White Ware	469
Mogollon Brown Ware—Decorated	469
Tsegi Orange Ware	470
Tusayan White Ware	470
White Mountain Red Ware	470
Utility Wares	470
Mogollon Brown Ware	470
Tusayan Gray Ware	472
Puerco Valley Utility Ware	472
Alameda Brown Ware	472
Little Colorado Gray Ware	472
Unknown Utility Ware	472
Comparing the Ceramic Assemblages	472

Figures

Part 1

Figure 1.1. Rock Art Ranch and other project areas in northeastern Arizona.	2
Figure 1.2. Petroglyph with figures and map (AZ P:3:117[ASM]) at Rock Art Ranch.	3
Figure 1.3. Comparisons of chronologies for the general Colorado Plateau.	6
Figure 1.4. Rock Art Ranch Archaeological Field School project areas.	16
Figure 2.1. Field botany with the Rock Art Ranch Field School.	28
Figure 2.2. Grassland plant community at Rock Art Ranch.	28
Figure 2.3. Sand dune plant community at Rock Art Ranch.	29
Figure 2.4. Washes and floodplains plant community at Rock Art Ranch.	30
Figure 2.5. Upper Chevelon Canyon.	31
Figure 2.6. "Feast of Foods" available from local resources.	33
Figure 3.1. Petroglyph panel and general setting at "The Steps."	40
Figure 3.2. Examples of clan symbols at The Steps.	41
Figure 3.3. Petroglyph gallery designations at The Steps.	45
Figure 3.4. Pictographs in Upper Chevelon Canyon.	47
Figure 3.5. Snakes and human figures holding things.	48
Figure 3.6. Snake symbolism.	49
Figure 3.7. Zoomorphic petroglyphs.	51
Figure 3.8. Water features.	53
Figure 3.9. Repatinated glyphs.	55
Figure 3.10. Superimposition.	56
Figure 3.11. Possible corn tassels.	57
Figure 3.12. Cinderella panel.	58
Figure 3.13. Rain priests.	59
Figure 3.14. Modifications to glyphs by grinding.	60
Figure 3.15. Pueblo Period flute players and breath lines.	62
Figure 3.16. Historic glyphs.	63
Figure 3.17. Water serpent carving from temple in Mexico.	65
Figure 4.1. Petroglyphs from The Herd at Chevelon Steps.	72
Figure 4.2. Hidden access "steps" to the Herd Panel at the Chevelon Steps	74
Figure 4.3. The Herd panel at the Chevelon Steps.	75
Figure 4.4. Concealed petroglyphs of The Herd.	76
Figure 5.1. Sites identified in the Rock Art Ranch Core and AZLAC-Adjacent Areas.	86
Figure 5.2. Distribution of isolated Little Colorado White Ware sherds in RAR-Core and AZLAC-Adjacent areas.	86
Figure 5.3. Distribution of isolated Tusayan Gray and White Ware sherds in RAR-Core and AZLAC-Adjacent areas.	87
Figure 5.4. Distribution of isolated Mogollon Brown Ware sherds in RAR-Core and AZLAC-Adjacent areas.	87
Figure 5.5. Distribution of isolated chert flakes in RAR-Core and AZLAC-Adjacent areas.	88
Figure 5.6. Distribution of isolated petrified wood flakes in RAR-Core and AZLAC-Adjacent areas.	88
Figure 5.7. Distribution of isolated quartzite flakes in RAR-Core and AZLAC-Adjacent areas.	89

    Ceramic Production Strategies
    Style and Type Considerations
    Basketmaker III/Early Pueblo I Assemblage (600-825CE)
    Pueblo I/Early Pueblo II Assemblage (825-1100CE)
    Pueblo II/Early Pueblo III Assemblage (1100-1225CE)
    Late Pueblo III Assemblage (1225-1300CE)
    Pueblo IV Assemblage (1300-1600CE)

Chapter 11. Summary and Conclusions *by E. Charles Adams*
  General Findings
    Temporal
      Paleoindian
      Relationships to Chevelon Pueblo
      Hopi Yellow Ware and Pueblo IV Use of RAR
      Radiocarbon and Ceramic Dating
      Shifting Ceramic Traditions
    Spatial
      Pre-Basketmaker II and Basketmaker II
      Ceramic Period
      Hopi Yellow Ware
      Petrified Wood
      Projectile Point Styles and Material
      Ceramic Distribution
    Cultural
      East/West Boundary
      North/South Boundary
      Regional Population Movement and Exchange
      Closure Practices
      Petrified Wood
    Environment
      RAR-South
      Rock Art Ranch (RAR-Core)
  Collaboration
  Continuing and Future Research
    Sourcing Project
    Community Project
    Petroglyph Project
    Paleoarchaic Project
  Conclusions

References

Appendix I

Figure 5.8. Distribution of isolated ground stone artifacts in RAR-Core
and AZLAC-Adjacent areas. 89
Figure 5.9. Distribution of preceramic sites in RAR-Core and AZLAC-Adjacent areas. 90
Figure 5.10. Distribution of Basketmaker III/Pueblo I sites in RAR-Core and
AZLAC-Adjacent areas. 90
Figure 5.11. Distribution of PuebloII/Pueblo III sites in RAR-Core
and AZLAC-Adjacent areas. 91
Figure 5.12. Distribution of Hopi Yellow Ware in RAR-Core
and AZLAC-Adjacent areas. 91
Figure 5.13. Reconstructed Awatovi Neck-banded jar with interior design 95
Figure 5.14. Distribution of obsidian artifacts in RAR-Core
and AZLAC-Adjacent areas. 99
Figure 5.15. Distribution of cores in RAR-Core and AZLAC-Adjacent areas. 99
Figure 5.16. Spear and arrow points recovered from the ground surface during
RAR survey 2011-2015. 100
Figure 5.17. Distribution of Paleoindian and Paleoarchaic period projectile points
in RAR-Core and AZLAC-Adjacent areas. 101
Figure 5.18. Distribution of Archaic period projectile points in RAR-Core
and AZLAC-Adjacent areas. 101
Figure 5.19. Distribution of Basketmaker period projectile points in RAR-Core
and AZLAC-Adjacent areas. 102
Figure 5.20. Distribution of Pueblo period projectile points in RAR-Core
and AZLAC-Adjacent areas. 102
Figure 5.21. Distribution of isolated basin manos and metates in RAR-Core
and AZLAC-Adjacent areas. 104
Figure 5.22. Locations of bedrock grinding features in Rock Art Ranch-Core area. 104
Figure 5.23. Photograph of bedrock grinding feature at AZ P:2:148(ASM) in
RAR-Core area. 105
Figure 5.24. Locations of petroglyphs in Rock Art Ranch-Core area. 105
Figure 5.25. Examples of petroglyphs recorded by the Rock Art Ranch Field School. 106
Figure 5.26. Ash and charcoal in burned feature at AZ P:3:137(ASM). 107
Figure 5.27. Sites in RAR-West, west of Chevelon Canyon. 113
Figure 5.28. Projectile points from sites and isolates in RAR-West. 115
Figure 5.29. Projectile points from AZ P:2:56(ASM) and other sites in RAR-West. 116
Figure 5.30. Map of features and excavations at AZ P:2:56(ASM). 117
Figure 5.31. Map of Feature 7, pit house, at AZ P:2:56(ASM). 119
Figure 5.32. Distribution of sites in RAR-South project area. 121
Figure 5.33. Isolated worked sherds from Rock Art Ranch-South. 124
Figure 5.34. Worked sherds from sites in the Rock Art Ranch-South project area. 124
Figure 5.35. Worked sherds from surface collections at Multi-Kiva Site, RAR-South. 125
Figure 5.36. Isolated projectile points from Rock Art Ranch-South. 126
Figure 5.37. Projectile points from sites in Rock Art Ranch-South. 126
Figure 5.38. Examples of flaked stone tools from Multi-Kiva Site, RAR-South. 127
Figure 5.39. Serrated petrified wood and chert tools from Rock Art Ranch-South. 127
Figure 5.40. Formal chert blade core from AZ P:2:174(ASM). 130
Figure 5.41. Radiocarbon dates from isolated and excavated features in the Rock Art
Ranch research areas. 132

Part 2

Figure 6.1. Plan map of Multi-Kiva Site and related features. 205
Figure 6.2. Grinding slicks at the Multi-Kiva Site. 205

Figure 6.3. Vandalized areas at Multi-Kiva Pueblo. 206
Figure 6.4. Surface collection units at Multi-Kiva Site. 207
Figure 6.5. Soil auger tests at Multi-Kiva Site. 211
Figure 6.6. Test units in Multi-Kiva Site midden. 213
Figure 6.7. Sterile caliche layer at bottom of midden. 213
Figure 6.8. Shallow midden profile, Multi-Kiva Site midden. 214
Figure 6.9. Rodent disturbance at base of Multi-Kiva Site midden. 214
Figure 6.10. S.100 testing, auger tests, and feature. 215
Figure 6.11. Bedrock in north trench, S.100. 216
Figure 6.12. North test trench, S.100, Multi-Kiva Site. 216
Figure 6.13. Feature in bottom of S.100, Multi-Kiva Site. 217
Figure 6.14. S.101 at Multi-Kiva Site, features and excavation limits. 219
Figure 6.15. S.101 ventilator shaft and floor; east half of structure. 219
Figure 6.16. Top of ventilator shaft, S.101. 220
Figure 6.17. Floor level ventilator shaft and clay coping for sandstone closing slab. 220
Figure 6.18. Hearth in center of S.101, Multi-Kiva Site. 221
Figure 6.19. Sandstone spall skirting around south end of S.102. 222
Figure 6.20. S.102, Multi-Kiva Site, testing and features. 222
Figure 6.21. Hearth area near center of S.102. 223
Figure 6.22. Top of Feature 1, S.102. 223
Figure 6.23. Feature 1, S.102, Multi-Kiva Site, views and details. 225
Figure 6.24. Possible post holes, S.102. 226
Figure 6.25. First version (2013) site map for Multi-Kiva Site. 226
Figure 6.26. Large patches of wall fall around Multi-Kiva Site. 229
Figure 6.27. Location of wall tracing units around Multi-Kiva Site. 229
Figure 6.28. Wall Tracing Unit #1. 230
Figure 6.29. Exterior of west wall of S.18. 230
Figure 6.30. Exterior east wall of S.17, looking west. 231
Figure 6.31. Wall Tracing Units #2 and #3. 231
Figure 6.32. Views of southeast corner and main east wall of Multi-Kiva Pueblo. 233
Figure 6.33. Wall Tracing Units #4, #5, and #6. 234
Figure 6.34. Wall Tracing Unit #7. 235
Figure 6.35. Wall Tracing Units #8 and #9. 235
Figure 6.36. Profile wall north of S.28. 236
Figure 6.37. Wall Tracing Units #10 and #11. 237
Figure 6.38. North pueblo wall, example of double-wide construction. 237
Figure 6.39. Foundation courses below north main wall. 237
Figure 6.40. North roomblock, S.15, S.16, and S.17. 238
Figure 6.41. Wall Tracing Units #12 and #13. 238
Figure 6.42. S.28, northeast corner, Multi-Kiva Pueblo. 240
Figure 6.43. North wall, S.28. 241
Figure 6.44. South wall and southwest corner, S.28. 241
Figure 6.45. Floor features in S.28. 243
Figure 6.46. Features 1 and 2 in northeast corner of S.28. 244
Figure 6.47. Features 3, 4, and 5, northwest corner of S.28. 245
Figure 6.48. Excavation units in S.16, S.17, S.18, S.19, and S.27, northeast corner of Multi-Kiva Pueblo. 245
Figure 6.49. Clay collar, S.16. 247
Figure 6.50. Plaster slump along east wall, S.16. 247
Figure 6.51. Corner of pit house below northeast corner of S.16. 248
Figure 6.52. Exterior east walls of S.17 and S.20. 248
Figure 6.53. Architectural details for S.17. 249

Figure 6.54. Reed impressions in roof daub, S.17. 250
Figure 6.55. Utility ware jar in place in roof of S.17. 251
Figure 6.56. Post holes in ramada area south of S.19. 253
Figure 6.57. Outlines show dismantled stone-masonry wall of S.27. 253
Figure 6.58. Feature 1 and south double walls, S.19. 254
Figure 6.59. Fill in S.19, north wall of S.19, and fill below S.19. 254
Figure 6.60. Fill below north wall of S.19. 255
Figure 6.61. Interior west double wall sitting on fill, S.19. 255
Figure 6.62. Double wall at southeast corner of S.19. 256
Figure 6.63. Double wall at northeast corner of S.18. 256
Figure 6.64. Fragment of a burned secondary beam on floor of S.18. 258
Figure 6.65. Padre Black-on-white sherd in floor context, S.18. 258
Figure 6.66. Burned roof beams on floor of S.18. 259
Figure 6.67. Circular feature in roof collapse of S.18. 259
Figure 6.68. Circular feature in floor of S.18. 260
Figure 6.69. Projectile points from surface collections at Multi-Kiva Site. 265
Figure 6.70. Projectile points from testing in the Multi-Kiva Site midden. 266
Figure 6.71. Projectile points from miscellaneous structures. 266
Figure 6.72. Drills (S.102) and projectile points from S.100 and S.101. 267
Figure 6.73. Projectile points from S.102. 267
Figure 6.74. Projectile points from S.28. 268
Figure 6.75. Examples of ground stone artifact types from Multi-Kiva Pueblo. 269
Figure 6.76. Abrader and mano fragment. 269
Figure 6.77. Igneous hammerstone, S.28. 270
Figure 6.78. Worked bone from Multi-Kiva Pueblo. 275
Figure 6.79. Worked bone—beads—from Multi-Kiva Pueblo. 275
Figure 6.80. Worked sherds from the Multi-Kiva Site midden. 278
Figure 6.81. Worked sherds from miscellaneous structures. 278
Figure 6.82. Worked sherds from S.100 and S.101. 279
Figure 6.83. Worked sherds from S.102. 279
Figure 6.84. Worked sherds from S.28. 280
Figure 6.85. Worked stone from Multi-Kiva Site. 281
Figure 6.86. Worked stone ornaments from S.28. 281
Figure 6.87. Crystals from RAR-South. 283
Figure 6.88. Marine shell from Multi-Kiva Site. 283
Figure 6.89. *Olivella* beads from Multi-Kiva Site. 284
Figure 6.90. Shell beads from S.28. 284
Figure 6.91. Freshwater shell from Multi-Kiva Site. 284
Figure 6.92. Examples of terrestrial snails. 285

Figure 7.1. Architectural features of Brandy's Pueblo. 334
Figure 7.2. Pit structure Kiva location with respect to Brandy's Pueblo. 335
Figure 7.3. Soil auger tests and metric grid at Brandy's Pueblo. 335
Figure 7.4. Pit House 1, Trench 4. 337
Figure 7.5. Locations of archaeological trenching of Brandy's Pueblo. 337
Figure 7.6. Structure 2, Basketmaker pit house at Brandy's Pueblo. 338
Figure 7.7. Feature 2 mano cache. 339
Figure 7.8. Backhoe trench showing teeth marks. 340
Figure 7.9. Walls of Structures 3, 4, and 6. 341
Figure 7.10. East wall of Structure 3. 342
Figure 7.11. South wall, Structure 3. 342
Figure 7.12. Locations of extramural features. 345

Figure 7.13. Row of postholes representing supports to a ramada in Structure 4. 345
Figure 7.14. Row of closely spaced postholes possibly representing a jacal wall on Structure 4, Surface 3. 347
Figure 7.15. South wall separating Structure 4 and Structure 4-exterior. 347
Figure 7.16. West profile to Structure 4-exterior showing three occupation surfaces. 349
Figure 7.17. Profile of fill under north wall to Structure 4-exterior. 349
Figure 7.18. Structure 4-exterior, plan view of Feature 8. 350
Figure 7.19. Structure 4-exterior, plan view of Feature 50. 350
Figure 7.20. Surface showing potholes west of Feature 50, Structure 4-exterior. 351
Figure 7.21. Structure 3-exterior wall fall covering Surface 1. 352
Figure 7.22. Structure 3-exterior Surface 1, showing ash stain. 353
Figure 7.23. Structure 3-exterior Surface 1, worked sherd-covering Feature 65. 353
Figure 7.24. Middden area showing large Basketmaker II storage features. 355
Figure 7.25. Midden area, Features 53, 60, and 61. 356
Figure 7.26. Midden area, Feature 127 profile. 356
Figure 7.27. Structure 8 wall fall from west wall. 359
Figure 7.28. Structure 8, west wall. 359
Figure 7.29. AZ P:3:132(ASM), Structure 2. 363
Figure 7.30. Ceramic types from Brandy's Pueblo. 366
Figure 7.31. Partial restorable vessels from S.3 and S.3-exterior, Brandy's Pueblo. 369
Figure 7.32. Projectile points from Brandy's Pueblo. 374

Figure 8.1. Location of the project area in northeastern Arizona. 392
Figure 8.2. Locations of Pueblo III sites and site groups used in this study. 395
Figure 8.3. Analagous sites to Multi-Kiva Pueblo. 397
Figure 8.4. Traditional archaeological culture areas. 399
Figure 8.5. Location of the Purcell-Larson research area relative to Homol'ovi and Rock Art Ranch research areas. 401
Figure 8.6. Locations of clay samples and ceramic samples from sites. 408
Figure 8.7. Plan map of AZ P:3:215(ASM), RAR-Far North project area. 409
Figure 8.8. Plan map of AZ P:3:216(ASM), RAR-Far North project area. 410
Figure 8.9. Plan map of AZ P:3:219(ASM), RAR-Southeast project area. 411
Figure 8.10. Plan map of AZ P:3:240(ASM), RAR-Southeast project area. 412
Figure 8.11. Bivariate plot of Factor 1 and Factor 2 scores for ceramics. 415
Figure 8.12. Bivariate plots of Factor 1 and Factor 2 scores for compositional groups. 416
Figure 8.13. Bivariate plots of Factor 1 and Factor 2 scores for ceramics and clays. 417

Figure 9.1. Paleoindian period projectile points from Rock Art Ranch. 435
Figure 9.2. Archaic period projectile points from Rock Art Ranch. 436
Figure 9.3. Basketmaker II period projectile point from Rock Art Ranch. 437
Figure 9.4. Distribution of projectile points in Rock Art Ranch-Core area. 438
Figure 9.5. Distribution of Paleoindian period projectile points in Rock Art Ranch-Core and AZLAC-Adjacent research areas. 439
Figure 9.6. Distribution of Archaic period projectile points in Rock Art Ranch-Core and AZLAC-Adjacent research areas. 440
Figure 9.7. Distribution of Basketmaker II period projectile points in Rock Art Ranch-Core and AZLAC-Adjacent research areas. 441

Figure 10.1. Ceramic types from the survey of the Rock Art Ranch-Core area. 455
Figure 10.2. Ceramic types from Multi-Kiva Pueblo (Z P:3:112[ASM]). 465
Figure 10.3. Ceramic types from Brandy's Pueblo (AZ P:3:114[ASM]). 471

Tables

Part 1

Table 1.1. Temporal Distribution of Loci in the Rock Art Ranch Core Area.	17
Table 1.2. Sites and Loci in The Rock Art Ranch Project Areas.	17
Table 2.1. List of Plants Previously Compiled Within the Rock Art Region.	34
Table 2.2. Plants Identified on Sand Dunes, in Upland Grasslands, and Within Bell Cow Canyon and Its Transitional Canyon Edge.	36
Table 3.1. Glyph Types by Gallery at The Steps.	46
Table 3.2. Water, Rain, and Snake-like Petroglyphs at The Steps.	52
Table 4.1. Statistical Trends Between the Visible and Concealed Groups of The Herd's Petroglyphs.	77
Table 5.1. Comparison of Ceramic Ware Distributions by Sites and Loci from Project Areas in Northern Arizona.	142
Table 5.2. Ceramic Wares and Types from Homolovi State Park Surface Collections.	143
Table 5.3. Ceramic Wares from Loci in the Rock Art Ranch-Core Area.	144
Table 5.4. Ceramic Wares Documented as Isolates in the Rock Art Ranch-Core Area.	146
Table 5.5. Ceramic Types from Loci in the Rock Art Ranch-Core Area.	148
Table 5.6. Comparison of Ceramic Wares from Homolovi State Park and Rock Art Ranch Project Areas.	156
Table 5.7. Comparison of Ceramic Wares and Types from Homolovi State Park and Rock Art Ranch Project Areas.	157
Table 5.8. Comparisons of Ceramic Wares and Types for Rock Art Ranch Loci and Habitation Types.	158
Table 5.9. Comparisons of White Ware Types from Homolovi State Park and Rock Art Ranch Project Areas by Time Period.	159
Table 5.10. Comparisons of White Ware Types for Rock Art Ranch Loci and Habitation Types by Time Period.	160
Table 5.11. Comparisons of Ceramic Type Ratios for Homolovi State Park and Rock Art Ranch Project Areas.	161
Table 5.12. Comparisons of Raw Material Types for Flaked Stone from Loci from RAR-Core Area and HSP and Various Quarries.	161
Table 5.13. Raw Material Types for Flaked Stone Cores from Rock Art Ranch-Core Area.	161
Table 5.14. Projectile Points from the Rock Art Ranch-Core Area.	162
Table 5.15. Comparisons of Ground Stone Artifacts from the RAR-Core Area, HSP Loci, and HSC Pueblos.	163
Table 5.16. Radiocarbon Results from NSF-Arizona AMS Laboratory for Testing at Rock Art Ranch-Core Loci.	164
Table 5.17. Ceramic Wares from Loci on Aztec Land and Cattle Properties.	165
Table 5.18. Comparison of Ceramic Wares at Pit Houses vs. Pueblos from Aztec Land and Cattle Properties.	166
Table 5.19. Selected Decorated Ceramic Types by Locus for Aztec Land and Cattle Properties.	167
Table 5.20. Selected Utility Ceramic Types by Locus from Aztec Land and Cattle Properties.	169
Table 5.21. Percentages of Selected Ceramic Types for Pit Houses and Pueblos on Aztec Land and Cattle Properties.	170

xv

Table	Title	Page
Table 5.22.	Ceramic Types for AZLAC Habitation Loci.	171
Table 5.23.	Flaked Stone Counts for Loci on Aztec Land and Cattle Properties.	173
Table 5.24.	Flaked Stone Material Types for Loci on Aztec Land and Cattle Properties.	174
Table 5.25.	Flaked Stone Artifact Types for Loci on Aztec Land and Cattle Properties.	175
Table 5.26.	Flaked Stone Artifact Type by Material Type for Loci on Aztec Land and Cattle Properties.	176
Table 5.27.	Flaked Stone Material by Size for Loci on Aztec Land and Cattle Properties.	176
Table 5.28.	Flaked Stone Artifact Types by Amount of Cortex for Loci on Aztec Land and Cattle Properties.	177
Table 5.29.	Flaked Stone Material by Amount of Cortex for Loci on Aztec Land and Cattle Properties.	177
Table 5.30.	Flaked Stone Size by Locus for loci on Aztec Land and Cattle Properties.	178
Table 5.31.	Flaked Stone Size by Material Type for Loci on Aztec Land and Cattle Properties.	179
Table 5.32.	Periods of Occupation for Loci West of Chevelon Canyon.	179
Table 5.33.	Ceramic Wares Present at AZ P:2:56(ASM) — 1989 HRP Collections.	180
Table 5.34.	Ceramic Types Present at AZ P:2:56(ASM) — 1989 HRP Collections.	180
Table 5.35.	Flaked Stone Material Type by Provenience at AZ P:2:56(ASM).	181
Table 5.36.	Flaked Stone Artifact Type by Provenience at AZ P:2:56(ASM).	182
Table 5.37.	Flaked Stone Material Type by Artifact Type at AZ P:2:56(ASM).	183
Table 5.38.	Size of Flaked Stone Artifacts by Provenience at AZ P:2:56(ASM).	184
Table 5.39.	Size of Flaked Stone Artifacts by Material Type at AZ P:2:56(ASM).	184
Table 5.40.	Projectile Points from Sites and Isolates from West of Chevelon Canyon (Figure 5.28).	185
Table 5.41.	Projectile Points from Surveys West of Chevelon Canyon after 1989 (Figure 5.29).	185
Table 5.42.	Mano and Metate Types from AZ P:2:56(ASM)—1989.	186
Table 5.43.	Loci on State Land and Aztec Land and Cattle Properties South and West of the Rock Art Ranch-Core Area.	186
Table 5.44.	Locus Type by Time Period South of the Rock Art Ranch-Core Area.	186
Table 5.45.	Ceramic Wares from Loci on State Land West and South of the Rock Art Ranch-Core Area.	187
Table 5.46.	Decorated Ceramic Types from State Land and Other Loci West and South of the Rock Art Ranch-Core Area.	188
Table 5.47	Utility Ceramic Types from State Land and Other Loci West and South of the Rock Art Ranch-Core Area.	189
Table 5.48.	Worked Sherds from Loci and Isolates from RAR-South (Figures 5.33 and 5.34).	190
Table 5.49.	Worked Sherds from Multi-Kiva Site (AZ P:3:112[ASM]) Surface Collections in RAR-South (Figure 5.35).	190
Table 5.50.	Flaked Stone Material Types for Isolates in RAR-South.	191
Table 5.51.	Flaked Stone Material Types for Loci in RAR-South.	191
Table 5.52.	Flaked Stone Artifact Types by Provenience for Loci in RAR-South.	192
Table 5.53.	Flaked Stone Artifact Types by Material Type for Loci in RAR-South.	193
Table 5.54.	Flaked Stone Material by Size for Loci in RAR-South.	194
Table 5.55.	Flaked Stone Artifact Type by Amount of Cortex for Loci in RAR-South.	195
Table 5.56.	Flaked Stone Material Type by Amount of Cortex for Loci in RAR-South.	195
Table 5.57.	Flaked Stone Size by Provenience for Loci in RAR-South.	196
Table 5.58.	Flaked Stone Size by Material Type for Loci in RAR-South.	197
Table 5.59.	Material Type by Time Period for Projectile Points from Loci in RAR-South.	197
Table 5.60.	Source Directions for Projectile Points on Loci in RAR-South.	198

Table 5.61. Isolated Projectile Points from RAR-South (Figure 5.36).	198
Table 5.62. Projectile Points from Loci in RAR-South (Figure 5.37).	199
Table 5.63. Other Flaked Stone Artifacts from Loci in RAR-South (Figure 5.38).	199
Table 5.64. Flaked Stone "Serrated" Tools from Loci in RAR-South (Figure 5.39).	200
Table 5.65. Ground Stone Artifact Types from Loci in RAR-South.	200
Table 5.66. Flaked Stone Artifact Types from Loci in the Rock Art Ranch-Core Area.	201

Part 2

Table 6.1. Ceramic Types by Surface Collection Units.	290
Table 6.2. Ceramic Types by Midden Collection Surface Collection Units.	292
Table 6.3. Summary Table of Ceramic Types from Surface Collections by Area.	294
Table 6.4. Flaked Stone Material Types by Surface Collection Units.	295
Table 6.5. Flaked Stone Artifact Types by Surface Collection Units.	296
Table 6.6. Flaked Stone Artifact Types by Material Types.	296
Table 6.7. Flaked Stone Material Types by Amount of Cortex.	297
Table 6.8. Flaked Stone Artifact Types by Amount of Cortex.	297
Table 6.9. Flaked Stone Sizes by Material Types.	297
Table 6.10. Flaked Stone Artifact Sizes by Collection Units.	298
Table 6.11. Soil Auger Hole Data.	299
Table 6.12. Multi-Kiva Pueblo Structure Locations and Dimensions.	302
Table 6.13. Floor Feature Data, S.28.	302
Table 6.14. Ceramic Ware Data by Structure.	303
Table 6.15. Ceramic Types by Structure.	304
Table 6.16. Comparisons of Selected Ceramic Types by Structure.	306
Table 6.17. Counts of Diagnostic Ceramic Types by Structure.	308
Table 6.18. Tree-ring Dates and Data from Multi-Kiva Site.	309
Table 6.19. Radiocarbon Dates from Multi-Kiva Pueblo.	310
Table 6.20. Flaked Stone Material Types by Structure.	311
Table 6.21. Flaked Stone Artifact Types by Structure.	312
Table 6.22. Flaked Stone Artifact Types by Material Types from Excavations.	313
Table 6.23. Flaked Stone Material Types by Amount of Cortex from Excavations.	313
Table 6.24. Flaked Stone Artifact Types by Amount of Cortex from Excavations.	314
Table 6.25. Flaked Stone Artifact Size by Material Types from Excavations.	314
Table 6.26. Flaked Stone Artifact Size by Structures from Excavations.	315
Table 6.27. Projectile Point Affinities for Projectile Points from Excavations.	316
Table 6.28. Projectile Points by Material Type and Time Period from Excavations.	316
Table 6.29. Projectile Points from Surface Collections and Auger Holes (Key for Figure 6.69).	317
Table 6.30. Projectile Points from Testing of Midden (Key for Figure 6.70).	317
Table 6.31. Projectile Points from S.5 to S.27 (Key to Figure 6.71).	318
Table 6.32. Drills from S.102 and Projectile Points from S.110 and S.101 (Key to Figure 6.72).	318
Table 6.33. Projectile Points from S.102 (Key to Figure 6.73).	319
Table 6.34. Projectile Points from S.28 (Key to Figure 6.74).	319
Table 6.35. Material Types by Artifact Types for Ground Stone.	320
Table 6.36. Ground Stone by Structures.	320
Table 6.37. Faunal NISP by Structure.	321
Table 6.38. Faunal Assemblage at Multi-Kiva Site.	321
Table 6.39. Lagomorph Index Comparisons for Faunal Assemblage at Multi-Kiva Site.	322
Table 6.40. Artiodactyl Index Comparisons for Faunal Assemblage at Multi-Kiva Site.	322
Table 6.41. Bone beads from Multi-Kiva Site.	323

Table	Page
Table 6.42. Comparing Bowl-to-Jar Ratios for Various Ceramic Wares from Three Collections.	323
Table 6.43. Comparing Bowl-to-Jar Ratios for Various Ceramic Types from Three Collections.	324
Table 6.44. Worked Sherd Counts by Ceramic Wares at RAR-South and at Multi-Kiva Site.	325
Table 6.45. Worked Sherds from the Midden (Key to Figure 6.80).	325
Table 6.46. Worked Sherds from Miscellaneous Structures (Key to Figure 6.81).	326
Table 6.47. Worked Sherds from S.100 and S.101 (Key to Figure 6.82).	326
Table 6.48. Worked Sherds from S.102 (Key to Figure 6.83).	327
Table 6.49. Worked Sherds from S.28 (Key to Figure 6.84).	327
Table 6.50. Time Periods and Diagnostic Ceramic Types for Worked Sherds.	328
Table 6.51. Worked Stone Ornaments from Multi-Kiva Site (Key for Figure 6.85).	328
Table 6.52. Worked Shell Ornaments (Key to Figure 6.88).	329
Table 6.53. *Olivella* Shell Beads from Multi-Kiva Site (Key to Figure 6.89).	329
Table 6.54. Shell Beads from S.28 (Key to Figure 6.90).	329
Table 6.55. Surface and Excavation Sherd Counts for Diagnostic Ceramic Types.	330
Table 6.56. Presence of Ceramic Types and Wares and Comparisons Between Habitation Loci and Scatters in RAR-South.	330
Table 6.57. Comparisons of Ceramic Types Between the RAR-Core, RAR-South, Multi-Kiva Site, and S.101.	331
Table 7.1. List of Extramural Features at Brandy's Pueblo.	377
Table 7.2. Radiocarbon Dates from Brandy's Pueblo.	381
Table 7.3. Decorated Ceramic Wares and Types by Proveniences.	382
Table 7.4. Utility Ceramic Wares and Types from Brandy's Pueblo.	384
Table 7.5. Ceramic Wares and Types from Extramural Surfaces.	385
Table 7.6. Raw Materials and Completeness for Ground Stone Artifact Types.	386
Table 7.7. Provenance for Ground stone Artifact Types.	386
Table 7.8. Raw Material by Artifact Type for Flaked Stone.	387
Table 7.9. Projectile Points from Brandy's Pueblo.	388
Table 7.10. Faunal Remains by Structure.	389
Table 7.11. Faunal Taxa from Brandy's Pueblo.	389
Table 7.12. Maize Recovered by Provenance.	390
Table 8.1. Late Pueblo III Ceramic Types on Rock Art Ranch Pit House Sites.	395
Table 8.2. Early Ceramic types (Basketmaker III through Pueblo II).	401
Table 8.3. Late Pueblo III Ceramic Types.	402
Table 8.4. Pueblo III Period Pit House Site Ceramic Assemblages.	403
Table 8.5. Pueblo III Period Pueblo Site Assemblages.	404
Table 8.6. Ceramic Totals by Site Group.	406
Table 8.7. Elements Retained for Statistical Analysis.	413
Table 8.8. Results of Principal Components Analysis.	414
Table 8.9. Ceramic Compositional Groups.	418
Table 8.10. Clay Sample Compositional Group Membership.	419
Table 8.11. Temper Characterization by Site Group.	419
Table 8.12. Temper Characterization by Site.	420
Table 9.1. Projectile Point Types from Rock Art Ranch.	447
Table 9.2. Frequency of Preceramic Projectile Point Distributions in Rock Art Ranch-Core Area.	448
Table 9.3. Projectile Point Associations in Rock Art Ranch Core Area.	448

Table 9.4. Distribution of Contemporaneous and Out-of-phase Projectile Points at Sites.	448
Table 9.5. Out-of-phase Projectile Point Types and Site Types.	449
Table 9.6. Chevelon Pueblo Projectile Points by Time and Provenience.	449
Table 9.7. Raw Materials by Time Period.	450
Table 9.8. Comparing Bifaces and Projectile Points by Raw Material.	450
Table 9.9. Chi-square Tests for the Projectile Point and Biface Assemblages.	451
Table 10.1. Ceramic Decorated Wares and Types from the Rock Art Ranch Project Areas.	480
Table 10.2. Ceramic Utility Wares and Types from the Rock Art Ranch Project Areas.	482
Table 10.3. Ceramic Wares from Survey of the Rock Art Ranch-Core.	484
Table 10.4. Ceramic Wares from Excavations at Multi-Kiva Pueblo (AZ P:3:112[ASM]).	484
Table 10.5. Ceramic Wares from Surface Collections at Multi-Kiva Pueblo (AZ P:3:112[ASM]).	485
Table 10.6. Ceramic Wares from Brandy's Pueblo (AZ P:3:114[ASM]).	485
Table 10.7. Date Ranges for Ceramic Types from Rock Art Ranch.	486
Table 10.8. Date Ranges for Ceramic Types at Multi-Kiva Pueblo and Brandy's Pueblo.	487
Table 11.1. Ceramic Trends in the Rock Art Ranch Area.	493

Chapter 1
Background and Introduction
E. Charles Adams

As with any undertaking in the field for an archaeology program, the effort is collaborative and only possible with the help of many individuals, institutions, and funding organizations. This is particularly true for the field school at Rock Art Ranch (RAR) located 32 km (20 miles) southeast of Winslow, Arizona, on the southwest edge of the Colorado Plateau (Figure 1.1). Research at RAR is an extension of the larger Homol'ovi Research Program (HRP) that was established in 1984 with a focus on the large fourteenth-century pueblos along the Little Colorado. Fieldwork on the pueblos of the Homol'ovi Settlement Cluster (HSC) wrapped up in 2006.

While conducting excavations at Chevelon Pueblo west of Chevelon Creek (E.C. Adams, ed. 2016) from 2003-2006, Randy Baird, a member of a local ranching family, came by for a visit and offered to show me some small pueblos on the east side of Chevelon Creek. Randy proceeded to show me five small pueblos dominated by Walnut Black-on-white and corrugated brown ware ceramics. These assemblages suggested they dated about 1200 CE, or 100 years earlier than Chevelon Pueblo. What caught my attention was the contrast with the core area of the HSC (Homol'ovis I-IV) where there is a virtual absence of such sites with one exception, Creswell Pueblo (AZ J:14:282[ASM]; Barker and Young 2017). The dominance of gray corrugated utility wares versus brown corrugated utility wares in the core area also suggested our research was missing part of the big picture of who lived along the middle Little Colorado River (MLCR) prior to establishment of the Homol'ovi pueblos and who might have contributed to their settlement.

In addition, during analyses of Chevelon pottery, which began in 2003 and continued to 2015, it was discovered that the most frequent utility ware type was in fact an obliterated corrugated version of Mogollon Brown Ware (Barker 2017; Cutright-Smith and Barker 2016). (The meaning of the term "Mogollon Brown Ware" will be discussed and debated in more detail in chapters devoted to ceramic analysis later in this volume.) This suggested that communities later than those shown to me by Randy Baird existed somewhere near enough to Chevelon Pueblo to have migrated there. In the 1980s Richard C. Lange directed the survey of state land around the core Homol'ovi pueblos, but also included land south and west of Chevelon Pueblo that revealed light prehispanic use from Archaic times forward and particularly during the Pueblo III (PIII) period preceding the founding of Chevelon Pueblo (Lange 1998). In contrast, with the exception of the transmission line from the Cholla power plant that was surveyed for cultural resources by Arizona State Museum (ASM) in the 1970s (Reid 1982), nothing was known about the archaeological record east of Chevelon Canyon and south of the LCR for

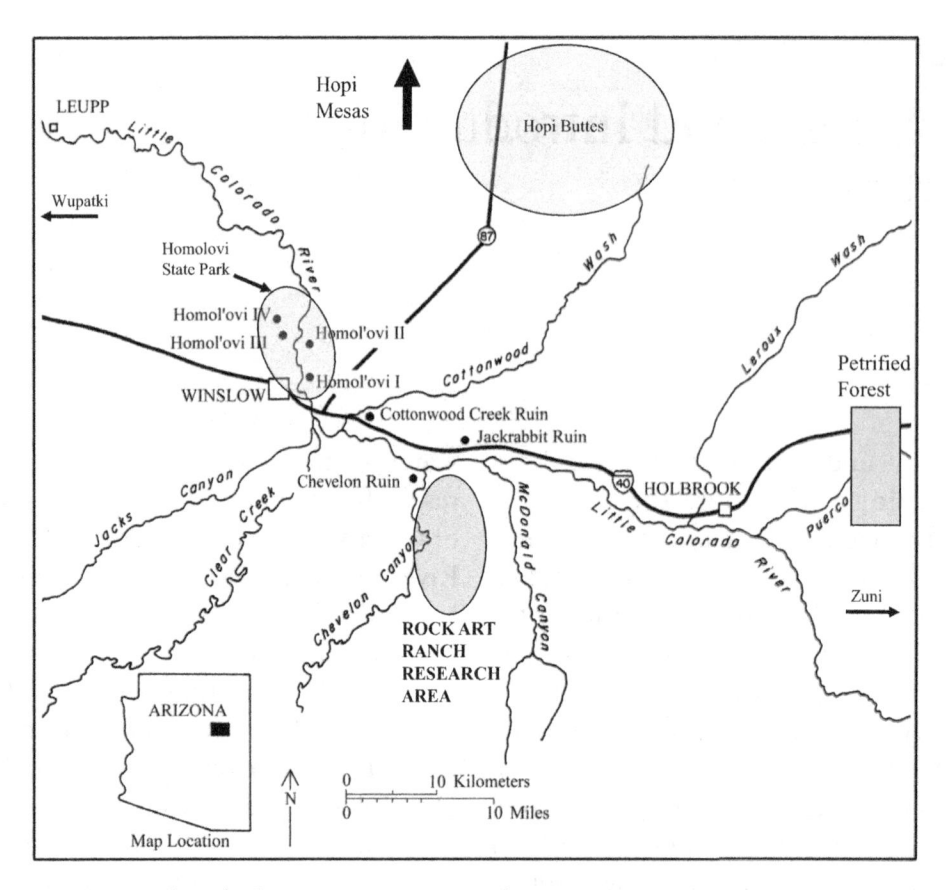

Figure 1.1. Rock Art Ranch and other project areas in northeastern Arizona.

the next 25 km. Compounding the problem was that virtually all of this land was privately owned.

To fill in this huge gap in our understanding of the prehispanic use of this region, in 2010 I, along with Richard C. Lange and Vincent M. LaMotta, embarked in search of potential locations for a field school focused on survey and low intensity excavations. Because Brantley Baird, Randy's father and owner of RAR, had built bunkhouses, a kitchen, and an eating area for hosting large events, logistically it seemed the most promising option. In addition, the extensive petroglyph locale in Chevelon Canyon on the Baird ranch, referred to as "The Steps," had been documented in the late 1990s and suggested Basketmaker II (Early Agricultural) and even Archaic group use of the ranch might be substantial (Kolber 2000; Weaver 2000). Brantley, who expressed interest in our working on his ranch, spent the morning showing us multiple small pueblos on and off his land. All had been vandalized to some degree but seemed to have intact architecture and deposits as well. Ceramics on the surfaces of these sites suggested they were more or less contemporary and dated PIII, ca. 1150–1250 CE. In size the four small pueblos we visited were generally smaller than those east of Chevelon Pueblo, but possibly a bit later based on decorated ceramics. Utility pottery was predominantly corrugated brown ware similar to those 5 km north near the LCR. The few rooms visible during our visit revealed they were constructed of thick stone masonry and were larger than rooms in later Homol'ovi villages also similar in size to the small pueblos near the LCR. All these attributes suggested the archaeology was exactly what we were interested in exploring. Only one of these pueblos, AZ P:3:114(ASM)—RAR-2, was on Baird land. Brantley had allowed a backhoe to probe the site in late 1970s or 1980s, and more recently an amateur archaeologist from Sedona had been doing small shovel tests in the trashy areas of the site and screening the dirt. Brantley shut down the backhoe work when he saw the destruction and allowed the amateur to keep the pottery; nevertheless, the small pueblo still had an extensive ceramic assemblage on the surface along with a medium-sized rubble mound indicating it was a viable locale for limited excavations.

On our visit Brantley also took us to a small petroglyph panel and storage cist comprised of upright vertical slabs at the bottom of Bell Cow Canyon (Figure 1.2). Areas around the slabs had some pottery, but we were more impressed with the extensive lithic scatters encountered on our way down to the panel. The panel itself appeared to have glyphs dating to the late pueblo period, certainly post-1100 and possibly post-1300. While excavating at Chevelon Pueblo, Fewkes (1898, 1904) published accounts by his Hopi crew of frequent visits to the Chevelon Canyon area to collect turtles, birds, reeds, and other riparian plants and animals to take back to the Hopi Mesas for ceremonial uses. This created the second primary focus of research at RAR—identifying how groups carving glyphs at The Steps or simply visiting the canyon for its resources used the surrounding landscape. In other words, what were the reasons groups visited the area other than to carve glyphs? This, along with identifying land use during the ceramic period, would be the focus of survey.

Brantley Baird and I agreed on a handshake that he would allow establishment of a University of Arizona, School of Anthropology field school based at ranch headquarters for a minimum of three years. Housing and

Figure 1.2. Petroglyph with figures and map (AZ P:3:117A[ASM]--RAR-5) at Rock Art Ranch (photograph by E. Charles Adams, enhanced by Robert Mark).

cooking would be provided by the Baird family, shower facilities would be built, and we would commence excavations at AZ P:3:114(ASM) and survey of ranch land in 2011. In addition, we could keep all artifacts recovered for one to two years after recovery to complete analysis, but in the end all artifacts would be returned to the Baird family except for small type collections to be used for documentation and potential future research. We also provided the Bairds with annual reports of our activities and produced posters, some presented at professional meetings, for their use in explaining our research. These were intended not only for the Bairds but also for the many visitors the Bairds host for tours of the ranch and especially the petroglyph panels.

Contexts Provided by Regional Research

Paleoindian through Middle Archaic

Paleoindian and Early/Middle Archaic (Paleoarchaic) traditions have been documented in the region by numerous researchers (Agenbroad 1967; Bartlett 1943; Briuer 1977; Burton 1991; Burton and Farrell 1993; Danson 1961; Gumerman 1988; Herr 2017; Huckell and Huckell 1999; Sims and Daniel 1967; Smiley 2002a; Tagg 1994; Wendorf and Thomas 1951). Surface remains occur as lithic scatters with diagnostic technology and projectile points. The nearest rock shelters having perishable material dating Early/Middle Archaic are in the vicinity of Chevelon Butte 40 km south-southwest, two of which were tested by Frederick Briuer for his dissertation (Briuer 1976b, 1977). Briuer (1977) focused on plant and animal remains in these rock shelters while collecting nearby plants for comparison to the archaeological record. Of particular interest is the presence of 26 native grasses of which 11 were recovered from the rock shelters, although rodents could be responsible for the presence of some of these remains (Briuer 1977: Table 2.1). Notably, grasses are present throughout the archaeological record of the rock shelters, which range from 6700 BCE to 1300 CE (Briuer 1976b, 1977: Table 4.5). Briuer (1976a) also reports that flaked stone artifacts uniformly had plant residues. These findings are significant in helping interpret the archaeological record at RAR.

The most recent research on remains dating to this lengthy period have been in and around Petrified Forest National Park (PEFO; Burton 1991; Tagg 1994). With the exception of a Clovis campsite near an ancient playa, the PEFO sites are represented by scatters of lithics with diagnostic projectile points (Burton 1991; Burton and Farrell 1993). Smiley (2002a) reports similar remains on Black Mesa with the absence of rock shelters having Paleoarchaic remains.

Although 87 projectile points diagnostically dated Middle Archaic and earlier were recovered from survey of RAR, none of these points is definitively associated with lithic scatters of the same age, although flakes likely resulting from Paleoindian biface production/reduction occur in greater frequency in the vicinity of the densest concentrations of Paleoindian points.

Thus, the points are either isolates or associated with later sites, especially Basketmaker II (BMII) sites, but also from the ceramic period (Soza 2018, and Chapter 9 this volume). An identical pattern was noted by Smiley (2002a:30) on Black Mesa where more than 20 Middle Archaic points were recovered from BMII or ceramic period contexts. Sliva (2017:209) reports the same practice below the Mogollon Rim of preceramic points recovered from ceramic period sites. Therefore, although it is likely some of the BMII sites overlay earlier sites, there is compelling evidence that later occupants collected earlier points (Medeiros 2016; Smiley 2002a; Soza 2018). Fully one-third of Paleoindian points are made from petrified wood, a frequency maintained throughout the preceramic sequence with the exception of Early Archaic when it dips to 18 percent. This suggests continuous movement of groups between the source of petrified wood 40 km east and RAR from Clovis until the appearance of ceramics. The Puerco River and associated well-watered side drainages are also present in the PEFO area that would have provided resources similar to RAR with the added presence of petrified wood (Burton 1991).

The Paleoindian occupation also has the only obsidian point (from the Government Mountain source) in the assemblage of 246 points, which includes points through the Pueblo occupation. This is notable because obsidian is common to dominant in lithic assemblages west of Clear Creek and on Black Mesa during this period (Lyndon 2005; Smiley 2002a) and totals an average of 4–5 percent of total flaked stone and 17–26 percent of projectile points on the Pueblo IV villages of the 1300s (Harry 1989; Lange 2020:402; Medeiros 2016; Young 2001). For example, Lyndon's (2005) data indicate that half of the points on the Coconino Plateau west and north of Flagstaff were made of obsidian and Smiley (2002a:31) noted 40 percent of Archaic assemblages on Black Mesa were obsidian. These material distributions underscore patterns observed for the BMII assemblages that suggest groups using the PEFO/RAR area were not the same as those using Black Mesa or areas to the west. In fact, a lengthy and purposeful lack of interaction between these areas is suggested.

The distribution of Paleoarchaic points on RAR is strongly associated with the canyons and particularly striking is their association with Bell Cow Canyon. Fully 79 percent of Paleoindian points occur there with 77 percent of Early/Middle Archaic points and "only" 68 percent of Late Archaic/BMII points. These match the 73 percent frequency of preceramic sites having features associated with Bell Cow Canyon.

Notably distinctive at RAR are the extensive Archaic petroglyphs resembling the Glen Canyon Style 5 or Linear Style (Turner 1963) or Palavayu Style (Malotki 2007)—dating as early as 6000 BCE (Malotki 2007; Weaver et al. 2000). Similar glyphs are also common in the PEFO area. Petroglyphs are strongly associated with place-making or the creation of combined natural and cultural landscapes denoting their sacred nature but also signaling the identity and possibly ownership by prior groups. Perhaps points made from petrified wood are also symbolic and expand the claim of the landscape and resources of RAR by groups who used the area for thousands of years (Soza 2018). Danielle Soza explores the role of projectile points in placemaking later in Chapter 9.

Late Archaic/Early Agricultural

Figure 1.3 shows date ranges that have been assigned to the Late Archaic, Early Agricultural, and BM II manifestations defined for the Colorado Plateau (Cole 1990; Malotki 2007; and Smiley 2002a), and as adapted for the RAR area based on radiocarbon dates, features, and petroglyphs. A brief summary of the chronology, settlement patterns, and petroglyph styles is provided here.

Over the past 50 years research has helped define and refine the chronology of the early agricultural period and the transition from the pre-agricultural Late Archaic. Excellent summaries of this transition are presented by Berry (1982); Irwin-Williams (1973), Matson (1991, 2007), Sliva (2015), Smiley (2002a, 2002b), and Vierra (2018). The introduction of

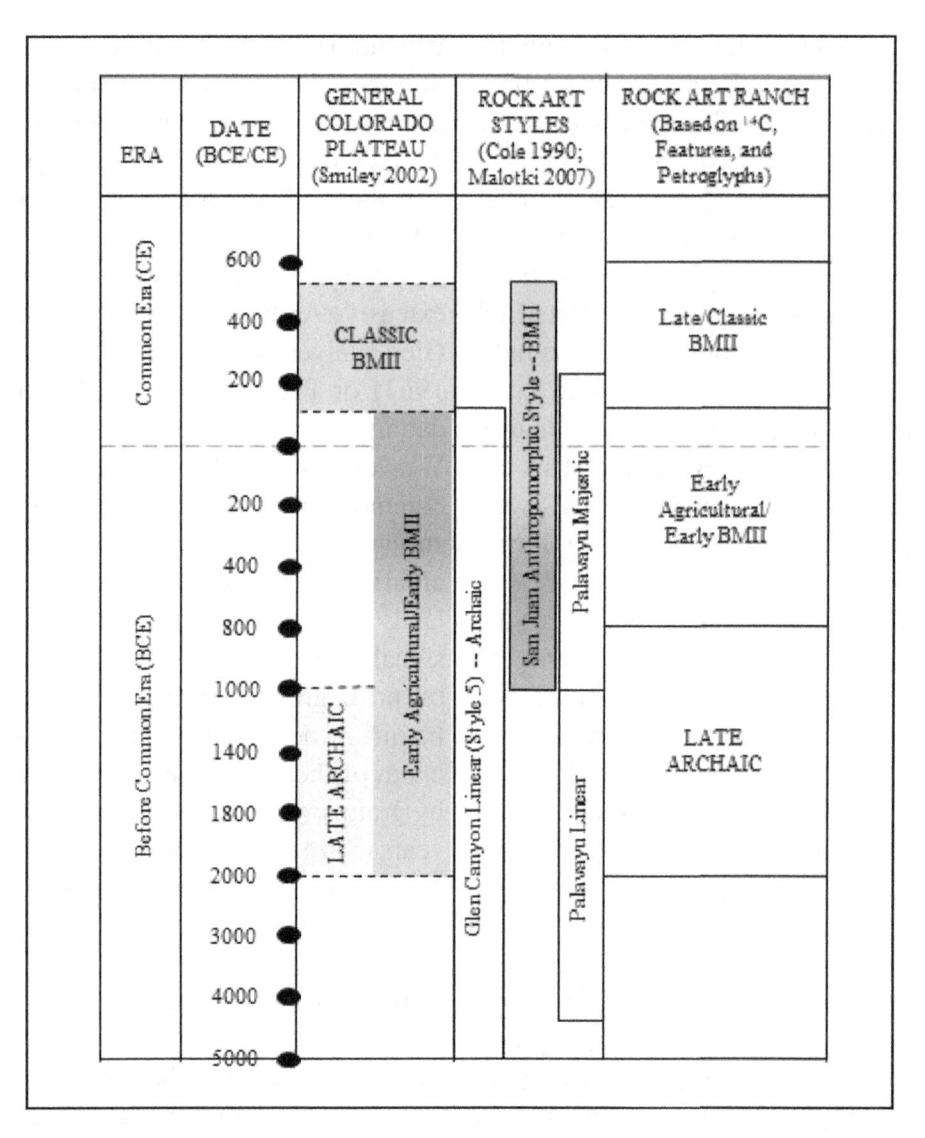

Figure 1.3. Comparisons of chronologies for the general Colorado Plateau, rock art styles, and the Rock Art Ranch project area.

maize to the US Southwest occurred between 2200–2000 BCE based on recent research in southeastern Arizona and refinement of AMS radiocarbon dates of maize from New Mexico and northern Arizona (Mabry 2009; Sliva 2015; Smiley 2002a, 2002b). In Herr's (2017) summary of regional archaeology, she notes that maize is present as early as 1400 BCE but is subsidiary to wild plants and animals throughout the period until the arrival of ceramics ca. 500 CE. Squash remains from this period are apparently indigenous gourds according to Sliva (2015) and edible squash does not appear in the region until after 400 BCE (Herr 2017).

Dependence on maize as a staple of the human diet seems to have occurred in three stages on the Colorado Plateau: pre-BMII or Late Archaic (1800–800 BCE); early BMII, regionally termed the White Dog Phase (1200 BCE–50 CE, and late BMII, regionally termed Lolomai Phase (50–500 CE; Smiley 2002b).

Generally, Late Archaic sites do not have pit houses but have numerous thermal and nonthermal features with evidence of structures from associated surfaces and postholes. Maize is present, but as an addition to a diet based in mobile hunting and gathering. White Dog Phase sites in northeastern Arizona are typically in rock shelters and display a commitment to maize agriculture (Berry 1985; Briuer 1977; Smiley 2002b). Shallow pit houses are common along with ubiquitous subsurface storage features. Lolomai Phase sites are much more varied and occur in the open (Smiley 2002b).

Four types of sites were identified by the Black Mesa Project: proto-village sites with multiple pit structures; earthen pit storage habitation sites with one or more formally prepared bell-shaped storage pits; non-storage habitation sites; and limited activity/campsites (Smiley 2002b: 52–61). At least two, the earthen pit storage habitation site and the limited activity/campsite have been documented at RAR. Although more than 100 Lolomai Phase BMII sites were recorded on Black Mesa, none involved rock art. This diversity and the increase in storage features indicates a more stable diet associated with farming maize on the Colorado Plateau where there are fewer subsistence options than in southeastern Arizona (Matson 1991; Smiley 2002b). Herr (2017) notes similar patterns along and below the Mogollon Rim 80 km south of RAR and at a similar elevation (5000–6500 ft [1824–1982 m]). The Lolomai Phase ends with the appearance of gray ware pottery and the introduction of the axe and bow and arrow, all occurring between 500–700 CE.

In 1992 and 1996, as part of regional research by ASM, Bruce and Lisa Huckell (Huckell and Huckell 1999) did a small survey west of Chevelon Canyon and 5 km south of RAR. They also excavated a BMII site (AZ P:2:56[ASM]) in a small side canyon to Chevelon Canyon that was first recorded as part of the HRP survey (Lange 1998). The excavations uncovered a shallow pit house and exterior work areas. A maize cob was AMS radiocarbon dated and calibrated at 2600+/-65 BP (815–500 BCE). The survey recorded more than a dozen deflated Middle and Late Archaic and Early Agricultural/BMII sites, most with diagnostic projectile points and some with considerable ashy deposits suggesting lengthy occupation. The presence of maize at AZ P:2:56(ASM) and its absence from six thermal features on RAR is intriguing. Given that White Dog and Lolomai Phases represent times when groups intensified the use of maize in their diet, its absence in flotation samples from RAR could signal that the area was involved more heavily in hunting and gathering than farming (Bohrer 2007). However, the small sample size of burned features from RAR means one cannot confidently assume it is absent during the preceramic period.

Further research on this important formative stage of Pueblo culture at RAR with the added bonus of abundant BMII petroglyphs has added significantly to our understanding of BMII White Dog and Lolomai Phase settlement and land use (see Chapter 5 for added detail). As noted earlier, given the greater diversity of sites documented elsewhere and the mobility of BMII groups (Smiley 2002a, 2002b), it is unlikely the sites at RAR represent the entire settlement system of White Dog or Lolomai society. At RAR, based almost entirely on surface remains, there are no traits that clearly distinguish the two phases. Sites with AMS radiocarbon dates ranging from 822 BCE to 567 CE are equally dominated by above ground, stone-lined storage cists, thermal features, and ubiquitous basin and flat metates with one-hand manos. Shallow pit houses and bell-shaped storage pits are also suggested based on excavations at AZ P:3:114(ASM)—RAR-2, Brandy's Pueblo. The absence of nearby alcoves might explain the similarity through time at RAR in contrast to White Dog Phase sites on and around Black Mesa; however, these may also be elements of the BMII seasonal round not represented at the ranch where nondomestic plants are the focus (Smiley 2002b).

The plant and animal remains upland and south of RAR suggest use in the fall in contrast to spring and summer use suggested at AZ P:2:56(ASM) (Herr 2017:338; Huckell and Huckell 1999). Circular pit houses similar to the one at Brandy's Pueblo are common elsewhere by 800 BCE. As with the RAR assemblages, there is little to differentiate the assemblages throughout the Early Agricultural period except settlement size increases from single pit houses to small groupings.

Peeples and others (2012) arrived at the same conclusion and suggest that shallow pit houses with or without central firepits were likely used during warmer weather and are frequently associated on the landscape with dense artifact scatters and features, a phenomenon observed at RAR where 33 of the 91 preceramic loci have features and one has a pit house (Table 1.1), all dating to the Early Agricultural Period based on projectile points and AMS dates. This is also consistent with the interpretation of AZ P:2:56(ASM) as occupied in the spring and summer (Huckell and Huckell 1999). Deeper pit houses found farther east in the Zuni area suggest colder weather use. None have been observed at RAR, although they could be buried. Another important element to the BMII sites with features at RAR is the high density of ground stone—especially basin and flat metates plus one-hand manos, all from local sources. Together these emphasize a strong commitment to gathering over hunting as the attraction to RAR where K. Adams and Smith (Chapter 2 in this volume) have recorded 14 native grasses with some available spring, late summer, and fall. Large game in the form of mule deer and antelope have also been observed on the ranch during warmer weather, but nutritionally would be more desirable in the fall. Their common representation on BMII style petroglyphs in Chevelon Canyon further suggests hunting large game animals was important to BMII groups using the area.

It is also likely the Black Mesa and RAR/LCR BMII populations are separate and did not share similar seasonal rounds, although no doubt they knew of each other. This conclusion is supported by the material in the flaked stone assemblages at RAR, which is dominated by local cherts and petrified wood from what is today PEFO more than 40 km east in the LCR drainage. The RAR assemblages are virtually devoid of obsidian. In contrast; flaked stone on Black Mesa BMII sites is dominated by local siltstones (Smiley 2002b:49) and to the west of RAR by obsidian (Lyndon 2005). Sliva (2017) notes Early Agricultural sites 80 km south and below the Mogollon Rim also preferred local lithic sources. It would appear the BMII and earlier archaic traditions represented at RAR are focused along the MLCR, although projectile point styles suggest interaction with nearby groups.

Another element to understanding differences in regions on the southern Colorado Plateau is projectile point style/morphology and resultant typology (Burton 1991; Justice 2002; Sliva 2015; Smiley 2002a, 2002b; Tagg 1994). On RAR a total of 26 San Pedro style points has been identified that fit within Sliva's (2015) expansive typology of subtypes, including 7 made on petrified wood. In contrast, only 10 points fall within classic BMII types of Durango (n = 2) or Black Mesa/White Dog (n = 8) styles (Justice 2002). Exactly half (n = 5) of these are petrified wood. Thus, 72 percent of Early Agricultural/BMII points on RAR are associated with the San Pedro Point tradition. This stands in stark contrast to those illustrated in Smiley (2002b: Figures 3.3 & 3.5) and above and below the Mogollon Rim (Herr 2017) where San Pedro point styles are rare. This suggests either the San Pedro style predates the BMII styles of White Dog and Lolomai phases or persists as a style or identity marker for groups using RAR. Given the presence of petrified wood in all types and their temporal overlap, it would appear the point types are at least partly a product of cultural choices rather than temporal differences. These differences in raw material preferences further underscore the likely existence of at least two BMII traditions, one along the LCR and another on Black Mesa, and a third, contemporary Early Agricultural tradition along the Mogollon Rim.

In a detailed comparison among point types present along the Santa Cruz River in southern Arizona, below the Mogollon Rim near Payson (80 km south of RAR), and Black Mesa to the north of RAR, Sliva (2017) identified styles remarkably consistent and similar from sites dating 810 to 30 BCE between below the Mogollon Rim and Black Mesa, including the presence of White Dog/Black Mesa Narrow Neck-style points. Three of the six projectile point styles are identical to those from the north (Black Mesa) and the other three are identical to styles to the south (Santa Cruz River) with neither the southern cluster nor the northern cluster overlapping in their respective areas. As Herr (2017) notes, this suggests the sub-Mogollon Rim was an area of contact and exchange between groups to the north and south. According to McBrinn (2005) such patterns in projectile point style are consistent with band-level social organization and mobility. Diversity of styles, such as below the Mogollon Rim, are likely locales where periodic gatherings of mobile groups took place to exchange knowledge and possibly marriage partners that would encourage cooperation rather than conflict.

The presence of so many San Pedro style points at RAR also suggests connections to the south—the Mogollon Rim/Transition Zone and Santa Cruz River (Sliva 2015). It seems possible that San Pedro points, which are dominant along the Santa Cruz from 1200–800 BCE were modified to create most, if not all, the styles found sub-Mogollon Rim and Black Mesa that appear about 800 BCE. Their dominance in Early Agricultural assemblages at RAR may indicate settlement during the Late Archaic, possibly predating BMII on the southern Colorado Plateau. Although this may be the reason maize is not present in the flotation samples, the uniform post-800 BCE calibrated AMS ^{14}C dates contradict this interpretation and support the idea that San Pedro points are associated with group identity.

One of the primary goals of the research summarized in this volume is its attempt to contextualize the role of rock art (petroglyphs) in creating a cultural landscape for preceramic groups (Brinkerhoff, Chapter 3, and Doery, Chapter 4, in this volume). The Chevelon glyphs have 3457 elements with 746 anthropomorphs, 526 zoomorphs, 827 geometric elements, and 1452 other elements (Kolber 2000; Weaver et al. 2000). These panels are dominated by BMII (aka San Juan Anthropomorphic style [Cole 1990, 1996; Malotki 2007; Schaafsma 1980; Turner 1963]) shared by groups throughout the Colorado Plateau that date 800 BCE to 500 CE (Weaver 2000). Malotki (2007) dates the San Juan Anthropomorphic style 1000 BCE to 400 CE, while Cole (1990) dates it 500 BCE to 500 CE. We have chosen a middle ground (750 to 500 BCE) based in part on AMS dates from burned features at seven BMII sites on RAR and AZ P:2:56(ASM) with extensive features and ground stone reported in detail later in the volume. Perhaps the petroglyphs are associated with specific uses of the landscape as suggested by elements within the panels. The large anthropomorphs often have elaborate personal decorations; the quadrupeds include recognizable bighorn sheep, antelope, and deer or elk (Cole 1990, 1996; Kolber 2000; Weaver et al. 2000).

An earlier petroglyph tradition in Chevelon Canyon is that of Glen Canyon Style 5 or Linear Style first defined by Turner (1963) in the Glen Canyon area of the San Juan River to the northwest of RAR. Although this style overlaps with BMII in time (dating 4500–250 BCE [Malotki 2007]), typically it predates depictions of BMII glyphs. This is true in Chevelon Canyon where all examples are either overdrawn by the San Juan Anthropomorphic style or show heavier patination. Malotki (2007) refers to this tradition as the Palavayu (Hopi for Little Colorado River) Anthropomorphic Style with shared traits to the Glen Canyon region, but still distinctive. In Chevelon Canyon this style is expressed by either simple anthropomorphic or geometric elements.

To summarize, RAR likely played a pivotal subsistence role for mobile hunter-gatherers who had added domestic plants to their subsistence base but were not relying on them. In this vein, early agriculturalists using RAR appear to focus on gathering and processing of seeds and wild plants supplemented by hunting during warm weather months. These groups' logistical moves focused on the LCR basin, however, they interacted with nearby groups, especially south near the Mogollon Rim, based on shared projectile point styles and complementary subsistence bases. In this sense, the early farmers may not be much different from their more sedentary ceramic period farmers who also practiced mobility and exchanged widely (Douglass 1987).

Ceramic Period (600–1400 CE)

The nearest and most relevant large-scale archaeological projects are those conducted in the Hopi Buttes by George J. Gumerman, III for his doctoral dissertation (Gumerman 1988) and by Amy Douglass (1987) for her dissertation on the local pottery tradition, Little Colorado White Ware. Closest to RAR is the survey directed by Richard C. Lange (1998) mostly focused near the pueblos of Homol'ovi I–IV, but also including sections of land west of Chevelon Canyon and 5 km south of RAR. A fourth large-scale project was in upper Chevelon and Clear Creek canyons initially under the direction of Fred Plog, James Hill and Dwight Read from UCLA between 1971–1974 (F. Plog et al. 1976) and later under the direction of Stephen Plog from the University of Virginia between 1997–2001 and known as CARP I and II (Solometo 2004).

Hopi Buttes/Little Colorado River

George Gumerman conducted dissertation research on the poorly understood Hopi Buttes area 30–40 km north of RAR combining survey of 25 sq mi with excavation of seven sites (Gumerman 1988). This work was made into a regional synthesis by including excavations on five sites conducted by Alan Skinner (Gumerman and Skinner 1968:185) along the Interstate 40 corridor 30 km east of RAR. This research defined the Winslow Branch of the Ancestral Pueblo tradition based on production of a distinctive decorated pottery named Little Colorado White Ware (LCWW; Colton 1955). Production of LCWW was centered in the Hopi Buttes, a volcanic field located between the LCR and Hopi Mesas (Douglass 1987; Figure 1.1 in this volume). Within this area settlements are typically small masonry pueblos of 5–20 rooms that have decorated ceramic assemblages consisting of nearly 100 percent LCWW dating between 1050 and 1250 CE. This decorated pottery tradition is associated with the distinctive environment of the region, which is extremely arid with few springs and ranges in altitude from 4500–6200 ft (1372–1890 m). Juniper is found on the highest elevations in an area dominated by Great Basin Desert Province vegetation

(Gumerman 1988). The only exception is the LCR, which was too unpredictable to farm regularly (Lange 1998; Van West 1996b).

Gumerman and Skinner (1968) also described the extensive history of the Hopi Buttes region prior to the introduction of LCWW. Prior to development of the Winslow Branch distinctive Little Colorado ceramic tradition, the Tusayan branch of Ancestral Pueblo culture was the dominant tradition in the Hopi Buttes region beginning in BM III, dating from about 500 CE to the mid-1000s (Daifuku 1961). Tusayan Branch settlements are characterized by pit house architecture with small, temporary pueblos of jacal. BMII sites, dating from about 100 to 500 CE, are quite rare in the Hopi Buttes region and are not particularly distinctive from settlements to the north or east. Also poorly known are the Early Agricultural and Archaic traditions predating 100 BCE, which are present only as surface lithic scatters with occasional diagnostic projectile points.

Amy Douglass conducted her dissertation research in the same region, focusing on production and exchange of LCWW (Douglass 1987). Despite Gumerman's definition of the area of pure LCWW as focused in the Hopi Buttes, sites having pure LCWW occur in the Flagstaff region on Sinagua sites and in the canyon country north of the Mogollon Rim, including the CARP projects, many miles outside the areas defined by Gumerman. As a result, many researchers claimed that LCWW was manufactured in these areas, so the focus of Douglass's research was to identify the production area for the ware and where, when, and why it was exchanged. Using X-ray diffraction and electron microprobe analysis, Douglass determined that production of LCWW was restricted to the northeast portion of the Hopi Buttes (Figure 1.1) and that directional long-distance exchange explained its occurrence outside the production area (Douglass 1987:225–26). She (1987:25–61) determined that LCWW in the Mogollon Region, along Chevelon and Clear Creek canyons south of RAR, was the product of direct exchange (see also Solometo 2004). She noted that sites with the highest percentages often had public architecture and sites close to one another had different frequencies of LCWW (1987:257, 263). Exchange also increased after 1130 when production of one particular pottery type, Walnut Black-on-white, began. Douglass (1987:271–72) attributes the intensive, long-distance exchange to social groups trading across environmental and cultural boundaries as a means to minimize risk by gaining access to resources not available in the area of production, an idea first proposed by S. Plog (1980:133).

Richard C. Lange conducted a 30 sq. mi survey of Homolovi State Park and adjoining areas on both sides of the LCR floodplain, including west of Chevelon Canyon, as part of the ASM's long-term study of the Pueblo IV HSC (Lange 1998; Figure 1.1 in this voume). Lange (1996, 1998) and Carla Van West (1996b) proposed that multiple short-term occupations of pit house villages along the LCR corresponded to stream flow in the river and precipitation patterns in the region. The pattern recurred from the early 600s to the early 1200s. This pattern of short-term settlement was confirmed by excavations conducted by Lisa Young at a site next to the Homolovi State Park visitor center (Young 1996). For the 600–1050 period, the occupants used Tusayan White Ware and Gray Ware (TWW and TGW), but from 1050–1230 they used LCWW and Gray Ware (LCGW) consistent with regional patterns identified by Gumerman and Skinner (1968). These assemblages suggested the occupants were migrating from the Hopi Buttes to the edges of the LCR floodplain during periods of drought and low stream flow. Major occupations occurred from 620–780, 820–890,

1000–1050, 1120–1225, and 1260–1400 CE (Lange 1998: 44, 147–161). Throughout these occupations, the dominant ceramics came from the north (from the Hopi Buttes and Black Mesa/Hopi Mesas areas), with Sinagua ceramics from the west (Alameda Brown Ware [ABW]) comprising 8.6 percent and Mogollon Brown Ware (MBW) from the east/southeast a comparable 7.6 percent, attributed to exchange with these areas (Lange 1998). Both brown ware traditions were common prior to 900 and after 1120.

Upper Chevelon and Clear Creek Canyons South of Rock Art Ranch

Julie Solometo (2001, 2004) focused her dissertation work on data gathered from long-term research by UCLA from 1971–1974 (Plog et al. 1976) and the University of Virginia under the guidance of Stephen Plog from 1997-2001 (Solometo 2004). The original Chevelon Archaeological Research Project (CARP) focused its research 30–40 km south of RAR east of Chevelon Canyon on Apache-Sitgreaves National Forest land (Figure 1.1). An intensive survey project covered 65 sq km, recording over 1000 sites, and was complemented by excavations in 24 sites (Solometo 2004:161). CARP II centered its research farther to the west of CARP to evaluate and test sites along Chevelon and Clear Creek canyons focusing on what Solometo (2001, 2004) terms "tactical settlements" (those that are defensive due to remote or inaccessible locations complemented by walls constructed to further limit access). CARP II recorded an additional 264 sites with excavations of four sites (Solometo 2004:169). The CARP study areas are dominated by pinyon-juniper at elevations of 6200–6700 ft (1890–2042 m).

Solometo (2004:207-11) presents the chronology as follows: Archaic: 7600–1000 BCE, whose remains are focused in rock shelters in deep canyons and likely exploited patches of the landscape with high plant diversity (Briuer 1977). Pre-Ceramic, Early Agricultural (BMII) on the Colorado Plateau: 1000 BCE–500 CE) remains are focused in the canyon and along its edges. Abundant ground stone is found in association with small arable patches of alluvial soils, suggesting early experimentation with maize (Briuer 1977:29). Solometo (2004:201) defined five ceramic time periods: 500–1000, 1000–1100, 1100–1150, 1150–1250, 1250–1320 CE.

From 500–1000 CE ceramic-producing, farming groups moved away from the canyons and their flood-prone patches and began farming on secondary and tertiary drainages in pinyon-juniper forests focused on Moenkopi Sandstone-derived soils. They constructed check dams and terraces to enhance these farm plots. Throughout the period these groups used brown wares for cooking and storage and traded for TWW with groups to the north. From 500–850 CE they traded for Lino Black-on-gray (B/g) from the north and ABW from Sinagua groups to the west. From 850–1000 CE or a little later, they built pit house villages and traded for Kana-a B/w from the north and ABW from the west.

From 1000–1150 CE stone masonry dwellings were built. TWW and LCWW were exchanged into the area with some sites having Cibola White Ware (CWW). To the east of Chevelon Canyon, CWW was dominant after 1100 while LCWW was dominant elsewhere west to Clear Creek Canyon. This was the period of highest population with many sites burned when people left. The typical site had 1–3 large rooms organized in a U-shape, suggesting occupation by a single family. Some sites, usually larger, have circular or square great kivas and/or rectangular enclosures, which were the focus of these dispersed communities.

From 1150–1250 CE the settlement

pattern shifted back to the deep canyons of Chevelon and Clear Creek where the sites are heavily fortified or near fortifications. These sites are dominated by Walnut B/w. There is no indication of occupation away from the aggregated pueblos near the canyons. The settlements also moved north for better defensible locations where it is more open, drier, and warmer. Defensive sites dominated by ABW are also on the west side of Clear Creek Canyon (Wilson 1967). Average site size during this period is 12–15 households, five times the size of the previous period. Solometo (2004:275) identifies four tactical site types: forts, proximate refuges, isolated refuges and defensive habitations.

From 1250–1320 CE the aggregated pueblos continue but are relocated away from the canyons and back to the pre-1150 CE locations. The ceramics are CWW types. The pueblos have large room blocks, more variable architecture, rectangular community rooms and possibly small square kivas. Many are burned. Occupation of the area ended about 1300–1320 CE.

The Cholla Project (Reid 1982) conducted by ASM in the late 1970s was to mitigate the effects on archaeological sites of the construction of a transmission line from the Cholla power plant near Joseph City to Phoenix. Mitigation along the Chevelon Canyon portion resulted in excavation of 14 sites just west of the CARP survey, and 25–30 km south of RAR. The sites are located in pinyon-juniper at elevations ranging from 6400–6900 ft (1951–2103 m). Sites with less than 15 rooms dated to 850–1275 CE. The Cholla Project research identified the same patterns similar to those summarized above by Solometo (2004). Sites prior to 1100 CE were dominated by TWW with LCWW dominant from 1100–1150 CE and CWW after 1250 CE. There was an occupational hiatus from 1150–1250 CE signified by the complete absence of Walnut B/w at any of the sites, when, according to Solometo (2004), settlements clustered along the rims of the canyons.

In the mid-1960s, John Wilson (1967, 1969) conducted extensive archaeological survey of Anderson Mesa to McDonald Canyon to determine the eastern boundary of the Sinagua, which Colton (1946) originally defined as Clear Creek/Chevelon Canyons. Wilson also visited areas around Meteor Crater, Clear Creek, Upper Canyon Diablo and Heber, all more than 30 km from RAR. He recorded a total of 92 sites and identified several boundaries based on the distribution of ceramics. ABW associated with Sinagua did not extend east of Clear Creek (but see the previous section). MBW did not extend west of Clear Creek. Mogollon Corrugated BW (MCBW), which postdates 1050, and CWW do not extend west of Clear Creek and Chevelon Canyon respectively. According to Wilson, sites were scarce between Chevelon Canyon and Clear Creek in the region 40 km south of RAR. This boundary was also observed by Solometo (2004).

The sites Wilson recorded in the vicinity of McDonald Canyon are of particular interest, given that his survey area is only 14 km south of RAR. The area is geographically similar to RAR with a canyon, tributary washes, sandy soils and sparse juniper vegetation. Wilson (1969: Figure 1) recorded several small pueblos ranging from 2-20 rooms dating 1100-1300 CE, all dominated by MCBW. He (Wilson 1969:160) also noted that the McDonald Canyon area was unique in having numerous sites predating 1100 CE, all pit house villages located in the deeper sandy soils of the area. Settlements were concentrated in upland areas and along the canyon and its tributary washes (Wilson 1969:166), settlements and geography that are similar to RAR. As described in later chapters, excavations at Multi-Kiva Site and Brandy's Pueblo provide needed context to patterns identified farther south—amplifying some while putting others into question.

Previous Research Within a 10 km Radius of Rock Art Ranch

Northern Arizona University (NAU), under the direction of Mike Andrews, surveyed land around and south of Chevelon Pueblo on the west side of Chevelon Canyon and south of the LCR (Andrews 1982). The survey is 6 km north of the study area at an elevation of 4900–5000 ft (1494–1524 m). The entire area is grasslands. Thirty-one sites were documented ranging from BMIII to PIV. The sites are dominated by TWW until 1050-1100 CE when LCWW is invented and completely replaces TWW. No CWW is present. Walnut B/w is the most common type dating most of the settlements to 1130–1230 CE. The area is densely settled and used due to the proximity of permanent water in Chevelon Canyon and abundant arable land at the confluence of Chevelon Creek with the LCR. An almost identical survey was done to the east of Chevelon Creek and south from its confluence with the LCR on Arizona Game and Fish Department land (Moses, Luchetta, and Larkin 2008). As with the Andrews study, the area is dominated by grasslands and sand dunes with several small pit house villages predating 1100 and small pueblos dating to the Walnut Phase. Lange (1998) also included parts of six sections west of Chevelon Creek and south of the LCR in his survey that otherwise focused on the area between Homol'ovis I, II, III, and IV. Due to the general lack of surface soil due to prevailing winds from the southwest, only sparse lithic or ceramic/lithic scatters were recorded that concentrated in PIII (Walnut B/w dominant) and preceramic periods. One preceramic site, AZ P:2:56 (ASM), was tested and is discussed later in this report.

The author (E.C. Adams 2002, ed. 2016) has directed the excavations at five of the seven pueblos in the HSC since 1985, with work at Chevelon Pueblo closest to RAR (6 km to the north). Chevelon Pueblo was occupied from 1290–1400 and consists of 500 rooms (E.C. Adams, ed. 2016). There are remains of two earlier settlements beneath and beside Chevelon Pueblo, one with abundant Lino Gray and discernible pit house depressions on the west side of the pueblo representing the BMIII occupation; the other with abundant Walnut B/w indicative of a PIII occupation that was beneath the pueblo. No features from either earlier occupation were excavated. Decorated ceramics from the PIV component are dominated by yellow- and orange-firing pottery. In contrast the corrugated utility wares are an equal mixture of northern styles (Tusayan Corrugated), southern styles (MCBW), and local copies named Homolovi Gray (HGW) and Orange Ware (HOW; Barker 2017; Cutright-Smith and Barker 2016). Chevelon therefore differs from its contemporaries at Homol'ovi I and II in having more corrugated ceramics with clear southern influence (Barker 2017). However, religious and domestic architecture are consistent with contemporary northern traditions at villages on the Hopi Mesas (E.C. Adams 2002, ed. 2016, 2016a).

THE ROCK ART RANCH ARCHAEOLOGICAL FIELD SCHOOL

The RAR Archaeological Field School, offered by the University of Arizona School of Anthropology and Arizona State Museum (ASM), and funded in part by a National Science Foundation Research Enrichment for Undergraduates (NSF-REU) Grant No. 1262184, was in the field for six summers during June and early July from 2011 through 2016. The RAR Field School was focused on the ranch properties east of Chevelon Canyon and south of Joseph City in northeastern

Arizona (Figure 1.1). The ranch property itself is the geographical center of various project areas that were also investigated and provided important information and perspectives on the RAR sites and materials. The other project areas are spatially and physiographically distinctive and involved different landowners. Thus, some of the geographically- and spatially-defined project areas have single landowners, others have multiple ownerships. Some of the project areas are under private ownership, others belong to the State of Arizona. The datasets generated by the RAR Field School and other projects operating earlier under ASM's Homol'ovi Research Program (HRP) are a mixture of formal surveys, collections, and analyses as well as informal, non-intensive surveys and field observations. Much of the RAR Field School and other projects' activities involved archaeological survey work that is the principal focus of sites and data reported here. However, some data from testing are also included in this report. Data presented in tables in this report represent only artifacts analyzed from formal collections made during the documentation of sites and loci or notes and proveniences recorded for isolates during survey, but all loci for which site numbers were assigned in AZSITE are counted in the tables summarizing sites and loci by project area.

The RAR research area is divided into five separate locations (see Figure 1.4): 1) the private RAR core area (the RAR-Core), including the parcels owned by the Rock Art Ranch/Baird Family and the private Aztec Land and Cattle Company (AZLAC-Adjacent) property just north of the ranch; 2) the private land to the north along the LCR east of Chevelon Canyon and north of Territorial/McClaws Road also owned by AZLAC (AZLAC-Far North); 3) an area west of Chevelon Canyon that has mixed ownership but includes two sections of State land (designated RAR-West); 4) an area southeast of RAR that includes two parcels with sites documented by the RAR Field School, one on State land, one on AZLAC land (designated RAR-Southeast); and 5) an area south of RAR with sites in a section of State land that was formally surveyed, plus other sites in the proximity that were documented that are either also on State land or on AZLAC land (designated RAR-South).

This report summarizes the survey findings, discussed within geographical subsets reflecting the research areas noted above. The report also presents data and analyses from the excavations at two pueblo sites conducted by the RAR Field School—one in the RAR-Core area on private land (AZ P:3:114[ASM]—RAR-2—Brandy's Pueblo), the other on State of Arizona Trust land in the RAR-South subarea (AZ P:3:112[ASM]—FN-37—Multi-Kiva Site). The archaeological survey work by the RAR Field School on State land was done under Arizona Antiquities Act (AAA) Blanket Permit 2011-029bl; the excavations on State land were done under ASM AAA Permit 2012-011ps. In addition, this report incorporates survey work west of the RAR-Core and Chevelon Canyon conducted by the HRP in 1989 and by Bruce and Lisa Huckell in the 1990s under AAA Permits 1993-035bl, 1994-70ps, and 1995-70ps. RAR Field school collections are under ASM Accession AP-2012-0321. The materials from the 1989 HRP survey are under ASM Accession 1994-3.

This report documents 147 sites added to AZSITE representing 193 original field sites having 247 loci from an area totaling 6.65 sq. mi (17.2 sq. km; Table 1.2 and Appendix I). A total of 88 sites in AZSITE representing 116 field sites and 158 loci was recorded by the field school in the RAR-Core area. Another 25 in AZSITE representing 32 field sites and 41 loci were recorded on AZLAC properties. A total of 25 in AZSITE representing 36 field sites and 38 loci is on land managed by the State of Arizona. Numbers for Other land ownership

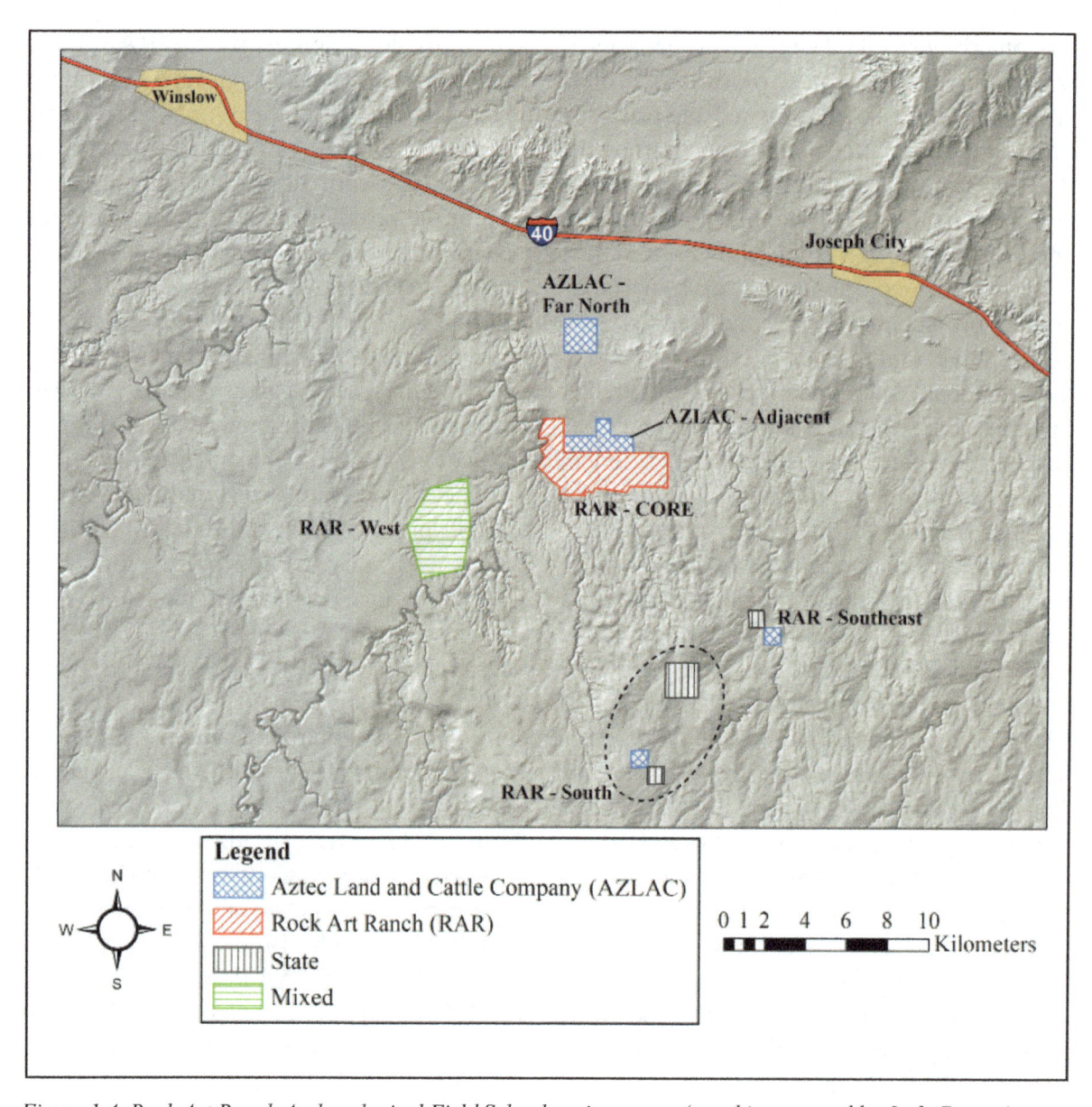

Figure 1.4. Rock Art Ranch Archaeological Field School project areas (graphic prepared by Josh Conver).

are 9, 9, and 10 respectively.

Research Goals

As noted, the decision to establish a University of Arizona field school at RAR was based on the complete absence of previous professional research in the area because it is surrounded by private ranches (some now purchased by the Hopi Tribe or Navajo Nation). As a result, major elements of regional research and the ability to contextualize the fourteenth-century pueblos has been seriously compromised. In addition to big picture concerns, the RAR field school had other specific research goals. The **first goal** was to conduct a survey to identify and locate all cultural resources on the ranch

Table 1.1. Temporal Distributions of Loci in the Rock Art Ranch Core Area.

Time Period	Date Range	Habitation	Features	Scatter	Total*	Percent
Preceramic	Pre-600 CE	1	33	57	91	42
BMIII/PI	600-1025 CE	13	10	29	52	24
PII/PIII	1100-1255 CE	16	8	45	69	32
PIV	1325-1700 CE	0	0	3	3	1
	Totals	30	51	134	215**	
	Percents	14	24	62	100	100

*Note: Several sites contained multiple temporal components resulting in the total (215) being larger than the total number of sites and loci identified in the Core area during survey (187).
**Total does not include 10 petroglyph sites.

Table 1.2. Sites and Loci in the Rock Art Ranch Project Areas.

Ownership	RAR Project Area	AZSITE SITES	FIELD SITES	LOCI	Notes*
AZLAC					N, S, & E of RAR Core
	Far North	3	3	7	
	Southeast	1	1	1	
	South	3	3	4	
	Subtotal	7	7	12	
OTHER					W of RAR
	West	9	9	10	
	Subtotal	9	9	10	
RAR	RAR Core	88	116	158	RAR Core Area
AZLAC	RAR Core	18	25	29	AZLAC-Adjacent (N)
	Subtotal	106	141	187	
STATE					W, S, & E of RAR
	West	4	8	8	
	Southeast	1	1	1	
	South	20	27	29	
	Subtotal	25	36	38	
	TOTALS	147	193	247	

*Note: AZLAC = Aztec Land & Cattle Company, RAR = Rock Art Ranch, N = north, S = south, E = east, W = west.

**Note: AZ P:3:176(ASM) has loci on both RAR and AZLAC properties. Three of the four loci are on AZLAC and are counted as 3 loci and 1 site (both field and AZSITE site) for AZLAC and as 1 locus and 1 site (both field and AZSITE site) for RAR.

and adjacent areas to further other research goals and to provide the Baird family with information to better contextualize the cultural programs they launched two decades ago. The **second goal** was to relate the sites to variables of the topography and environment. The **third goal** was to place these sites within regional spatial and temporal frameworks according to their material culture. The **fourth goal** was to relate the groups who created the surface archaeological record to the petroglyphs panels in Chevelon Canyon. These will primarily be pre-ceramic groups, especially early farmers. The **fifth goal** was to relate the later occupation of the area when small pueblos are present to the large, nearby members of the HSC that were founded about the time settlement ceased in the study area. The nearest is Chevelon Pueblo less than 6 km north. The **sixth goal** was to reconstruct cultural landscapes based on settlement patterns, environmental variables, natural features, and ethnographic reports. The **seventh goal** was to place the history of RAR within the broader social and cultural landscapes of the MLCR Valley to better understand how the people identified themselves by analysis of their material remains and changing relationships with their near and far neighbors as measured through exchange. Progress on achieving these goals can be measured by results reported in this volume.

ORGANIZATION OF THE VOLUME

The volume is organized into five sections: background (Chapters 1 and 2), petroglyphs (Chapters 3 and 4), survey (Chapter 5), excavations (Chapters 6 and 7), and regional patterns (Chapters 8 to 10). Chapter 2 by Karen Adams, Susan Smith, and E.C. Adams summarizes the geology and the natural environment of the ranch. Brinkerhoff describes the petroglyphs in Chevelon Canyon in comparison to regional styles in Chapter 3, while Doery focuses on a significant central panel to imagine how it was used to manipulate social power in hunting and gathering groups in Chapter 4. Chapter 5 takes on the task of summarizing the data from survey to consider the striking patterns of changing land use through time expressed through sites and objects. Chapter 6 summarizes the excavations at Multi-Kiva Site. Chapter 7 summarizes excavations at Brandy's Pueblo on the ranch. These summaries include those of architecture and material culture. The volume wraps up with three regional studies focused on the meaning and interrelationships among clusters of pueblos (Chapter 8), projectile points—focused on the preceramic era (Chapter 9), and ceramics (Chapter 10). All three highlight the one constant for the region—population movement. Chapter 11 provides some concluding thoughts and offers recommendations for future research.

Editorial Note: Many original photographs used in this report have been adjusted through cropping and changes in brightness and contrast to show the subjects of the photographs more clearly. Such edits have been done by Bill Burkett, Bob Mark, Evelyn Billo, Chuck Adams, Rich Lange, and others, particularly in the grayscale editions.

Chapter 2

The Rock Art Ranch Area: Physical Environment, Geology, and Native Plant Communities

Karen R. Adams, Susan J. Smith, and E. Charles Adams

Physical Environment

The Rock Art Ranch (RAR) research area is located south of the Little Colorado River (LCR) near Joseph City in northeastern Arizona (Figure 1.1). A major tributary, Chevelon Canyon, is prominent in the landscape, and an extensive series of ancient petroglyph panels located there (known as The Steps) is the cultural feature from which the ranch takes its name. Chevelon Canyon forms the western boundary of the RAR.

Within the RAR research area it is important to note the significant barrier that Chevelon Canyon poses to the east-west movement of populations south of the LCR. Although there is permanent water in Chevelon Canyon, fed by springs along the canyon as well as an extensive watershed originating to the south along the Mogollon Rim, it is a deep, mostly inaccessible canyon. It is possible to get into the canyon near its mouth, in the area between Chevelon Pueblo (AZ P:2:11 [ASM]) and Territorial/McClaws Road, at The Steps (approximately 5 km to the south), and not again until around the McCauley Ranch 13 km south of The Steps. The restricted access and limit to movement influenced the landscape use of prehispanic peoples, and affected the exchange of resources such as ceramics from the east and west, obsidian from the west, and petrified wood from the east.

The survey area is located in the Great Basin Desert Grassland, with the RAR-Core area 5-6 mi (8-10 km) south of the LCR, while the State of Arizona Trust land (RAR-South project area) is 19 km south in juniper-dominated grassland (Figure 1.4). The RAR-Core area is near the boundary of the grasslands to the north and juniper-dominated uplands located 2-6 km to the south. Between the ranch and the LCR are several ridges and valleys that drain to adjacent named canyons rather than directly into the river. The ridges and higher terrain, most prominently Apache Butte, effectively direct the flow either east to McDonald Canyon or west to Chimney Canyon before reaching the river. Sand dunes, including several large, active dunes, occur on the ranch and in the area north and west of the ranch, predominantly along the east sides of Chimney and Bell Cow Canyons, a result of sand being redeposited from the canyon bottoms by the prevailing southwest winds. These dunes and small side valleys seem to be preferred locations for dry farming based on artifact density.

The 3.5 mi (5 km) east-west width of the RAR-Core area straddles three drainage systems with McDonald Canyon draining the eastern third, Chimney Canyon the central third, and Chevelon and its tributary, Bell Cow Canyon, receiving runoff from the western third. At times all three convey large amounts of water into the LCR from the highlands to the south that rise to the Mogollon Rim. Through the ranch property, the other canyons are much shallower than Chevelon Canyon and are therefore more accessible to get water and to potentially use interior terraces and bottomland for farming. McDonald Canyon lies outside the survey area, so it is not considered in the following discussion.

Where Chimney Canyon traverses the ranch property it is 5-10 m wide with low sandstone walls ranging to 10 m high; however, less than a kilometer north of the boundary between RAR and AZLAC, the canyon walls are eroded away opening the next 2 km to a 1 km-wide floodplain fed by seasonal runoff from snowmelt and summer monsoon storms. The canyon reforms with a broader bottom for the remainder of its journey to the LCR. On the RAR portion of Chimney Canyon, there are eight natural "dikes" where the Coconino Sandstone bedrock rises up in small ridges running across the canyon, restricting the flow of water. The basins created by these dikes are filled with loose sand.

Bell Cow Canyon has similar natural catchment basins in the lower kilometer before it intersects Chevelon Canyon. It is a deeper, narrower canyon on the southern boundary to the ranch with walls up to 20 m high and bottom 5-10 m wide. Below its intersection with a major unnamed side drainage from the east, about 2 km prior to its intersection with Chevelon Canyon, the canyon broadens and becomes shallower losing its walls altogether before reforming 0.5 km before Chevelon Canyon. Artifact and site density increase to the highest levels in the study area in this section of Bell Cow Canyon dominated by Basketmaker II (BMII) assemblages.

Soil auger testing in 2012 probed the deep pockets of sand held behind the natural dikes in Chimney and Bell Cow Canyons. Deposits in both canyons were augured to 1.8 m to determine if there was stored water as well as intact stratigraphy that might preserve the geologic and archaeologic history of the region during the Holocene. Although the tests revealed a complete lack of stratigraphy, they did locate pools of water which collected in the auger holes beginning at 1.65 m. Given that the region has suffered a nearly continuous drought since 1999, it is likely the sand-filled basins in Chimney and Bell Cow Canyons held permanent water readily accessible to the prehispanic peoples using this area by digging shallow wells. The bedrock also naturally forms shallow basins along the canyon edges that collect and hold water from rain or snowmelt and could have been seasonally used to supplement more permanent sources. The canyon sides and bottoms were also loaded with artifacts from farther upstream eroded into the canyon from the dunes along the edges. In addition to the smaller canyons, Chevelon Canyon has a permanent water flow available at the surface, but, as noted, the canyon can be difficult to access.

The natural catchment of the canyons also supports significant riparian communities in the otherwise fairly homogeneous grasslands covering the research area. Riparian plants in Chimney Canyon include coyote willow, narrow-leaf cottonwood, and hackberry. Chevelon and Bell Cow Canyons also have black walnut. These would provide materials for house construction and edible fruits. The resulting plant diversity and water clearly attracted earlier non-farming human populations to the canyons. The locales of arable land were of more interest to groups who possessed pottery and practiced small-scale farming.

In addition to the sand dunes on the east sides of Chimney and Bell Cow canyons, grassland areas farther from the canyons had ceramic scatters suggestive of farming locales. The highest density of these farming sites lay between Chimney and Bell Cow Canyons where sands eroding from Coconino Sandstone were 20-50 cm deep overlying a 30-cm thick layer of caliche in contact with either Coconino or Moenkopi Sandstone bedrock. Where the sands were shallower or covered Moenkopi Sandstone bedrock, such as most of the land between Chimney Canyon and the main ranch house, very few artifacts and fewer sites were identified. Similarly, the diversity of native plants, especially grasses, was more varied and larger with deeper sand and substrates of Coconino Sandstone than shallow sands and Moenkopi Formation substrates, which were often quite clayey. Distribution of juniper trees on the ranch was strongly associated with deeper sand and Coconino Sandstone bedrock.

West of Chevelon Canyon, the area has numerous smaller drainages. They are shallow, like the drainages east of Chevelon Canyon, but the soils west of Chevelon Canyon are extremely thin or non-existent with bedrock at or just below the surface. The drainages also typically end in hanging canyons that do not provide actual access into Chevelon Canyon. These factors likely explain lower site density and diversity than noted for the loci east of the canyon.

North of the RAR-Core (AZLAC-Far North) the sites are on Moenkopi Sandstone terraces overlooking the LCR. These terraces also have thin soils and lag gravels. Water and better arable land would be available just to the west at the mouth of Chevelon Canyon or to the north in the LCR floodplain.

Areas surveyed to the east and south of the RAR-Core area are in locations higher in elevation and with denser stands of juniper trees. There are deeper soils as in the core area between Bell Cow and Chimney Canyons overlying the Coconino Sandstone. The main drainages of McDonald and Lard Bucket Canyons are shallow and accessible for water and farming similar to the RAR Core area. The edge of the pine forest is only 10-15 km south from these areas. Elevations are around 5400 to 5700 ft, approximately 300-600 ft higher than the RAR Core. The headwaters of Chimney Canyon are in the extreme northwest quarter of the State Land section where surveys were conducted in the South project area.

Higher elevations in the RAR research area meant that, even in early June, nighttime temperatures were cooler than lower elevation areas and broader expanses of floodplain in the vicinity of Winslow. At 5000 ft, RAR is 250 ft (75 m) higher in elevation than the Homol'ovi area near Winslow. It also receives cooler air that flows downslope from the Mogollon Rim to the LCR via the canyons in the evenings as part of the typical diurnal cycle. These factors shortened the growing season in and next to the canyons likely making the areas between the canyons better suited for farming.

GEOLOGY OF ROCK ART RANCH
E. CHARLES ADAMS

The geological record of RAR is quite straightforward and has a significant impact on the availability of water on or near the surface, the resulting plant and animal communities and, ultimately, human use of the landscape. The lowest formation is the Coconino Sandstone, which is overlain in sections of the ranch by the Holbrook Member of the Moenkopi Formation, which in turn is overlain by remnants of the Shinarump Conglomerate, often assigned as the basal member of the Chinle Formation. The Chinle is the primary member of the painted desert in the region and higher units include the Petrified Forest Member, which is most prominent in the Petrified Forest National Park 60 km east of RAR.

Descriptions of the Geologic Formations

Coconino Sandstone

The Coconino Sandstone dates to the early middle Permian and is typically buff to white. It consists primarily of fine, well-sorted quartz grains, with minor amounts of potassium feldspar grains deposited by eolian processes approximately 260 million years ago (Blakely 1990). Several structural features such as ripple marks, sand dune deposits, rain patches, slump marks, and fossil tracks are not only well preserved within the formation, but also contribute evidence of its eolian origin. At the ranch the formation has occasional unconformities marking brief interruptions of wind deposition that create dense, better-cemented layers 1-5 cm thick. The Coconino Sandstone is more than 100 m thick in the ranch area and comprises nearly the entire walls of Chevelon, Bell Cow, and Chimney Canyons. The Coconino Sandstone is the basal formation to the entire ranch and is overlain by the Holbrook Member of the Moenkopi Formation due to a local unconformity that is manifest by the complete absence of the Kaibab Limestone, as well as the lower Wupatki and Moqui members of the Moenkopi Formation (Stewart, Poole, and Wilson 1972). Wind and water erosion of the Coconino Sandstone has produced sand 30 cm to over 5 m deep covering nearly all the ranch west of Chimney Canyon.

Holbrook Member, Moenkopi Formation

On RAR the Moenkopi Formation is represented by its uppermost layer—the Holbrook Member—which dates to the lower and middle Triassic around 240 million years ago (Stewart et al. 1972). Typically, it is composed of interspersed layers of red sandstone and siltstone/claystone, but also contains localized layers of green and gray siltstone with ripple layers. These layers represent coastal, marine, and mixed environments (Stewart et al. 1972). In RAR the Holbrook Member lies in direct contact with the underlying Coconino Sandstone and, where exposed in canyon settings, is less than 5 m thick. These exposures are typically underlain by gray and green clays and silts less than 1 m thick. Multi-Kiva Pueblo sits on top of a shallow exposure of Moenkopi Sandstone overlying Coconino Sandstone. The Moenkopi Formation is the surface formation over the eastern third of the ranch beginning just east of Chimney Canyon. West of Chimney Canyon it is covered with moderate to deep sand derived from the Coconino Sandstone. Elsewhere on the ranch there are intermittent exposures 50-100 m wide and 100-200 m east of Chevelon Canyon. These are the only exposures overlain by the Shinarump Conglomerate

Shinarump Conglomerate

The early-late Triassic formation called the Shinarump Conglomerate, formerly the Shinarump Member of the Chinle Formation, was deposited about 225 million years ago (Evensen 1958). It is a highly resistant coarse-grained sandstone and pebble conglomerate, sometimes forming a caprock because of its hardness, cementation, and erosion resistance. This is true along parts of Chevelon Canyon where it rests directly on the Coconino Sandstone. East of the canyon no cemented portions of the Conglomerate exist; it is represented only by erosion-resistant pebbles ranging from pea- to cobble-sized. It rests unconformably over the Holbrook Member of the Moenkopi Formation and is present northeast of the Chevelon Steps petroglyph site and east of Deer Canyon where it intersects Bell Cow Canyon. Cobbles visually identified or collected from these locales include quartzite, chert, igneous rhyolite and basalt, and petrified wood, in order of ubiquity. A wide range of colors of all material types is also represented.

Effects on Plant Communities

Multiple student projects during the field school compared plant density and variety by parent geology and found significant results (Comstock-Ross and Berghausen 2012). Five-meter square samples compared Moenkopi Formation (Holbrook Member)-derived soils to those derived from the Coconino Sandstone. Moenkopi Formation soils had significantly fewer plants and significantly less diversity than plant communities in Coconino Sandstone soils. Not surprising, only five archaeological sites were recorded on Moenkopi Formation soils east of Chimney Canyon, which covers an area of approximately 2 sq. km. In contrast, a comparable sized area immediately to the west covered with soils from the Coconino Sandstone has 30 sites. Notably, several of these sites are ceramic period and likely involved farming domestic plants, especially maize.

Effects on the Availability of Water

The most important resource available on RAR is the local and abundant availability of water either on the surface or accessible through shallow wells. The Coconino Sandstone is the primary aquifer in the LCR Basin. It is designated the C-Aquifer (after Coconino) by the Arizona Department of Water Resources (ADWR 2009). It is recharged by rain and snow on the Mogollon Rim to the south. Because the Coconino Sandstone dips west and northwest from the rim, moisture pools in the vicinity of the LCR. As a result, large springs from the C-Aquifer in Chevelon Canyon are present five km upstream from RAR and provide permanent flow in the canyon and in turn into the LCR. This flow is joined by comparable flow from similar springs in Clear Creek Canyon to create a permanent stream flow in the LCR extending 20 miles (32 km) downstream. This permanent flow allowed the Homol'ovi/Chevelon pueblos to be established and the City of Winslow to be created to serve the fledgling Santa Fe Railroad route completed in 1881. Smaller springs and runoff from rain and snow also replenish subsurface water in Chimney and Bell Cow Canyons. The reliability of water in these seasonally dry canyons is visible in established willow, cottonwood, hackberry, and black walnut trees in the canyons. Sand dunes covering exposed sandstone also provides microclimates for the growth of sand sage, mountain mahogany, squaw/skunk bush, cliffrose, and various cacti that are rare to nonexistent in upland areas. These resources would be valuable to all prehispanic occupants of the area with sites having architecture, features, and ground stone concentrated within 150 m of the canyons.

Other Resources

Each geologic formation provided unique and important resources to prehispanic groups and especially preceramic groups who used the RAR-Core area. Basin and flat metates were uniformly manufactured out of layers within the Coconino Sandstone caused by unconformities in the deposition of the dominant eolian sands. Several of these layers are present where the sandstone is exposed in the canyons. Circular pockets infused with iron oxides are also present in some areas and strata within the Coconino Sandstone. Where sufficiently hard and hand-sized, these were used for one-hand manos. The Holbrook Member of the Moenkopi Formation provided stone and likely clay/silt used as mortar in the construction of stone walls by pueblos, such as Brandy's and Multi-Kiva, constructed during Pueblo III (PIII; 1050-1225 CE).

In addition, clay bedding at the base of the Holbrook Member has adequate plasticity to make pottery. Sands from both Coconino Sandstone and the Holbrook Member were used as temper in manufacture of corrugated jars at Brandy's Pueblo and Multi-Kiva Pueblo (Ownby 2016, 2017). Cobble-sized gravels derived from the Shinarump Conglomerate were used extensively for raw materials in the manufacture of flaked stone with larger cobbles, usually quartzite, also converted to one-hand manos. High densities of flaked stone tools, debitage and debris, and tested cobbles in two areas (AZ P:2:161[ASM] and AZ P:2:153[ASM]) resulted in their being recorded as sites by the RAR survey. Chert and quartzite were predominant in the flaked stone artifacts on each site, although basalt and petrified wood were also used (Kat 2014; Soza 2018).

Modern Plant Studies: Insights into Ancient Plant Communities and Resources at Rock Art Ranch
Karen R. Adams and Susan J. Smith

Introduction

Interpretations of past plant use by ancient groups generally rely on analysis of plant parts from archaeological sites (K. Adams and Smith 2011). Archaeobotanists specialize in various components of the archaeological plant record, for example K. Adams analyzes and interprets charred plant parts from macrobotanical and flotation samples. Macrobotanical samples are hand-picked during excavation from site strata and screens for species identification and description; they often include maize (*Zea mays*) cobs/kernels/ears and other domesticates, as well as larger wild plant specimens and charred fragments of wood.

Flotation samples are site sediment samples processed via water to a buoyant "light fraction" of plant materials that are examined under a microscope. Plant specimens recovered are identified in comparison to an extensive modern collection of regional plant materials backed by herbarium specimens deposited in accredited herbaria. Data are generally presented as taxon ubiquity, which tallies the number of samples in which a given plant and its parts occur within all samples analyzed, and which provides insight into the frequency of use of a plant resource in prehistory.

Pollen samples, analyzed by Smith, consist of additional site sediment samples chemically processed until only the durable pollen grains remain to be identified and counted. Results are presented by sample, as the percentage of the grains of each taxon counted of 200 total grains, or as the relative density of each pollen type when compared to counts of a known number of spores added at the start of the extraction process. These two methods provide different perspectives on the usage of plants that have left pollen grains as evidence. Additional analyses of micro-remains such as phytoliths and starch grains can also contribute insights into plant uses in the past.

Another perspective on ancient plant availability can be acquired via studies of plant communities. We acknowledge that the relative proportions of individual species within modern plant communities may be dramatically changed from the prehispanic era. Yet despite the passage of centuries and notable impacts from historic land use (grazing, plowing, fire suppression, introduction of plants from other continents), modern plant assessments can still provide insights into many native plants that still prefer the same local landforms and plant communities they occupied in the past. When picked and pressed as herbarium specimens, modern plants voucher the collections of seeds/

fruit, pollen grains, wood, and other plant parts that provide the comparative specimens useful for accurately identifying ancient plant parts via side by side comparisons.

This chapter discusses botanical reconnaissance in the region and adds new information on three modern plant communities near RAR archaeological sites that were surveyed, tested, or partially excavated. Each of these plant communities differ to some extent in their available resources. The ethnobotanical potential of many of these plants, as recorded in historic documents (see K. Adams and Fish [2006: Table 2] and K. Adams and Fish [2011]), offers important insights into subsistence and non-subsistence resources likely of interest to ancient groups as well. The ethnographic literature on plant uses by historic Hopi groups living to the north, including the publications of Colton (1974), Hough (1897, 1898), Kuhnlein and Calloway (1977), Nequatewa (1954), Vestal (1940) and Whiting (1966), reveal a comprehensive knowledge of plants and their importance as foods, medicines, tools, and for other everyday needs, as do generalized publications on Southwest U.S. groups (Bell and Castetter 1941; Castetter 1935). A searchable on-line database provides an entrance into this historic literature (Rainey and Adams 2004).

One important trait of interest to human groups is the season(s) in which they can gather reproductive fruit and seeds as food, and other useful plant parts such as new-growth lemonade berry (*Rhus*) stems needed for making baskets (Bohrer 1983). A thorough assessment of resource seasonality would require visits in multiple seasons, preferably over at least a two-year period. Although seasonality data was not acquired during this research, generally mid-summer through fall seasons provide the highest diversity of plant reproductive parts for human groups (K. Adams 1988; K. Adams and Bohrer 1998).

Historic Land Use and the Analog Problem

Interpretation of modern ecosystems as analogs for archaeological landscapes must acknowledge that present conditions may not precisely predict the past. The LCR region has a long history of use by diverse cultures including Native Americans, Mexicans, and Euro-Americans, each leaving a legacy of environmental change. Human imprints are visible in some cases as faint traces of artifacts, trash, and trails. One of the more dramatic examples of historic impact is the overstocking of range land throughout the western United States during the late 1800s CE (Fleischner 1994; Nabhan et al. 2004:9-13) and continuing into the present.

Colton (1937) summarized some of the early written records of Little Colorado River explorers, who reported that groves of cottonwoods and willows lined the region's narrow-channeled river and drainages. Prior to the mid-1800s, the nearly permanent Little Colorado River was occupied by beaver colonies. Heavy sheep and cattle grazing in the 1870s through 1880s, plus drought, shifted the balance of vegetation. Grazing continued through the 1900s, and at the time of the RAR field school a small herd of bison were still being grazed as a novelty on RAR property.

Climate Considerations

Another important historic factor is shifting climate patterns of precipitation and temperature in the US Southwest. Winter and early spring storms originate in the eastern North Pacific and summer thunderstorms push north from the Gulf of California, or occasionally the Gulf of Mexico (Barron et al. 2012; Sheppard et al. 1999). Extreme rainfall events can occur from late summer through early fall when the edges of tropical Pacific cyclones brush across the US Southwest. These rare hurricane rains have been linked to alluvial fan and flood deposits in the Southwest (Bacon et al. 2010; Ely 1997). Winter storms in the Southwest cycle through wetter (El Niño) or drier (La Niña) winters approximately every two to ten years in response to shifts in Pacific Ocean temperature gradients (Sheppard et al. 1999:10). Arizona climate over the past decade is characterized as moderate to extreme drought as measured by the Palmer Drought Index (NOAA 2017), and the persistence of this drought is changing vegetation.

Previous Studies of Modern Plant Communities

A compilation of previous research resulted in a long list of plants at five locations within the LCR drainage (Table 2.1). Although common names are utilized throughout this chapter, in Table 2.1, their scientific equivalents are also reported. Modern plant reconnaissance during visits in the summers of 2003, 2004, and 2005 resulted in comparisons between a heavily grazed landscape near Chevelon Pueblo (adjacent to both Chevelon Creek and the LCR) and a protected riparian zone approximately 7 km to the south that is naturally secluded from grazing animals (K. Adams 2016). These two locations, Location 1 (grazed floodplain and adjacent uplands) and Location 2 (ungrazed riparian area in middle Chevelon Creek) highlight the dramatic historic changes that have occurred within native plant communities.

Most drainages in the region are now covered with non-native tamarisk trees and shrubs so thick they generally out-compete indigenous vegetation. The adjacent low river terraces host species of saltbush and plants of importance to human groups, including cattail and bulrush, native grasses, cacti and yucca, and a variety of herbs and forbs. Juniper trees also grow in the region. Records of travelers from the nineteenth century report a heavier grass cover, including grama grass, on the low hills above the LCR floodplains (Colton 1937; Miksicek 1991). Currently, non-native camelthorn from Asia aggressively occupies streams, canals, fields, and rocky hillsides (Kearney and Peebles 1960:471) in the region.

In contrast, the secluded upper Chevelon Creek area has protected a wide range of native plants important to historic groups. Lacking tamarisk, this area instead supports cottonwood, willow, walnut, netleaf hackberry, New Mexican privet, and box elder trees or shrubs, species of bulrush, rush, reedgrass, and other native grasses, and many other valuable plant resources representing foods, medicinal/ceremonial plants, or plants providing other daily needs such as fuelwood and raw materials for tools and construction elements.

During June of 2011, K. Adams recorded plants within Chimney Canyon and along the eastern edge of Chimney Canyon near AZ P:3:124(ASM)(Table 2.1, Locations 3 and 4, respectively; tables are at end of chapter). One additional set of plant observations was made at the same time near Brandy's Pueblo (AZ P:3:114 [ASM]; Location 6). Many of the plants observed in these locations had been previously noted on the landscape in Locations 1 and 2.

Finally, plants were recorded in an area around AZ P:2:56 (ASM) four miles southwest of RAR (Location 5 in Table 2.1). This area, because of its location some distance away, contained a number of unique resources. Although Table 1 reveals that many plants are widespread in the region, from one to eight species are unique to nearly every location visited, suggesting that human groups would need to know the region well in order to collect those plants with relatively limited distributions.

Composition of Three Plant Communities

Each summer between 2014–2016, RAR field school students took an active part in assessing three plant communities, in researching and reporting on the ethnobotanical uses of the plants within these plant communities, and in tasting products made from wild and domesticated plants that would likely have been available in the past. These botanical assessments included sand dunes, a grassland, and a wash (Bell Cow Canyon), including a transitional area at the edge of the canyon. RAR fieldschool students were grouped into pairs and sent in various directions within each plant community. They were given approximately 30 minutes to observe and collect small pieces of every different kind of plant they encountered as they walked around; these included trees, shrubs, perennials, and annuals. Students were required to actually look closely at plants they gathered and to keep moving to maximize their totals. Then, all groups re-assembled under a canopy, and laid their plant parts out on a tarp into organized piles (Figure 2.1). Many groups had collected duplicates, but groups also collected plants that no other pair of students had seen. The piles of plants were discussed, one by one. For each plant collected, students were given the common names, scientific names, something about the ecology of the plants, and some of the plant uses based on historic ethnographic accounts. The results of these collections are presented in Table 2.2. Observations on the relative dominance of each plant population were based on estimations of overall size and population density: D (dominant), CD (co-dominant), C (common, > 25 plants), S (sparse, 11-24 plants), and R (rare, 1-10 plants). Again, historic factors have likely altered the relative dominance of these plants, but perhaps not their preferred landforms.

Grasslands

Grasses dominate the rolling hills of the region (Figure 2.2). Based on observations in Table 2.1 (Locations 1 and 6) and Table 2.2, grains (fruit) of at least ten grass species could have been harvested in quantity by human groups. These include grains of three-awn, two species of grama grass (side oats, blue), galleta/tobosa, ricegrass, muhly, dropseed, squirreltail, New Mexico feather grass, and needle-and-thread grass. These diverse grasses ripen at different times during the spring through fall growing season, offering important dietary components that include fats, proteins, and carbohydrates. Additional subsistence resources found within grasslands included fruit/seeds of members of the sunflower family, among them sagebrush, snakeweed, asters, paper flower, groundsel, native thistles, and young *Thelesperma* plants for making Indian tea. The goosefoot family offered saltbush fruit and a source of food known as winterfat that would have drawn deer and other browsers close to human occupations and activity areas. The mustard family offered abundant seeds of pepperweed and spectacle pod, some of them ripening in spring along with woolly wheat and species of globemallow. Berries of widely scattered juniper trees would have ripened in summer/fall, along with cholla and prickly pear cactus fruit, cliffrose fruit, and seeds of wild buckwheat plants.

Sand Dunes

Sand dunes offer unique conditions for plants, including shifting sands and deep water easily accessible to penetrating roots (Figure 2.3). Despite these unique conditions, the sand dunes visited by student groups supported many of the same plants (Table 2.2) observed within the region's grasslands, reported

Figure 2.1. Field botany with the Rock Art Ranch Field School, June 2015.

Figure 2.2. Grassland plant community at Rock Art Ranch, June 2015.

Figure 2.3. Sand dune plant community at Rock Art Ranch, June 2015.

above. Among these were a number of grasses (ricegrass, three-awn, galleta/tobosa, muhly, and squirreltail). Ricegrass thrives in sand dune locations, able to cover them in abundance. As spring-ripening resources, ricegrass and woolly wheat would have drawn human groups to sand dunes during a relatively food-stressed time of the year. Plants within the sunflower family, including species of sagebrush, paper flower, and Indian tea, would have also attracted people to sand dunes. Mustards (pepperweed, others), cactus fruit (cholla, prickly pear), globemallows, stickleaf (*Mentzelia*), wild buckwheats, and the occasional juniper tree, lemonade berry, wolfberry, cliffrose bushes, and yuccas all offered subsistence resources or fibers and wood for daily needs. Aromatic dune broom plants that especially favor sand dunes in the region were used historically by the Hopi for snow brooms and basketry, ceremonial objects such as katsina masks, a toothache medicine, and as ashes for coloring piki bread (Whiting 1966:26, 28, 33, 80).

Washes/ Floodplains

In the arid west, washes and floodplains contain two critical human resources: water and those plants that require mesic (damp) habitats. These locations are like magnets for animals including birds, and for human groups. Because precipitation and flooding are on-going, large stretches of mesic habitats are often devoid of plants, washed out in the most recent flooding. But, those plants that thrive in these locations are generally robust and are also often historically introduced plants such as tamarisk trees (Figure 2.4). In Table 2.1, Locations 2-5 represent riparian environments protected from historic impacts due to limited

Figure 2.4. Washes and floodplains plant community at Rock Art Ranch, June 2015.

access, for example upper Chevelon Creek (Figure 2.5). In Table 2.2, Bell Cow Canyon and its canyon edge transition were inventoried for plants. Many noted in drier locations include plants in the sunflower and mustard families, cholla and prickly pear cacti, globemallows, woolly wheat, and grasses. Two additional grasses, fluffgrass and rabbit's foot grass are unique to these damp locations. Spiderwort, Mormon tea, Indian paintbrush, milk wort and datura were inventoried only in these damp locations, although they likely grew away from them as well. Members of the Agave family (narrow-leaf yucca, broad-leaf yucca) also did well in mesic locations in addition to mountain mahogany and cliffrose. Other plants unique to these washes and floodplains include walnut, cottonwood, willow, hackberry, box-elder and historically introduced tamarisk trees.

Hands-On Learning Experiences

The value of such hands-on learning experiences is high. After returning to base camp, students researched a library of ethnobotanical literature so that they could prepare short oral reports on the plants they had just collected in the field. Each student summarized the variety of uses (food, medicine, ceremonial/ritual, tools, construction elements, etc.) and diversity of native groups known to have utilized these plants in the historic period, using ethnobotanical resources provided to them (Curtin 1984, 1997; Dunmire and Tierney 1995, 1997; Kearney and Peebles 1960; Mayes and Lacy 1989; Moerman 1998; Rainey and Adams 2004; Stevenson 1993). By the end of the exercise, each student had acquired direct knowledge of some local plants and their useful

Figure 2.5. Upper Chevelon Canyon.

parts from three different plant communities in the vicinity of numerous RAR archaeological sites. Students gained direct knowledge of the specific plant resources available in the June/July period of the field school and perspectives into the seasonal availability of plants in one short section of a calendar year. At the end of each field session, a feast of foods, each one containing at least one wild or domesticated plant ingredient that would have been available to the ancient occupants of the region, was enjoyed by all (Figure 2.6).

Closing Thoughts

The value of understanding the modern plant communities surrounding archaeological sites is high, especially when an archaeological plant record is not available. This information provides a more holistic perspective on some of the plants likely available as food and for other daily needs of ancient groups. Despite the many historic impacts to Southwestern U.S. landscapes, many native plants still grow in their preferred habitats. When archaeological plant evidence is available, modern plant community perspectives both complement and expand the list of important plants in the past.

At the RAR Archaeological Research Project, field reconnaissance of plant communities, ethnographic research on plants, and taste-testing converged as multiple teaching methods for field school students. Students learned to canvass the plant communities in areas where people once lived. And, when provided with ethnographic literature resources, they became acquainted with one or more plants of historic importance to indigenous US Southwest groups. Students acquired lasting impressions of eating cattail pollen muffins and sliced/roasted prickly pear pads, while drinking Mormon tea. Importantly, students took away some understanding of the realities of food gathering faced by ancient groups.

Figure 2.6. "Feast of Foods" available from local resources.

Table 2.1. List of plants previously compiled within the Rock Art Ranch region by K.R. Adams and S.J. Smith. Locations explained below. K.R.A. terminology follows Kearney and Peebles (1960), Correll and Correll (1975), and Christy (1998). S.J.S. terminology follows the USDA Plants Database. Shaded cells indicate plants observed only in a single location.

Family	Common Name	Taxon	Locations					
Aceraceae	Box-elder	*Acer negundo* L.*	1	2				
Agavaceae	Banana yucca	*Yucca baccata*					5	
Agavaceae	Narrowleaf yucca	*Yucca angustissima*					5	
Anacardiaceae	Lemonadeberry	*Rhus trilobata*					5	
Asclepiadaceae	Milkweed	*Asclepias* sp.	1	2				
Asteraceae	Brickellia	*Brickellia* sp.	1	2				
Asteraceae	Cocklebur	*Xanthium* sp.	1	2				
Asteraceae	Goldonrod	*Solidago missouriensis* Nutt.*	1	2				
Asteraceae	Hopi tea	*Thelesperma megapotamicum* (Spreng.) Kuntze*	1	2				
Asteraceae	Indian tea	*Thelesperma subnudum*				4		6
Asteraceae	Paperflower	*Psilostrophe* sp.					5	6
Asteraceae	Rabbitbrush	*Chrysothamnus* sp.					5	
Asteraceae	Ragweed	*Ambrosia* sp.	1	2				
Asteraceae	Sagebrush	*Artemisia* sp.						6
Asteraceae	Sagebrush	*Artemisia carruthii* Wood*	1	2				
Asteraceae	Sagebrush	*Artemisia ludoviciana*		2				
Asteraceae	Sand Sagebrush	*Artemisia filifolia*					5	6
Asteraceae	Snakeweed	*Gutierrezia* sp.				4		6
Asteraceae	Telegraph plant	*Heterotheca villosa* (Pursh) Shinners*	1	2				
Brassicaceae	Mustard Family	spp.					5	
Cactaceae	Cholla	*Opuntia* (Cylindropuntia)			3	4	5	6
Cactaceae	Hedgehog cactus	*Echinocereus*			3			
Cactaceae	Prickly pear	*Opuntia* (Platyopuntia)			3	4	5	6
Chenopodiaceae	Saltbush	*Atriplex* sp.				4	5	6
Chenopodiaceae	Winterfat	*Krascheninnikovia lanata* (Eurotia lanata)	1	2		4		
Cleomaceae	Rocky Mountain beeweed	*Cleome serrulata* Pursh*	1	2				
Commelinaceae	Spiderwort	*Tradescantia* sp.	1	2				
Cupressaceae	Juniper	*Juniperus* sp.				4	5	
Cupressaceae	Juniper, one seed	*Juniperus monosperma*						6
Cyperaceae	Bulrush	*Scirpus acutus* Muhlenberg*	1	2				
Cyperaceae	Bulrush	*Scirpus americanus* Persoon*	1					
Cyperaceae	Bulrush	*Scirpus maritimus* Linnaeus*	1	2				
Cyperaceae	Bulrush	*Scirpus pungens* Vahl*	1	2				
Cyperaceae	Sedge	*Carex* sp.					5	
Ephedraceae	Mormon tea	*Ephedra* sp.			3	4		
Equisetaceae	Horsetail	*Equisetum* sp.	1	2				
Fabaceae	False-indigo	*Amorpha fruticosa* L.*	1	2				
Fabaceae	Locoweed	*Astragalus* sp.				4		
Fabaceae	White clover	*Melilotus albus***	1	2				
Juglandaceae	Walnut	*Juglans major* (Torr.) Heller*	1	2				
Juncaceae	Rush	*Juncus ensifolius* Wikstr.*	1	2				
Juncaceae	Rush	*Juncus tenuis* Willd.*	1	2				
Juncaceae	Rush	*Juncus torreyi* Coville*		2				
Malvaceae	Globemallow	*Sphaeralcea* sp.			3	4	5	
Moraceae	Hop	*Humulus americanus* Nutt.*	1	2				
Nyctaginaceae	Desert 4-O'clock	*Mirabilis linearis* (Pursh) Heimerl*	1	2				
Oleaceae	New Mexican privet	*Forestiera neomexicana*	1	2	3			
Plantaginaceae	Indian wheat, woolly wheat, plantain	*Plantago major* L.*, **	1	2			5	
Poaceae	Bent grass	*Agrostis stolonifera* L.*	1	2				
Poaceae	Cheatgrass	*Bromus tectorum***	1	2				
Poaceae	Dropseed grass	*Sporobolus* sp.				4		6

Table 2.1. List of plants previously compiled within the Rock Art Ranch region by K.R. Adams and S.J. Smith. Locations explained below. K.R.A. terminology follows Kearney and Peebles (1960), Correll and Correll (1975), and Christy (1998). S.J.S. terminology follows the USDA Plants Database. Shaded cells indicate plants observed only in a single location, *cont'd*.

Family	Common Name	Taxon	Locations					
Poaceae	Galleta, tobosa	*Pleuraphis jamesii* Torr. (*Hilaria jamesii*)				4		6
Poaceae	Grama grass, blue	*Bouteloua gracilis*				4	5	
Poaceae	Grama grass, sideoats	*Bouteloua curtipendula*						6
Poaceae	Indian ricegrass	*Achnatherum hymenoides (Oryzopsis)*				4	5	6
Poaceae	Needle n' thread grass	*Stipa comata*						6
Poaceae	Rabbit's foot grass	*Polypogon monspeliensis* (Linnaeus) Desfontaine*	1	2				
Poaceae	Reedgrass	*Phragmites australis* (Cav.) Trin. Ex Steudel*	1	2				
Poaceae	Three-awn grass	*Aristida* sp.				4		6
Polygonaceae	Buckwheat	*Eriogonum* sp.					5	6
Primulaceae	Water-pimpernel	*Samolus floribundus* HBK.*	1	2				
Rosaceae	Antelopebrush, bitterbrush	*Purshia tridentata*					5	
Rosaceae	Mexican cliffrose	*Purshia mexicana (Cowania)*			3			6
Rosaceae	Mountain mahogany	*Cercocarpus* cf. *montanus*					5	
Rosaceae	Wild rose	*Rosa* sp.	1	2				
Salicaceae	Cottonwood	*Populus* sp.	1	2				
Salicaceae	Fremont cottonwood	*Populus fremontii*						
Salicaceae	Narrowleaf cottonwood	*Populus angustifolia*			3			
Salicaceae	Willow	*Salix exigua* Nutt.*	1	2				
Salicaceae	Willow	*Salix monticola* Bebb ex Coult.*	1	2				
Solanaceae	Thorn-apple	*Datura* sp.	1	2	3			
Solanaceae	Wolfberry	*Lycium* sp.				4		
Tamaricaceae	Tamarisk	*Tamarix pentandra***	1	2				
Typhaceae	Cattail	*Typha latifolia* L.*	1	2				
Ulmaceae	Netleaf hackberry	*Celtis reticulata*	1	2	3		5	
Vitaceae	Wild grape	*Vitis* sp.	1	2			5	

Locations: (1) Adams 2007, Table 1. Chevelon Pueblo, floodplain and drier upland grassland near ruin; (2) Adams 2007, Table 2. Within and adjacent Chevelon Creek, and 5.5 miles south at protected riparian location known as middle Chevelon Creek; (3) Chimney Canyon, KRA field visit June 2011; (4) RAR-12: along the eastern edge of Chimney Canyon, KRA field visit June 2011; (5) God's Pocket, 4 miles SW of Rock Art Ranch, Bruce and Lisa Huckell, 750 B.C.; petroglyphs in area range from Archaic to BMII, plus God's Pocket SJS observations over several visits; (6) Brantley's Site, KRA field visit June 2011.

* Plants with herbarium specimens verified by Kathryn Mauz and deposited in the University of Arizona Herbarium (ARIZ).
** Plants considered historically introduced from another continent.

Table 2.2. Plants identified on sand dunes, in upland grasslands, and within Bell Cow Canyon and its transitional canyon edge. Based on visits with Rock Art Ranch field school students in June of 2014, 2015, and 2016. Supervised by Susan J. Smith and Karen R. Adams. Dominance rankings are given as a general guide to the relative presence/dominance of the plants documented.

Life Form*	Family	Common Name	Genus	Species	Dunes	Upland, Grasslands	Bell Cow Canyon	Canyon Edge Transition
S	Agavaceae	Banana yucca	Yucca	baccata				R-S
S	Agavaceae	Narrowleaf yucca	Yucca	angustissima	R			
S	Anacardiaceae	Lemonadeberry, Squawbush	Rhus	trilobata	R			R-S
H	Asclepiaceae	Milkweed, broad leaves	Asclepias	speciosa (?)	R	C	S-C	S
	Asclepiaceae	Milkweed, type 2	Asclepias	?		R		
S	Asteraceae	Big sagebrush	Artemisia	tridentata (severly grazed)	S-R	S-R		C
DS	Asteraceae	Sand sagebrush	Artemisia	filifolia	C-D			
S	Asteraceae	Brickellia	Brickellia				S	S-C
H	Asteraceae	Thistle	Cirsium		R-S	S-C	S	R
H	Asteraceae	Small aster	Erigeron or Leucocene			C		S
S	Asteraceae	Snakeweed	Gutierrezia			C		R
H	Asteraceae	Purple aster	Machaerantha	sp.		S-C	R-S	
H	Asteraceae	Paperflower	Psilotrophe		R	R-C		
H	Asteraceae	Groundsel	Senecio			C		
H	Asteraceae	Indian (Hopi, Navajo) tea	Thelesperma		S	S		S-C
AH	Brassicaceae	Spectaclepod	Dimorphocarpa (Dithyrea)	wislizeni		R		S-C
AH	Brassicaceae	Pepperweed	Lepidium		S	R-S	R-S	R
AH	Brassicaceae	Mustard	Unk. Mustard yellow flowers		R			
Cactus	Cactaceae	Whipple's cholla	Opuntia (Cylindro)	whipplei	R	R		R-S
Cactus	Cactaceae	Prickly pear - peach flower	Opuntia (Platy)		R			R
Cactus	Cactaceae	Prickly pear - bristly	Opuntia (Platy)		C			C
Cactus	Catacae	Prickly pear - pink rose flower	Opuntia (Platy)			S-C		
S	Chenopodiaceae	Fourwing saltbush	Atriplex	canescens		C		
S	Chenopodiaceae	Winterfat	Krashenimikovia (Eurotia)	lanata	R	R		
S	Commelinaceae	Spiderwort	Tradescantia	occidentalis				R
T	Cupressaceae	Juniper	Juniperus			S		
S	Ephedraceae	Mormon tea	Ephedra	monosperma	R			S-C
H	Euphorbiaceae	Croton, Doveweed	Croton	texensis		R	S	S
AH	Euphorbiaceae	Spurge	Euphorbia			R- browsed		
H	Fabaceae	Locoweed	Astragalus		R			
H	Fabaceae	Hog potato (woody stem = subshrub?)	Hoffmanseggia	jamesii	R-S	R		
DS	Fabaceae	Dune broom	Parryella	filifolia	R			
H	Hydrophylllaceae	Scorpion weed	Phacelia		S	R		
T	Juglandaceae	Walnut	Juglans				R	

Table 2.2. Plants identified on sand dunes, in upland grasslands, and within Bell Cow Canyon and its transitional canyon edge. Based on visits with Rock Art Ranch field school students in June of 2014, 2015, and 2016. Supervised by Susan J. Smith and Karen R. Adams. Dominance rankings are given as a general guide to the relative presence/dominance of the plants documented, *cont'd.*.

Life Form*	Family	Common Name	Genus	Species	Dunes	Upland, Grasslands	Bell Cow Canyon	Canyon Edge Transition
H	Linaceae	Yellow Linum	*Linum*	*aristatum*	S-C			
AH	Loasaceae	Stickleaf	*Mentzelia*	*albicaulis?*	S-C			R-S
H	Malvaceae	Globemallow	*Sphaeralcea*		R-S	R-S		R-S
H	Malvaceae	Threadleaf globemallow	*Sphaeralcea*		C	R-S		
H	Onagraceae	Evening primrose	*Oenothera* spp. (2 different spp?)			S		S
	Orobancheceae	Broomrape (saprophyte)	*Orobanche*	*ludoviciana?*		R-S		
AH	Plantaginaceae	Indian wheat, woolly wheat (early spring flowering)	*Plantago*		R	R		R
G	Poaceae	Indian ricegrass	*Achnatherum* (*Oryzopsis*)	*hymenoides*	R	R-S		R
G	Poaceae	Three-awn grass	*Aristida*		R	S-C		S-C
G	Poaceae	Blue grama grass	*Bouteloua*	*gracilis*		S		R
G	Poaceae	Side Oats	*Bouteloua*	*curtipendula*		S		R
G	Poaceae	Galleta, tobosa	*Hilaria*	*jamesii*	R	R		S-C
G	Poaceae	Muhly grass	*Mulenbergia*		S-C	S-C		S-C
G	Poaceae	Unkown Dominant Grassland	*Muhlenbergia?*		C			
G	Poaceae	Squirreltail	*Sitanion*	*hystrix*	R	C		
G	Poaceae	Dropseed grass	*Sporobolus*			S-C		
G	Poaceae	New Mexico feather grass	*Stipa*	*neomexicana*			R	S-C
G	Poaceae	Fluff grass	*Tridens*				R	
G	Poaceae	Rabbit's foot grass	*Polypogon*					
DS	Polygonaceae	Buckwheat dune stabilizer	*Eriogonum*		S-C			
H	Polygonacae	Winged Buckwheat basal leaves (dead), tall stalk	*Eriogonum*	*alatum*	S-C			S-C
H	Polygonaceae	Buckwheat	*Eriogonum*	*umbellatum*		C		
H	Polygonaceae	Milk Wort small white flowers in spike /grey green leaves	*Polygala*	*alba*	R-S		R-S	R-S
DS, S	Rosaceae	Cliffrose	*Purshia* (*Cowania*)	*mexicana*				S
S	Rosaceae	Mountain mahogany	*Cercocarpus*				R-S	
T	Salicaceae	Cottonwood	*Populus*				R-S	
T	Salicaceae	Willow	*Salix*					
H	Santalaceae	Bastard toad flax	*Comandra*		S-C			
H	Scrophulariaceae	Bird's beak	*Cordylanthus*		S	R	R 1 plant	S
H	Scrophulariaceae	Indian paintbrush	*Castilleja*					R
H	Scrophulariaceae	Penstemon	*Penstemon*		S	S		
H	Solanaceae	Datura	*Datura*				R-S	R-S
S	Solanaceae	Wolfberry	*Lycium*		R			S

Table 2.2. Plants identified on sand dunes, in upland grasslands, and within Bell Cow Canyon and its transitional canyon edge. Based on visits with Rock Art Ranch field school students in June of 2014, 2015, and 2016. Supervised by Susan J. Smith and Karen R. Adams. Dominance rankings are given as a general guide to the relative presence/dominance of the plants documented, *cont'd.*.

Life Form*	Family	Common Name	Genus	Species	Dominance rankings**			
					Dunes	Upland, Grasslands	Bell Cow Canyon	Canyon Edge Transition
T	Tamaricaceae	Tamarisk – introduced	*Tamarix*	*pentrandra*			in Chimney Wash	
T	Ulmaceae	Hackberry	*Celtis*	*reticulata*	R		R	
H	Asteraceae (unknown 1)	pink flowers	possibly *Stephanomeria*			R		
H	Asteraceae (unknown 2)	pink flowers different from above				R		
H	Polemoniaceae (unknown 3)	light pink/purple tubular flower	possibly Polemoniaceae Family		R	R		R
H	Nyctaginaceae (unknown 4)	Unknown	*Abronia*-like		R			
	Mushroom	Puff Ball			C			

*Life Form: T (tree), S (shrub), DS (dune stabilizer shrub), H (perennial herbaceous plant), AH (annual herbaceous plant), G (grass, sedge, rush).
**Dominance: D (dominant), CD (co-dominant), C (common, > 25 plants), S (sparse, 11-24 plants), R (rare, 1-10 plants).

Chapter 3
Chevelon Canyon & "The Steps" Petroglyph Site at Rock Art Ranch

It's All About Water – Life's Blood Source

Darlene L. Brinkerhoff

INTRODUCTION

The Steps, named for its natural access into Chevelon Canyon, is one of the most phenomenal petroglyph sites in Arizona. The Steps petroglyph site is also known as Baird's Chevelon Steps and has been given site designations AZ P:2:62 (ASM) and NA25,474 (MNA). The Steps and Chevelon Canyon host one of the longest time sequences of rock carvings in the region, from the Archaic through Basketmaker (BM) and Puebloan times (6000/4500 BCE–1400 CE) (Malotki 2007; Weaver 2000). Although numerous Clovis and later Paleoindian projectile points have been found within 500 m of Chevelon Canyon, Clovis and later Paleoindian inscriptions have yet to be verified in the canyon, although they have been located in other parts of the US Southwest. They may be present and just have not been found or recognized (Figure 3.1).

According to Ekkehart Malotki (2003:237; 2007:76-83), The Steps and the general region of the middle Little Colorado River (LCR) have a distinctive petroglyph tradition that he named *Palavayu* (Hopi word for "red river" applied to the Little Colorado River) Anthropomorphic Style. Unique to the Palavayu Anthropomorphic Style is the dominance of anthropomorphic (human) forms in comparison to nearby contemporary traditions (Malotki 2007:77). He divides this style into an earlier "Linear" version equivalent to Middle and Late Archaic dating 4500–1000 BCE and a later "Majestic" version associated with Basketmaker II (early farmers) dating 1000 BCE–250 CE (Malotki 2007:77)

Petroglyph symbols may have esoteric meanings and associations with religion, hunting, earth, sky, water, fire, pottery and textile designs, and may have multiple purposes. For example, Hopi katsinas, shamans, or deities such as Maasaw, Koyemsi (Mudhead), and Fluteplayers may be depicted at The Steps and in the Chevelon vicinity. Hopi Maasaw is the god of the upper world and is encountered during life and death (Parsons 1936; Titiev 1944). The Zuni have a similar supernatural being who is called Koko, and they believe they migrated from the Grand Canyon, traveling and subsisting along the LCR and on east to the Zuni area. (Dongoske 2017). The prehistoric people who created the majority of the petroglyphs at The Steps, along the LCR, and in surrounding tributaries in NE Arizona are hunters and gatherers and early farmers whose

Figure 3.1. Petroglyph panel and general setting at "The Steps," Chevelon Canyon, in northern Arizona (photograph by Chris Rhoads).

descendants include the Hopi and Zuni. Some of the petroglyphs may represent clan symbols (Bernardini 2007). A clan name often results from encounters on migrations, with each clan having its own stories about its migrations through the Southwest and their arrival into their present-day villages (Bernardini 2007; Lyons 2003). Clan symbol petroglyphs at The Steps can denote the identity of social groups as well as migration accounts. Examples in the canyon are the bear track, image of the bear, fluteplayers, water, parrot, badger, crane, lizard, eagle, snake, coyote, owl, and ants (Figure 3.2). The Water and the Tobacco clans are indicated from The Steps according to Eric Polingyouma (2018).

Many of the glyphs are similar in style, execution technique, and location on the panel and some may have been produced by the same artist. These may represent their journey to spiritual enlightenment (Malotki 2007). Others are diverse and with different levels of re-patination and superposition and provide evidence of people accessing this area for a very long period of time.

LOCATION

The watershed of Chevelon Canyon geographically lies in East Central Arizona at the Mogollon Rim and flows approximately 165 km (100 miles) toward the northwest to its confluence with the LCR 7 km north of The Steps. Millions of years of water channeling and flooding have created Chevelon Canyon beginning with the uplift of the Colorado Plateau 5-10 million years ago (see Chapter 2). This uplift also created the LCR, which begins near the town of Greer, Arizona at Mount

a. bear paw (photograph by Darlene Brinkerhoff).

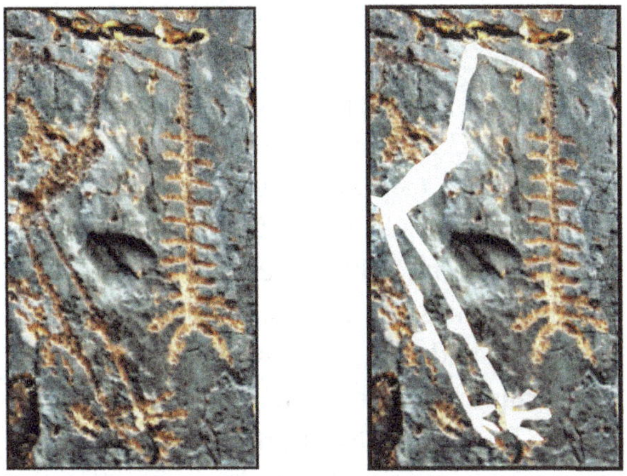

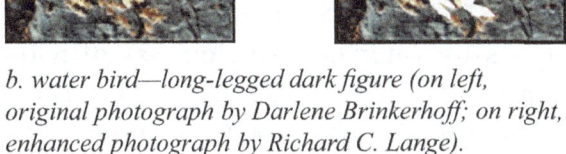

b. water bird—long-legged dark figure (on left, original photograph by Darlene Brinkerhoff; on right, enhanced photograph by Richard C. Lange).

c. owl (on left, original photograph by Darlene Brinkerhoff; on right, enhanced photograph by Richard C. Lange).

d. eagle (photograph by Patti Mozillo).

Figure 3.2. Examples of clan symbols at The Steps.

Baldy in the White Mountains and continues to the Colorado River into the Grand Canyon a distance of 394 km (245 miles; Lange 1998:1). The LCR region is located in the southern half of the Colorado Plateau and The Steps is situated in the middle Chevelon Canyon area. Snow melt and summer monsoons can unleash flood waters filling the canyon to approximately one-third to one-half its depth at The Steps. Flows up to 24,700 cfs have been recorded (USGS 1993).

Chevelon Canyon is one of several tributaries to the LCR from the south that includes Jacks, Clear Creek, and McDonald Canyons. In addition, the Zuni River and all washes among the Hopi Mesas flow into the LCR. Thus, the LCR creates a cultural landscape connecting Hopi to Zuni and both to its confluence with Chevelon Canyon and the Colorado River at the Grand Canyon. The general location of petroglyphs covers an area of over four acres and is situated in a U-shaped bend of the canyon about 250 m long, 15 to 30 m wide, and approximately 15 to 20 m high.

I believe there are a multitude of reasons why Chevelon Canyon and The Steps location were frequented for millennia. The lower Chevelon Canyon area has a greater amount of riparian area than upper Chevelon (Megdal and McKay 2007:2). Thus, the most obvious reason is the access to water. Even during periods of dry weather Chevelon Canyon's perennial stream harbors what is called a hyporheic flow, evident when there is a coarse substrate of gravels and rocks, and water flows beneath the surface through these particles (Meinzer 1923:57). Various Hopi attest to the fact that access to water in Chevelon was of main importance and religious significance. These "perennial streams, snow melt, springs, and seeps are what brought the Hitsat'sinom into this area" (Fredericks 2018). Eric Polingyouma (2018) from Second Mesa mentions that The Steps petroglyph site contains water symbols, including clouds, frogs and snake figures, as well as shamanistic figures to ascend or descend into the earthly realm, and that Chevelon was a place of Hisat'sinom (Hopi for *ancestors*), which includes the Mogollon Tradition. Additionally, water is used for purification and sanctification in most cultures. Other benefits of water in the canyon were access to the natural resources, that is the flora and fauna, including turtles and cattails used for religious purposes (Fewkes 1898). Chevelon Canyon creates a rich natural landscape, due to the presence of water, making it an oasis that served as a magnet for human use of the canyon, as indicated by the variety of rock iconography and archaeological remains present from Clovis to historic times.

Another resource is wood for fuel and architecture, which travels down Chevelon Canyon from the higher elevations when flooding occurs. Log jams can occur from The Steps to the confluence with the LCR. Before the addition of lakes and dams in Arizona and its Rim Country, the prehispanic people probably viewed and experienced a different environmental landscape with a more diversified and extensive list of resources (see Chapter 2). Access to these natural resources was of great importance, thus making The Steps a significant and revered spiritual place for the present-day Hopi and Zuni people and their ancestors. Thus, the Steps were likely visited on a seasonal basis for access to its various resources and for religious pilgrimages (see Chapter 1; Fewkes 1898, 1904). The petroglyphs are mainly on the western and eastern sides of the canyon, with some on the lowest areas of sandstone near the drainage zone.

History

Chevelon was also spelled *Chevalon* by the Civilian Conservation Corps (CCC) Camp participants from 1939 to 1942. The name Chevelon was derived from a trapper and scout during the 1800's who "found himself at a creek that ran through a narrow canyon on present-day Arizona's Mogollon Rim" (Austin 2018). The scout succumbed at the creek from eating a poisonous plant that grew along the bank, perhaps poisonous hemlock for which there is no antidote.

The natural access to water provided by The Steps attracted other historic people. During the late 1930's and 1940's my grandfather, Tomas Ortega, a Spanish sheep rancher, utilized The Steps area when sheepherders came to settle parts of Northern Arizona, such as Concho, St. Johns, Springerville, Holbrook, and Winslow. They moved to the Holbrook and Winslow areas to be closer to the train stations so that they could send their shipments of wool back East during war times.

These sheep ranchers came from the historical Spanish towns of San Mateo, San Rafael, Cubero, Cebolleta (Seboyeta), Albuquerque, and Santa Fe, New Mexico. Many of these Spanish ancestors married women from the Zuni and Isleta tribes before settling into Northern Arizona towns. The Steps area was one of my grandfather Tomas Ortega's "*partido* ranches." A *partido* was a partnership in which the owner paid the sheepherders in shares of new lambs for their income (Justia 1996:1). My grandfather told us that this was done to give people jobs during the Depression Era. He ran partido ranches in Concho, Springerville, St. Johns, across the border into western New Mexico, and one along Arizona Highway 180, which included an area in the current Fitzgerald Ranch. He would drive from one ranch to another to check on his employees and his sheep, which numbered in the thousands at certain times of the year, while bringing the employees and family supplies and food on a stake truck. This included the partido area at Rock Art Ranch.

On October 21, 1944, Tomas Ortega sold his land leases from the Aztec Land and Cattle Co. Ltd., and one from the New Mexico and Arizona Land Company to Thomas Baird, whose family came to settle in the Shumway, Snowflake, and Joseph City, Arizona, areas. They were originally from Texas and came to cattle ranch in the Arizona Territory. The ranch and The Steps have been passed down in the family to the present-day owners, Brantley Baird, son of Thomas, and his family.

Frequenting The Steps area from the nineteen sixties through the nineteen seventies, The Steps remained an enigmatic place for me, without knowing the significance of the canyon or the petroglyphs. Years later I finally realized that this was a very special and religious place to the previous inhabitants. For many years the petroglyph site was known and was frequented by local neighbors, artisans, photographers, archaeologists, and casual visitors who were also intrigued with these ancient drawings. With this heavier impact to the site, increasing human destruction became apparent, with vandals shooting at the glyphs with rifles and pistols, not realizing the uniqueness, age, or cultural aspects of the glyphs. This destruction prompted a conversation with Brantley Baird, with both of us in agreement as to how significant these panel etchings were, and on the need to preserve them for future generations and for the associated tribes of Northern Arizona. This conversation evolved into Mr. Baird controlling access to the canyon below with fences, gates and signs. This deterred the vandals, and within a year you could see the natural flora and fauna returning to the canyon below and becoming a riparian area. Additionally, there was no more broken glass in the creek, nor gun shots onto the petroglyphs.

During the period of 1989 to 1991, archaeologist Doug Johnson, who was employed at Homolovi State Park, instructed archaeology and petroglyph recording workshops through Northland Pioneer College in Winslow. One of our endeavors was to begin a rock art recording workshop at The Steps. At that point we began drawing to scale the first string-grid elements to get a proportional size of the Anthropomorphic figures. Subsequently, Mr. Johnson had to move on to pursue other obligations and opportunities, so the recording project was not completed at that time.

The documentation project we started with Northland Pioneer College was far from a complete assessment. Such a project would be an enormous undertaking. At this juncture I became interested in becoming a certified petroglyph recorder under the auspices of the Arizona Archaeological Society (AAS). Under the direction of Jane Kolber, Don Weaver, and Donna Yoder, I became certified while recording various petroglyph sites on the Coconino National Forest for forest archaeologist Peter Pilles.

To continue The Steps petroglyph recording in 1995 I began to use the recording methodology used by AAS in the Coconino National Forest. I made 10 and 20 cm square string grids in order to draw the petroglyphs to scale and began this venture by placing a string grid on the panel, ultimately it was immediately apparent that with the multitude and size of the anthropomorphs that this would create an overwhelming project. With the human and natural deterioration in mind, at the next AAS recording session on the Coconino National Forest, I asked the directors and the recording group if they had an interest in recording a site that was unique. Soon a survey was scheduled with Weaver, Kolber, Yoder, other volunteers, and me–slated to descend into the canyon to assess the petroglyphs. Everyone was completely in awe of the immense number and style of petroglyphs, including the size of the panels, the height of some of the glyphs on the canyon walls, and the quantity of superimposition. Without much coercion they agreed to assist, which was the catalyst in scheduling a meeting with the landowner, Brantley Baird.

Upon receiving permission and a written agreement to record the petroglyphs, we came up with a plan to record the glyphs in totality. This would include recording data, such as facing, inclination, element content, count, dimensions, visibility, condition, number of stylistic differences, mapping, photographing, and drawing the petroglyph galleries, panels and elements to scale. This full-scale recording was initiated in 1996 and completed in 2000. On April 5, 2000, Weaver submitted materials to the National Register of Historic Places for inclusion of the Baird's Chevelon Steps on the register. It was designated on the National Register on January 23, 2003. This designation was to assist in stopping any future possible destruction of the ancient glyphs by the canyon being dammed upstream, which at the time was a possibility.

The mapping and recording were performed by many competent and experienced AAS petroglyph recording volunteers, with the assistance of Don Weaver Jr., Evelyn Billo and Robert Mark (now with Rupestrian CyberServices, Flagstaff), Jane Kolber, Donna Yoder and myself. Upon completion of the recordings, it was determined that Chevelon Steps contained 40 galleries, 251 panels, and at least 3,457 glyphs. The galleries were numbered horizontally; and due to the height of many of the panels, we further divided the galleries alphabetically vertically, with (A) starting at ground level (Figure 3.3; Table 3.1).

The images consist of mainly anthropomorphic, zoomorphic, and geometric figures, as well as abstract and unidentifiable elements. Each gallery usually contained several panels.

PALAVAYU ANTHROPOMORHPIC STYLE AND THE PETROGLYPHS AT THE STEPS

As previously noted, The Steps and other early rock art sites in the middle LCR are dominated by anthropomorphic forms. Malotki (2003, 2007) named this tradition the Palavayu Anthropomorphic Style with an early Linear phase and later Majestic phase. Characteristic traits that distinguish this style from surrounding areas are differences in the type of dress (expressed as torso decorations), headgear (headdresses, horns, antlers, antennae, and feathers), items held in hands (fending sticks, spears, hoops, crooks, staffs, and canes), body shape, body size, and technique and style. Zoomorphs are second in frequency and are dominated by hoofed animals with birds and snakes also common. Plants (including datura) and insects, especially dragonflies, are also present (Malotki 2007:78).

No pictographs have been found at Chevelon Steps to date; however, pictographs in other parts of Chevelon and the LCR tributaries feature the colors of red, black, white, orange, green, blue, and gold (Figure 3.4).

Figure 3.3. Petroglyph gallery designations at The Steps, Chevelon Canyon (photograph by Rupestrian CyberServices).

Human Figures and the Amphitheater

The large human figures appear to be looking down, adorned with headdresses and decorated torsos, and holding either weapons, staffs, snakes, lightning motifs, or prayer wands/pahos (Figure 3.5).

The majority of these human-looking

Table 3.1. Glyph Types by Gallery at The Steps, Chevelon Canyon.

Gallery	Panels	CenterInt*	Superposition	Anthropomorphs	Zoomorphs	Bios**	Other Representations	Geo	Non-Representational	Unidentifiable	Total/Gallery	StyleDiff***
1	9	59	47	42	14	6	60	132	0	38	292	4
2	2	6	0	1	8	0	8	0	0	0	17	2
3	8	0	3	7	12	2	10	5	9	0	48	2
4	4	0	0	7	4	0	4	19	5	12	51	2
5	8	56	7	40	40	0	7	51	67	87	292	5
6	7	21	5	47	10	0	71	5	115	0	248	3
7	6	15	2	28	2	0	7	0	2	2	41	3
8	13	14	5	34	22	2	48	3	40	17	166	4
9	8	82	14	46	64	0	1	26	36	3	176	4
10	13	12	5	33	12	0	4	23	18	18	108	3
11	4	0	0	10	3	0	0	7	0	19	39	2
12	14	22	24	87	54	0	16	8	5	0	170	3
13	10	14	13	33	38	0	38	15	0	17	141	4
14	8	6	1	13	12	0	2	47	2	5	81	3
15	4	4	10	20	20	1	13	49	0	16	119	2
16	9	7	0	32	41	2	19	90	0	24	208	4
17	4	0	0	9	11	0	0	5	21	9	55	3
18	6	0	0	0	2	0	0	0	2	0	4	2
19	17	25	2	22	15	0	0	31	23	23	114	5
20	0	0	0	0	0	0	0	0	0	0	0	0
21	0	0	0	0	0	0	0	0	0	0	0	0
22	3	1	0	1	0	0	0	3	0	0	4	3
23	12	1	1	15	1	0	14	15	0	30	75	4
24	1	24	0	18	1	0	0	8	0	20	47	4
25	3	22	7	35	13	0	2	30	0	17	97	3
26	3	0	1	2	0	0	1	0	21	0	24	1
27	11	1	0	13	6	0	2	11	9	10	51	3
28	8	3	1	57	52	0	0	66	99	2	276	4
29	14	6	3	47	36	0	1	88	0	43	215	3
30	2	1	0	3	4	0	0	6	0	4	17	2
31	7	8	4	17	13	1	24	18	2	12	87	3
32	7	5	0	3	4	0	2	22	1	11	43	4
33	2	7	0	3	1	0	0	14	1	7	26	4
34	6	0	0	3	1	0	0	0	2	0	6	2
35	2	0	0	1	1	0	0	2	0	0	4	3
36	5	1	2	14	5	0	0	14	0	22	55	3
37	5	0	0	1	1	0	6	9	2	17	36	2
38	2	0	0	0	0	0	0	0	0	0	0	0
39	2	0	0	0	2	0	0	5	0	1	8	1
40	2	0	0	2	1	1	8	0	1	3	16	1
Totals	251	423	157	746	526	15	368	827	483	489		

Notes: * CenterInt = Center intrusions on anthropomorphs and zoomorphs; ** Bios = plant-like glyphs; *** StyleDiff = differential patination.

Figure 3.4. Pictographs in Upper Chevelon Canyon (photograph by Darlene Brinkerhoff).

figures appears to be males, although females are also represented. Only six were definite, as determined by exhibiting genitalia or hair whorls. Designs of migration or emergence spirals, clouds, rain, snow patterns, lightning, and clan symbols are also displayed on both sides of the canyon and appear to be situated in conspicuous areas for all to see, mimicking an amphitheater.

This presentation may have been the original intent and today evokes a similar reverence in all visitors. A ceremony of ritual passages may have been performed here, accented by the acoustic reverberation from the canyon walls. These supernatural beings evoke the feeling that you have just entered a spiritual place, one not of our realm or time period. This theatrical "stage" of human and animal figures watching the stream waters flow by torrentially or calmly give a sense of peace in this place (Figure 3.5e; see Chapter 4).

Snake Figures

The Steps contain a large number of snake-like figures, which the Hopi and Zuni believe are carrying prayers to the underworld (Parsons 1939). Snakes represent the belief they bring forth rain, clouds, and snow for prosperity and fertility in all things. There are various snake-like petroglyphs with a head, some are sinuous, coiled, spiraled, mouth open, and some are near natural cracks or holes appearing to be traveling in or out (Figure 3.6a,b). Some snake-like figures are held by anthropomorphs although some could be fending sticks (Figure 3.6c). In many cases it is hard to discern what object is being held because fending sticks can

48 Brinkerhoff

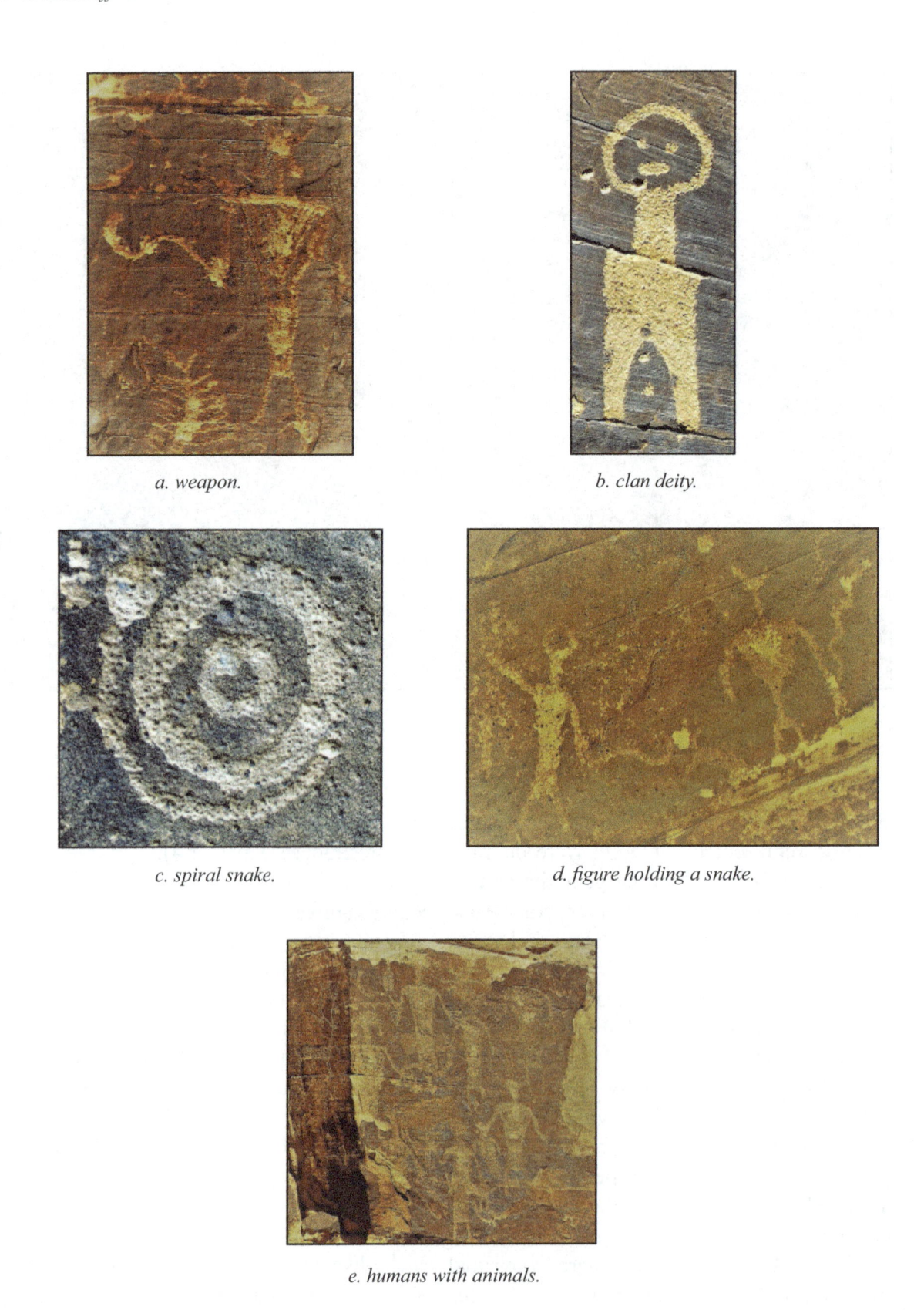

a. weapon.

b. clan deity.

c. spiral snake.

d. figure holding a snake.

e. humans with animals.

Figure 3.5. Snakes and human figures holding things (photographs by Darlene Brinkerhoff)..

3: Chevelon Canyon and "The Steps" 49

a. snakes emerging from a crevice (photograph by Chris Rhoads).

b. snakes in many forms (photograph by Chris Rhoads).

c. fending sticks.

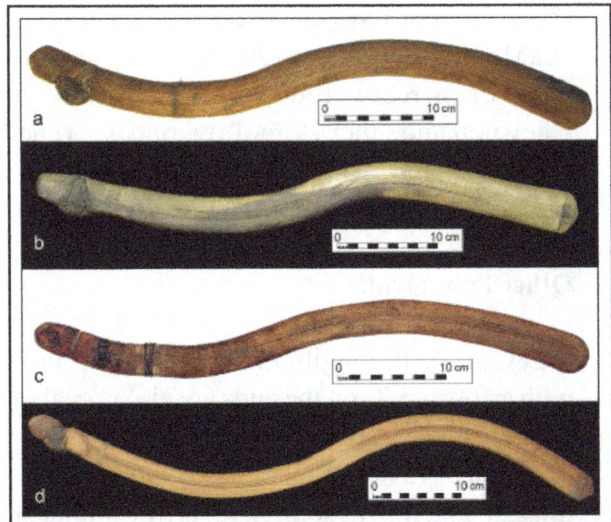

Figure 10.8. Four examples of typical Basketmaker II S-shaped flat curved sticks from the Four Corners area of the Colorado Plateau: (a) Cave 2, Moqui Canyon, Utah (Geib 5, MEVE 1857); (b) Battle Cave, Canyon del Muerto, Arizona (Geib 269, AMNH 29.1/8598); (c) Cave 9, Prayer Rock, Arizona (Geib 14, ASM 1183, A-13,388); (d,) unknown site in Grand Gulch, Utah (Geib 460, NMAI 051421). (Collections of Mesa Verde National Park [a], American Museum of Natural History [b], Arizona State Museum [c], and the National Museum of the American Indian [d]; photos by Phil R. Geib.)

Figure 3.6. Snake symbolism.

be shaped in sinuous form with a protuberance at one end (Curtis 2017:15). The items being held by these figures that appear to be snake-like are sinuous with some representation of a head-like protrusion, while the hunting sticks appear to be like curved hooks. Geib (2016:1; 2018:45-62) states that flat curved fending sticks were used in Basketmaker II (BM II). Other BM anthropomorphs at The Steps appear to be holding snake-like figures as in the Hopi snake dance (Figure 3.5a). When the snakes are released at the end of this ceremony, they carry prayers to the underworld (Parsons 1939).

Using element types from the recording project that may be considered snake-like symbolism, the results included element counts of curvilinear meander, s-curved, squiggle w/ outlined circle, squiggle with dot, appendage spiral, zigzag, tailed disk, tailed circle, appendage disk, spirals, squiggle w/appendage, and appendage circle (Figure 3.6a,b; Table 3.2). Zigzags could also represent lightning or an indication of snakes that propose bringing the rain, because snakes do not procreate until the rainy season. Lightning, rain, hail, snow, thunder and snakes likewise have an association in Mesoamerica with springs, caves, and mountains.

Zoomorphs

The zoomorphic figures (Figures 3.3, 3.7, 3.15a) include elk, deer, pronghorn antelope, dogs/coyotes, bighorn sheep, bears/prints, cats/prints, birds (eagles, herons and crane), fish, reptiles (snakes, lizards and frogs), and insects (butterflies, dragonflies, centipedes, and ants). Many of these animals were found to be in the Homol'ovi and Chevelon areas' faunal remains (Diaz de Valdes and Adams 2016; Pierce 2001; Strand and McKim 1996). This biodiversity continues to frequent this riparian body of water as all of these animals are still present in the vicinity of The Steps except the Merriam elk and bighorn sheep.

The Merriam Elk (*Cervus canadensis merriami*) was most likely the species that lived in the area prehistorically and with their enormous antler rack are the figures that appear on the canyon walls (Figure 3.7a). They have been extinct since 1908. In areas of the southern United States earlier archaeological evidence of the Merriam elk was recovered from stratigraphic units dating to approximately 1000 to 500 BCE. Other specimens from this species were discovered at sites dating to Archaic occupations from 4000 to 1000 BCE and from 6000 BCE to 1500 CE (Curren 1977:230-232; Hall and Kelson 1959). According to Curren, "the reduction of the range of the elk appears to have occurred within the last 2500 years." One of the largest galleries at The Steps reveals a hunting scene that may have been a record of an event, a supplication, a metaphor for water attracting animals, or a prayer of gratitude.

The nearest historic bighorn sheep are in the Grand Canyon more than 150 km from Chevelon Canyon, although herds closer to the area may have been present in the past (LaMotta 2006; Sheets 2019). Their remains have been recovered from excavations at Chevelon and other Homol'ovi pueblos (Diaz de Valdes and Adams 2016; LaMotta 2006; Strand and McKim 1996).

Other Petroglyphs

Wavy, straight, longitudinal, and zigzag lines with arrow points on the ends are also prevalent on the sandstone walls at The Steps (Figure 3.8a). Tawavaya (2017) believes that radiating lines up and down, some with arrow points on the end, can indicate the power of rising water and replenishment. They may indicate water replenished to the earth stream in the canyon. Some of these lines are over three meters long and have been carefully pecked leading down

a. deer, antelope, and Merriam elk.

b. deer.

c. antelope superimposed over anthropomorph.

Figure 3.7. Zoomorphic petroglyphs (photographs by Chris Rhoads).

52 Brinkerhoff

Table 3.2. Water, Rain, and Snake-like Petroglyphs at The Steps, Chevelon Canyon.

Gallery	Tailed Circle	Tailed Disk	Appended Circle	Appended Disk	"S" Curve	Squiggle	Squiggle with Dot	Curvilinear Meander	Squiggle Appended	Spiral	Appended Spiral	Parallel Lines	Zig Zag	Rakes *	Rain Symbol**	Stepped Pattern	Water Birds***	Totals
1	0	2	1	0	4	21	10	1	1	3	1	1	34	3	1	14	2	99
2	0	0	0	0	0	0	0	1	0	0	0	0	0	0	0	0	0	1
3	1	0	0	0	0	2	3	3	0	1	0	0	2	0	0	2	0	14
4	1	1	0	0	2	0	0	2	0	1	1	0	4	0	0	1	0	13
5	2	2	0	0	2	14	0	3	0	3	7	4	16	1	0	0	0	54
6	0	1	0	0	0	5	1	1	1	0	1	0	4	5	3	0	0	22
7	0	0	0	0	0	2	0	0	0	0	0	0	0	0	0	0	0	2
8	1	1	0	0	0	9	0	1	0	1	0	0	2	0	0	0	0	15
9	0	0	0	0	0	3	0	1	0	1	0	2	3	2	0	0	0	12
10	1	1	0	0	0	0	0	0	0	0	0	0	1	0	0	0	0	3
11	0	0	0	0	1	0	0	0	0	0	0	0	0	0	0	0	0	1
12	0	0	0	0	3	3	0	2	0	0	0	0	2	1	0	1	0	12
13	0	0	0	0	0	3	1	0	0	0	0	2	13	2	1	0	0	22
14	3	0	0	0	1	3	0	0	0	1	1	2	12	1	1	0	0	25
15	0	1	0	0	0	3	0	1	0	1	0	2	5	0	3	0	3	19
16	1	0	0	0	0	23	1	1	0	0	1	3	6	1	1	0	4	42
17	3	0	0	0	0	4	0	0	0	0	0	4	0	1	0	0	0	12
18	0	0	0	0	0	0	0	0	0	0	0	0	0	0	0	0	0	0
19	2	0	0	0	1	5	0	2	1	0	0	6	3	1	1	0	0	22
20	0	0	0	0	0	0	0	0	0	0	0	0	0	0	0	0	0	0
21	0	0	0	0	0	0	0	0	0	0	0	0	0	0	0	0	0	0
22	0	0	0	0	0	15	0	0	0	0	0	0	2	1	1	0	0	19
23	0	0	0	0	0	0	0	0	3	0	0	0	1	0	0	1	0	5
24	1	0	0	0	0	1	0	0	0	0	0	0	0	0	1	0	0	3
25	0	1	0	0	0	0	2	0	0	1	0	2	3	0	0	0	0	9
26	0	0	0	0	0	0	1	1	0	0	0	0	0	0	0	0	0	2
27	0	1	0	0	0	3	0	2	1	2	1	0	0	0	0	0	1	11
28	3	1	0	0	0	2	0	0	1	3	1	2	10	1	0	0	4	28
29	0	0	0	0	1	3	6	1	1	5	1	0	5	2	0	0	0	25
30	0	0	0	0	0	0	0	1	0	0	0	0	5	2	0	0	0	8
31	0	0	0	0	0	4	1	0	0	0	0	0	0	0	3	0	0	8
32	0	0	0	0	0	5	0	0	0	0	0	3	8	0	1	0	0	17
33	0	0	0	1	0	0	0	0	0	0	0	2	0	0	0	0	0	3
34	0	0	0	0	0	0	0	0	0	0	0	0	0	0	0	0	0	0
35	0	0	0	0	0	2	0	0	0	0	0	0	0	0	0	0	0	2
36	0	1	0	0	0	2	3	0	0	0	0	0	10	0	0	2	0	18
37	0	0	0	0	0	1	0	1	0	0	0	0	0	0	0	0	0	2
38	0	0	0	0	0	0	0	0	0	0	0	0	0	0	0	0	0	0
39	0	0	0	0	0	1	0	0	0	0	0	0	3	0	0	0	0	4
40	0	0	0	0	0	0	0	0	0	0	0	0	0	0	0	0	0	0
Totals	19	13	1	1	15	139	29	25	9	23	15	35	154	24	17	21	14	554

Notes: * Rakes = horizontal line with shorter perpendicular lines; ** Rain symbol = horizontal line with downward radiating lines; *** Water Birds = herons, cranes, ducks; Galleries 18, 20, 21, 34, 38, and 40 have no elements.

3: Chevelon Canyon and "The Steps" 53

a. lines with arrows (photograph by Patti Mozillo).

b. waterfall (photograph by Rupestrian CyberServices).

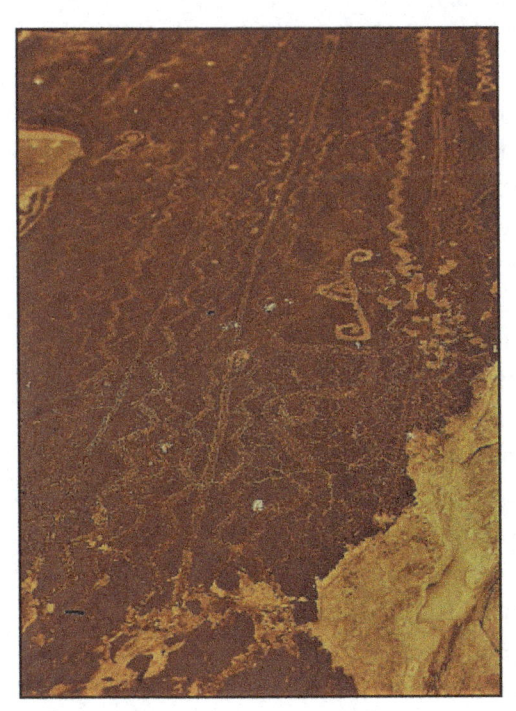

c. rain lines (photograph by Rupestrian CyberServices).

d. water lines (photograph by Patti Mozillo).

Figure 3.8. Water features.

to the waterway. Many of these "water lines" exist in what I have termed the "waterfall" area, while others lie on the sides of the highest and lowest cliff faces depicted vertically (Figures 3.8b-d). With careful observation, you can see that at one time there were a greater number of these "water lines" at the lower levels, but they have deteriorated due to the flood waters.

Dating of Petroglyphs

The chronological sequence of the rock images at The Steps begins at a time of foraging and continues through an agricultural subsistence period. Foraging was seasonal, while hunting occurred throughout the year. Palavayu Anthropomorphic Style has gained acceptance as a way to classify petroglyphs in the Southern Colorado Plateau area, which includes the Petrified Forest National Park (PEFO) area and the middle LCR tributaries west to Chevelon and Clear Creek Canyons (Malotki 2007; McCreery and Malotki 1994:1).

Presently, there are no absolute petroglyph dating techniques, so dating petroglyphs has relied on the relative techniques of patina differential (color change) on the rock surface, historical geologic sediment levels, superposition (one petroglyph on top of another), by association (an archaeological site nearby), by content (such as a depiction of a bow and arrow that can be dated), and lastly by petroglyph styles. Cole (1990:9) states that Paleoindian Period glyphs may exist, but that they are difficult to determine because they are generally found at the same locations with later petroglyphs. The Steps contain an extended chronology of petroglyphs, comprising at least Archaic through Pueblo Periods with the possibility of Paleoindian yet to be discovered. At the present time standard relative dating methods of petroglyphs will be used.

One relative dating technique is patina differential or re-patination, formed by hydrous iron and manganese oxide. The process of a chemical reaction with biological matter in which a recently pecked or scratched area of light color turns darker through time, eventually becoming totally blackened or darkened to the original color of stone, suggests older glyphs. However, different areas of a rock surface can display differential patination due to facing and variable amounts of sun, moisture, or mineral content. Different rocks may contain varying amounts of minerals and have different saturation qualities like a sponge. Nonetheless, the re-patination has value as a relative dating technique for petroglyphs on the same surface (Figure 3.9).

Although it is possible that the very dark patina figures, with no contrast to the surrounding rock, are from a late Paleoindian period, the abstract elements, meanders, curves, lines, hatching, mesh looking figures and scratching are consistent with the Palavayu Linear Style (Figure 3.9b; Malotki 2007). These enigmatic figures may be entoptic symbols used in ritual, a visible effect that originates through the observers' optic system and visual cortex and can be associated with altered states of consciousness usually involving plants producing this effect (Berrocal 2011).

Superposition is another form of relative dating that occurs frequently at The Steps (Figure 3.10a,b). Figures have been pecked over other figures, making it easy to determine which is older. The latest figure may have been placed over an older one—either at the same time or a different time, which may provide a different meaning due to context. Such cases are examples of when patina differential can aid in determining the intended association.

a. Basketmaker Linear Style.

b. Basketmaker Majestic Style.

c. Basketmaker Majestic and Pueblo Styles.

Figure 3.9. Repatinated glyphs (photographs by Chris Rhoads).

a. Late over Early Basketmaker anthropomorphs (photograph by Rupestrian CyberServices).

b. Basketmaker over Archaic anthropomorphs (photograph by Patti Mozillo).

Figure 3.10. Superimposition.

Comparing Stylistic Traditions

The word "style" refers to the subject matter and technological attributes of differences in characteristic expression of petrographic symbols (McCreery and Malotki 1994:5). These style differences can be associated with heterogeneous cultures and clan symbols in various locations, leaving evidence of migration patterns and frequency of occupancy. Such styles have been used to relatively date the rock art in the Southwest.

Petroglyphs can be abstract or representational, establishing regional styles and patterns. As discussed in detail below, The Steps petroglyphs start from the early to middle Archaic period, are dominated by BMII glyphs, and continue through all Pueblo periods, or ca. 4500 BCE to 1400 CE. There are also historic glyphs dating to the twentieth century. The Archaic period in the Chevelon area has been verified by previous work with archaeological remains and profoundly by projectile point dating analyses reported in Chapters 5 and 9. It is inferred that the earlier style of petroglyphs, such as rain, lightning, abstract, and snake symbols, which exhibit total re-patination are earlier than the BM II figures or that this was a transitional stage from the Archaic to the BM II period (Figure 3.9a).

Archaic

The Archaic age Glen Canyon Linear Style 5 was first proposed by Christy Turner's research in the Glen Canyon Dam area along the Utah/Arizona border (Turner 1963). The name Glen Canyon Linear (GCL) Style later was proposed

a. figures with corn tassel antennae (photograph by Darlene Brinkerhoff).

b. corn tassels (photograph by Karen Adams).

Figure 3.11. Possible corn tassels.

by Schaafsma (1980). Many researchers agree that the skeletonized anthropomorphs and zoomorphs in the middle LCR valley are Archaic and may be transitional to BM Linear Style, similar to the Glen Canyon Linear Style, (Cole 1990, 1996; Ferg 1974; Pilles 1975; Shaafsma 1980:72). However, there is a difference between the GCL Style and the LCR Linear Style—many of the GCL Linear Style anthropomorphs do not exhibit arms. McCreery and Malotki (1994) and Malotki (2007) have named the local tradition the Palavayu Anthropomorphic (PA) Style for the middle LCR area due to its distinctive and unusually high frequency of anthropomorphs with body, head, and face details that differentiate it from the GCL. The Archaic expression, dating 4500–1000 BCE is the "Linear" version of PA, while the Majestic style, dating 1000 BCE to 250 CE, is associated with BMII. Recently, however, McNeil and Shaul (2018) have argued, based on extensive analysis of head style and ornamentation, that the PA Linear expression and GCL are of the same Archaic tradition (Figure 3.9b).

Basketmaker II

McNeil and Shaul (2018) argue that the GCL Style is not related to the Basketmaker-era Glen Canyon Anthropomorphic Style and in fact is related to the later "Majestic" expression of PA Style (see Malotki 2007). The implication of their analysis is that groups from the Glen Canyon region along the Arizona/Utah border of today migrated to the middle LCR sometime around 1000 BCE.

While the Archaic style human-looking

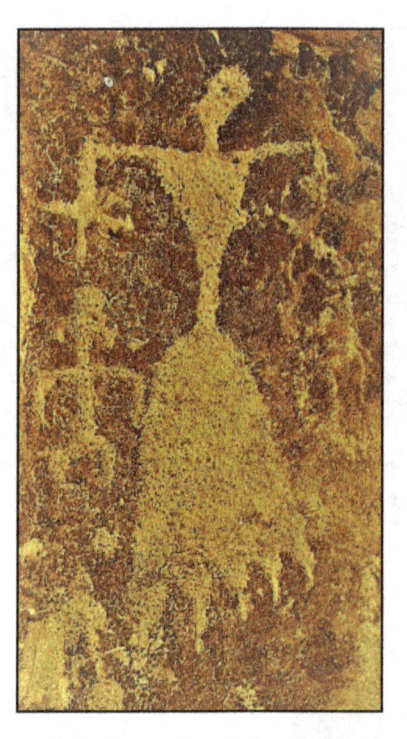

Figure 3.12. Cinderella Panel (photograph by Rupestrian CyberServices).

figures consist of straight horizontal or vertical parallel lined bodies, the Majestic Style anthropomorphs in the LCR area are much more elaborate (Malotki 2007; McCreery and Malotki 1994; McNeil and Shaul 2018). The majority of the human figures at The Steps are from this BM Majestic Style period, which associates them with the middle LCR area. The Majestic Style is expressed by broad triangular shoulders, decorated torsos, headdresses, horns, antlers and hair, and the figures holding fending or rabbit sticks, or snakes. It also appears that the anthropomorphic heads of this latter style exhibit ear bobbles/earrings, horns like a mask/headdress of an ungulate, or a plant like protuberance such as a tassel of a corn stalk. The earlier PA Linear style figures do not display these features (Figures 3.5e, 3.9c, 3.11; and see McNeil and Shaul [2018] for more examples).

The extensive archaeological record recovered at RAR and PEFO make it apparent the BM people were living and traveling throughout the middle LCR valley. Thus, the BM Majestic Style is earlier than the smaller undecorated anthropomorphic figures from the Puebloan period, and later than the Archaic Linear Style anthropomorphs and zoomorphs with cross hatched skeleton-style bodies. In much of the Southwest it has been suggested that these decorated figures are shamanistic (Hedges 1985; Malotki 2007; Schaafsma 1980:10; Vastokas and Vastokas 1973; Wellmann 1975), who are spirit helpers or deities carrying prayers from their communities for rain, fertility, and prosperity in all animate and inanimate subjects. For example, at The Steps, the "Cinderella Panel" may imply a human transforming into a bear or a bear into a human (Figure 3.12). This is also called therianthropic, a spiritual change or transformation exhibiting part animal and part human, to possibly rise above and beyond the ordinary realm. Dayton (2001:1) states that "Paintings of ...animal-human hybrids are among the oldest surviving art ever produced."

Tacon (2001:1), a rock art expert from the Museum of Sydney, Australia, believes that a combination of animal-headed and human figures goes back to the dawn of humanity, and has found such examples in rock painting and carvings that could date back more than 10,000 years. The Steps also contain bird- and rabbit-headed anthropomorphs and some human figures in flight or bird-like associations. There is one large figure in the canyon that is likely an eagle figure due to its pronounced beak, talons, large wings, and feathers in flight. Tawavaya (2017) concurs and observes that there are many snake figures and anthropomorphs with round bellies that signify pregnancy and fertility. The majority of snake figures is on the east side wall, which is closest to the stream bed.

Some human-looking figures in other areas of the canyon and at The Steps may be Rain Priests, shamans who underwent a spiritual transformation in order to bring rain. Unequivocally there appears to be a strong relationship with humans, animals, and water at The Steps and at most petroglyph locations. The rake, streaks, zigzag lines, wavy lines, lightning, clouds, water serpents, snakes, frogs, turtles, and tadpoles can be rain or clan symbols or both to Hopi. Many rain symbols denote power and prayer to Native Americans (Figure 3.13). The Hopi word *Yoyleki* means "falling rain," which would be depicted as lines radiating downward like a rake pattern. *Yoytatawlawu* translates as "Keep singing songs for rain" (Sekaquaptewa, Hill, and Washburn 2015:165).

The ubiquity of petroglyphs at The Steps predating the introduction of pottery (about 250 CE) is understood and explained by the evidence of Archaic and BMII visitation and occupation. These long-term visitations are manifest as projectile points, archaeological sites with features and ground stone, and radiocarbon dates recovered from burned features in these sites located within 1 km of the east side of Chevelon Canyon and along its

a. (Photograph by Darlene Brinkerhoff).

b. (Photograph by Rupestrian CyberServices).

Figure 3.13. Rain priests.

major tributary, Bell Cow Canyon. These are summarized in Chapters 5 and 9. Such detailed archaeological context connecting petroglyphs to other archaeological material is not present in such abundance anywhere else.

Modifications

Many of the Majestic Style figures are modified by additional grinding of circular shapes 2–4 cm deep and 2–6 cm in diameter, making them lighter in color compared to the image. With their depth and the presence of three or more degrees of re-patination on and around the cupule areas, grinding was apparently repeated over hundreds of years. These modifications are typically in the chest, stomach, hand and foot areas, and occasionally on the head or horns (Figure 3.14). Most researchers believe these are intended to extract the power of the image for the benefit of powerful individuals (perhaps shamans) or groups (Berrocal 2011). For example, extensive grinding on a large Majestic Style image of a woman giving birth may have been intended to transfer its power to a human in need of help by prayer.

Pueblo Period

From 1000–1150 CE (Pueblo II) a new petroglyph tradition is apparent in the LCR area and at The Steps. These human and animal figures are smaller and more solid-looking, sometimes outlined and not as decorated as in the BM Majestic Style figures. The less ornate forms depicting humans during this period may be due to a time necessitating more social interaction among larger groups, a more sedentary lifestyle, which included an increase in farming, construction of dwellings, and changing religious practices. It is likely religious specialists declined in significance or disappeared altogether and were replaced by farming groups where individual power was not emphasized. Images from this period depict flute players, parrots, other birds, snakes, cloven-hoofed animals, more female figures with Hopi hair whorls, and anthropomorphs

a. regrinding of zoomorphic glyphs (photograph by Darlene Brinkerhoff).

b. regrinding of anthropomorphic glyphs (photograph by Rupestrian CyberServices).

Figure 3.14. Modifications to glyphs by grinding.

that exhibit extended hair, with a decrease in headdresses, and some with bow and arrows instead of atlatls and masks/headdresses. These pueblo period style petroglyphs are not prevalent when compared to the earlier Basketmaker Majestic style representations at The Steps. To the east in the PEFO region, the PII period was a time of expansion and population growth, which may have started in the BM III Period (McCreery and Malotki 1994:33). The recent survey of RAR found little evidence of this period locally, perhaps explaining its relative absence at The Steps.

Between 1150 and 1250 CE (the PIII Period), the middle LCR area experienced significant population growth that was accompanied by a highly stylized petroglyph tradition (Cole 1990; Schaafsma 1980). These petroglyphs include highly decorated human and animal forms, as well as complex geometric iconography, which was probably associated with the increase of stylized pottery and textile designs during this period. This practice continued through the Pueblo IV (PIV) Period (1275-1400 CE), and also included an increase in katsina and deity depictions. A majority of katsinas and deities are considered to be spirit guides and messengers, links between earth and the spiritual world (Parsons 1939).

It is evident that the earlier style petroglyphs are primarily upstream of The Steps in Chevelon toward the Mogollon Rim and that the glyphs appear to be more recent as one travels north toward the LCR, which could be indicative of the migration of early farmers to their current locations, manifested at Chevelon and the Homol'ovi Pueblos.

Clan symbols began to appear during the PIII and PIV Periods, at a time of increased population, settlement size, agriculture, and social and political ceremonialism (Bernardini 2007). The Lower Chevelon area features PIV late style petroglyphs, including a bird figure with a spirit line or breath, fluteplayers, and a complex geometric, which may have been depicted by the Chevelon Pueblo occupation inhabitants from 1290–1400 CE (Figure 3.15). The occasional PIV style glyphs at The Steps and discovery of Jeddito Yellow Ware pottery at several nearby sites confirms the continued significance of the canyon and its resources (Figure 3.5b). This tradition was noted by Hopi working for Fewkes at Chevelon Pueblo in 1896 (Fewkes 1898, 1904).

Historic

Historic glyphs occur, many as names with dates, and attempts were made to identify the individuals, for example, "Dietz's - 33." Frank Robert Dietz was born between May 21-23, 1912 in Winslow, Arizona to Frank and Hattie Dietz (Figure 3.16a). The elder Frank Dietz was born in Germany in 1882 and moved to Winslow in the early 1900s. He worked for the Santa Fe Railroad and married Hattie May Mooney of Winslow in 1905. They had four children (Arizona Memory Project 2019 [Winslow Mail, 1921]). Frank Jr. was about 21 years old in 1933 and is the probable person of this inscription. Frank Jr. was listed in the Winslow High School yearbook at age of 16 and was listed as a dish washer in the 1930 U.S. Federal Census. At age 28, Frank was employed at AT&SF Railroad, like his father, and is then listed in a U.S. WWII draft card from 1940 to 1947. Frank passed away on February 23, 1976 in Contra Costa, California (Ancestry.com 2019: Arizona Births and Christenings, 1909-1917; U.S. School Yearbooks,1900-1999, Winslow, Arizona, 1929; U.S. Federal Census, Winslow, Arizona; U.S. WWII Draft Cards, 1940-1947); California Death Index, 1940-1997).

"Henry Anzures 5/7 1942," is another historical marker located at The Steps (Figure 3.16b). Henry G. Anzures was born February 16, 1905 in Bernalillo, New Mexico and died in

a. breath line within bird (photograph by Darlene Brinkerhoff).

b. flute player (photograph by Darlene Brinkerhoff).

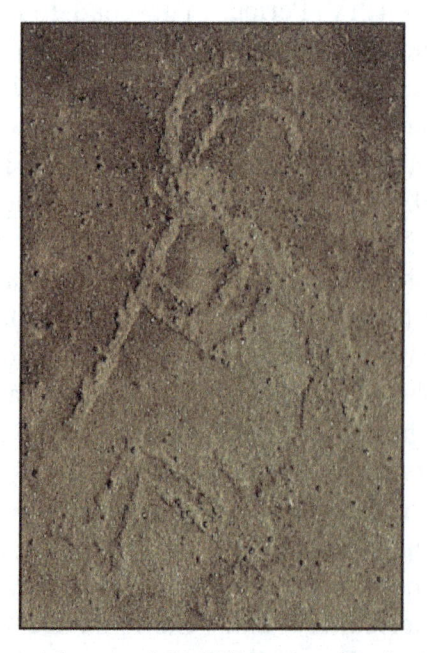

c. flute player (photograph by Will Tapp and Leslie Wertz).

Figure 3.15. *Pueblo Period flute players and breath lines.*

a. Dietz's -33-.

b. HENRY ANZURES 5/7/1942.

c. CE CARMACK July 4/.1941.

Figure 3.16. Historic glyphs (photographs by Darlene Brinkerhoff).

1969 and is buried in the Holbrook Cemetery. He would have been about thirty-seven years old at the time of this marking in the canyon, and he may have worked for or with my grandfather during this time (Ancestry.com 2019: US Find a Grave Index, 1600-current). More information about Henry as a student in nearby Holbrook, Arizona was found in the Arizona Memory Project (2019): Holbrook News in Navajo County, dated November 7, 1914, Vol.6, Issue 23, pg. 1: "The interest taken even by the fourth-grade pupils is truly encouraging, while playing in the common before the south school, Juan Garcia and Henry Anzures chanced to find a ten-dollar bill and checks amounting up in the thousands of dollars. The boys promptly gave their find to Mrs. Trammel, their teacher, who reported the fact to William Morgan who had lost the little sum. Mr. Morgan felt so elated over the recovery of his lost wealth that he set up treats to the entire school." In 1940 Henry registered for the draft in WWII. He listed his employer as Manual Candelaria whose family was also from the New Mexico and Concho and St. Johns, Arizona areas. Many of the Candelarias and Ortegas married and retained land and stock together as well as business ventures.

The name of "CE CARMACK July 4/. 1941" has been harder to identify as no one by that name lived in the general vicinity of The Steps (Figure 3.16c). There is a Charles Earl Carmack, also called Charles Earl, born about 1886 in St. Louis, Missouri. He lived in Denver, Colorado, married Mary L. Higson in Greely, Colorado on May 18,1910, and lived in several places in California. He died on July 9, 1954 and is buried in Redondo Beach, California. He was a veteran in WWI according to his Draft registration card of 1917-1918. In one occupation he is listed as a truck driver and in another he is listed as a chauffeur in California. This would make Charles Earl 55 years old at the time of inscription. (Ancestry.com [2019]: Birth, Marriage, and Death Records,1849-1980; Colorado, County Marriage records and State Index, 1862-2006; US Headstone Applications for Military Veterans, 1925-1963).

There was also a Charles Edgar Carmack born about March 1, 1901-1902 in Crocker, Missouri, USA, and was one of six children. He was registered on a WWII Draft card on February 16, 1942 at the age of 40, with his spouse as Dora Ann, father Jesse Carmack and mother Tressie Jane Carmack, as well as a son, Donald Clay Carmack. He died on July 29, 1977 and is buried in Crocker, Missouri; he would have been 39 or 40 years old at the time of the 1941 inscription. His occupation was not found.

A Charles Edward Carmack was born on May 2, 1892 in Orange Co. California married Bonnie Hope on July 11, 1939. He died on March 16, 1956 in Orange County according to the Ancestry.com (2019): Find a Grave Index, 1600's–current. He would have been 49 years old at the time of inscription.

Finally, a Charles E. Carmack was born on June 2, 1912-1913 in Denton, Missouri to James Edward Carmack and Sarah Jane Carmack. He was one of seven children in the 1930 U.S. Federal Census and resided in Rural, Oklahoma during the 1940 Census. He died on March 2, 2000 and is buried at Anutt, Missouri. His spouse is listed as Mary M. Carmack. He would have been 29 years old at the time of etching in Chevelon Canyon. That presents four possible Carmacks, but if I were to guess which one, there is a good possibility that the first one, Charles Earl, sketched his initials and date in the canyon, because he was a truck driver and chauffeur and probably traveled from Colorado and Missouri to California along Route 66.

Conclusions

We may never acquire absolute dating techniques to date these images. Similarly, we may never know their actual purpose, but descendant communities and groups who still make petroglyphs can provide insights. It seems likely the petroglyphs were left for both descendants and spiritual beings who inhabit the canyon. Anschuetz and others (2002:3.5) mention a poem written by Acoma poet, Simon J. Ortiz that "examines the spiritual connections that Native Americans have with special places in their lives and on their landscapes." Native Americans respect their petroglyph cultural landscapes. Cajete (in Anschuetz et al. 2002:3.25) commented that petroglyph areas are a center and healing place which "serves to transmit the energy of the peoples' thoughts and learning into the underworld and across time into the future." And, it is here that the Pueblo people wrote down their visions and messages to be communicated to the spiritual world. (Anschuetz et al. 2002:3.25; Slifer 1998:129-130). It is further believed that petroglyph rocks are keepers of a message and are alive (Anschuetz et al. 2002:3.25). Cole (1990)

Figure 3.17. Water serpent carving from temple in Mexico (photograph by Darlene Brinkerhoff).

states that many "Western Pueblo petroglyphs have ritual significance, depicting ceremonial personages and religious symbols" (see also Fewkes 1892; Parsons 1939:359-360). The association of petroglyphs and their sacred places is vital to Western Pueblo culture, and "dense concentrations of petroglyphs often are interpreted as special places in the landscape" ... "they validate the continuity between the ancient past and contemporary ceremonies, thus reinforcing the connections between the landscapes and petroglyphs" (Schaafsma 1992:13-14).

As non-Pueblo observers, we continue to call these etchings "petroglyphs," "sites," and other likely inappropriate names, and can only make inferences about their meanings. However, descendant communities offer the best interpretation of these enigmatic images. By themselves or in combination these symbols may indicate territory, clans, maps, food storage, water location, vision quests, hunting, seasons, ceremonies, altars, shrines, prayers, warfare, astronomy, proper balance in the universe, and probably metaphorical meanings. Serpents in Hopi are believed to bring about renewal and fertility in nature, including rain (Parsons 1939). Water serpent symbolism is widespread and are of religious significance in Aztec and Mayan cultures (Figure 3.17). Many other water icons such as waves, lightning zigzags, clouds, water birds, rake patterns, frogs and water serpents, which can be evident or metaphysical appear to be highly represented at The Steps. What appear to be water lines leading vertically down to the water source in various locations are frequently deep and heavily worn. These types of petroglyphs allude to rain and water and may have been invoked upon by later groups who passed this way.

The physical location of the stone images on the landscape in the canyon were no doubt crucial to the people who made them. No doubt their placement, size, and associations were meaningful (see following chapter by Doery). The choice to place them in the canyon with a permanent stream and associated plants and animals is most significant as a referent. The continued visitation and addition of images to The Steps suggests it was a significant and known place on the landscape for millennia.

The fact that preceramic groups left the area for lengthy periods yet retained memory of this place further underscores its significance and the sharing of knowledge when these groups gathered with others. Their location in a canyon also means the glyphs were not visible until literally at the canyon's edge. If necessary or desired, this location could have hidden The Steps from members of the group, if the images were too powerful or harmful.

The Steps and similar places preserve the legacy of people who traveled from many directions and stayed to pay homage and add to the narrative on the walls. By accessing and paying homage to these areas today, present cultures can promote preservation of these places, which offer the opportunity for transmitting knowledge and meaning to their descendants.

We can deter human-caused destruction but not natural degradations, although many Hopi believe that natural deterioration was set forth for a purpose and should continue. If the ancestors will it, then it must be accepted. At present these images have been documented for future generations in order to instill reverence, gain enlightenment and understanding, and as a significant learning tool to be interpreted by the successors of the people who made them and appreciated by all.

I believe that there were a substantial number of additional glyphs at the Steps at one time, but many have already been erased by floodwaters carrying very large timbers and debris. This action has made the white patina-less walls more evident on the eastern side of the canyon bends, which continues to wear away. It is remarkable, however, that the majority of petroglyph images have withstood the ravages of time and weathering over the centuries.

It appears that the vast majority of anthropomorphic petroglyphs at The Steps are of BM Majestic Style and by archaeological evidence in this region date to 1000/800 BCE to 250/500 CE (Cole 1990; Malotki 2007; Schaafsma 1980; Weaver et al. 2000). Presently, I am not aware of another place within the middle LCR area that reveals so many human or animal figures that exhibit the degree and depth of additional grinding modifications. I was informed that there are some glyphs with this additional cupule modification on the Hopi Reservation (Berggren 2018). The modifications on "The Mother of Game" (previously called birthing scene), the glyph of a rain cloud with lightning and other modified figures, confirms that a continual practice was taking place. This modification may be a shamanistic prayer for rain, water, game, and welfare, and a tribute to the ancestors made through pilgrimages and prayer. This would give credence to the theory that The Steps is of main importance to the pueblo people as a monumental and enigmatic place of worship, as well as being a tabloid of cultural migration and interaction. Chevelon Canyon and the "LCR area does not stop being significant to the associated tribes and continues to be a place of worship to this present day" (Polingyouma 2018).

The runoff, seeps, and springs in Chevelon not only provide life as vital sources of water and as natural cleansers but invite all the flora and fauna which culminate in provision of the essentials of food, clothing, and other natural sources for existence. Water is essential for all people and cultures to nourish and sanctify life. In the parched landscape within which it resides the water in Chevelon Canyon serves as a divine life energy that deserves to be coveted, prayed for, and payed homage to.

FUTURE WORK

The life stories of many occupants of the LCR areas and north to the Hopi Mesas are exhibited on the petroglyphs and recorded for future generations, but there are other petroglyph areas in Chevelon Canyon and its tributaries which have not been recorded. Such recording would help us to better understand the regional history and add to the ancient footsteps that represent migration in Hopi culture and are of historical importance. Additional work on clan symbols at The Steps and elsewhere could increase the cultural understanding of their migration patterns.

A vital task will be continual protection from vandalism to preserve the landscape for all cultural associations. These images have survived eons and hopefully will survive into the future so that they can chronicle who created them, and reflect the people who hunted, gathered, farmed, and subsisted on this plush environment. It seems imperative to continue to bring descendant groups to these areas to inform the present successors or ritual leaders about their past, to help reveal their futures, and to teach their progeny the need to succeed and carry on their practices.

Acknowledgments

My acknowledgments are numerous; however, I am most grateful to the many who helped with knowledge, editing, photography, suggestions, files sharing of data and patience on my behalf. I will list my family first and utmost, especially my spouse, Terry, for without him my work would have been impossible. A special thanks to E. Charles Adams for giving me an opportunity to assist in researching the Chevelon and LCR projects and to Richard C. Lange for his endless patience and instruction in many archeological facets. An additional thanks to Adams and Lange for the many years of research that they have performed in this Northeastern section of Arizona while directly and indirectly educating me for 30 years about this unique area along the Middle Little Colorado River. An appreciation and thank you goes to Doug Johnson for opening my eyes to petroglyph variations, to Don E. Weaver Jr. for his archaeological tutelage of mapping, to Brantley Baird and Family for their continued support through the years and opening up their home to us, Peter J. Pilles Jr. for expanding my development of archaeological theory, to Krystal Britt, Jaye Smith and Danielle R. Soza for their work and friendship in the advancement of Rock Art Ranch investigations, to Evelyn Billo and Robert Mark with Rupestrian CyberServices for their sharing of data and stewardship of rock art locations, to William Reitze and Melyssa Huston, (archaeologists of Petrified Forest National Park) in sharing information, to Jon Harman for his invention and curation of his D-Stretch Program, Diane E. Souder, Management Assistant of Petroglyph National Monument, William Collins, Program Coordinator (National Register of Historic Places, SHPO, Arizona State Parks), Dr. Miles Gilbert, Ken Zoll, Bernie Jones, Darrell Fillippe, and Eugene Verin for their assistance in the field. A special thank you to Francie M. Payne for editorial assistance and to Yolanda Lincoln for computer assistance. To Dennis & Sky Roshay and Gloria Kurtzhal for many years of their brother/sisterhood in the field, while trekking to new and old locations. And to all the photographers that contributed to my research photos, which credits are listed below. If I have failed to remember someone, it wasn't intended, so please accept this extra special thank you.

Photo Credits

Darlene L. Brinkerhoff
Sandy Haddock
Patti Mozillo
Chris Rhoads
Dennis Roshay
Rupestrian CyberServices, Evelyn Billo & Robert Mark
Will Tapp & Leslie Wertz

Chapter 4
Accessing the Audience: An Interpretation of Panel Seven at The Steps
Mairead K. Doery

Introduction

The petroglyphs of Rock Art Ranch (RAR) have fascinated generations of visitors to The Steps (or, Baird's Chevelon Steps). Likewise, the images have been the subject of years of archaeological inquiry, with many scholars presenting unique ideas about their significance (Hays-Gilpin 2003; Kolber 2000). Works that examine petroglyphs and pictographs across the Colorado Plateau, in the greater Southwest, and beyond, often focus on interpreting petroglyphs in terms of iconographic imagery, forming speculations about the role of petroglyphs in societies past based primarily on their visual design (Malotki and Weaver 2002). Considered far less frequently in the search for meanings of these images is the influence of environmental context and how petroglyph placement relates to a landscape's role in facilitating social actions.

In the preceding chapter, Darlene Brinkerhoff reviews the time frame and iconographic traditions of the petroglyphs at The Steps. In this chapter, I examine one petroglyph panel at the site to interpret the social activity of its Archaic and Basketmaker residents. Approaching The Steps and the greater RAR study area from a cultural landscapes perspective, I view the canyon's petroglyphs as important aspects of the site's landscape which play a role in turning the natural space into a cultural place. By analyzing the landscape-based visibility and accessibility patterns of these petroglyphs, as well as their iconographic design, I produce an understanding of the relative publicity of the images that make up the panel. I use the term "publicity" to describe the relative size and scale of the audience able to view each petroglyph. I then employ data about that audience in conversation with ethnographic information to present a series of interpretations for the panel's role in the cultural landscape of The Steps. I also provide suggestions for future research at RAR to extend current understandings of the use and meaning of these treasured images. Though a complete understanding of the original meaning of these images will never be achieved, by using a combination of iconographic documentation, landscape-based analysis, and ancestral ontology, I argue that detailed, evidence-based interpretations of the petroglyphs at Chevelon Canyon can provide important information about the inhabitants of the RAR area.

Petroglyphs and the Cultural Landscape

Archaeologists use cultural landscapes theory to cast light onto the ways that landscapes situate and shape social activity (Kuwansisiwma and Ferguson 2004). Human alterations to natural landscapes—including the creation or modification of a petroglyph—construct environments that influence the actions of those who view and interact with them. The reasons for these alterations have often been lost by the passage of time, making the role of petroglyphs in cultural landscapes difficult to comprehend. However, the physical placement and landscape context of petroglyphs can be made measurable in ways that add to understandings of their function and meaning. Wright (2014), for example, has operationalized petroglyph audience size in terms of landscape visibility, making the argument that images situated in very visible contexts were meant to be viewed often, which positions them as representative of community-level knowledge.

Building on this approach, I operationalize petroglyph publicity as a landscape variable defined by visibility *and* accessibility. Like Wright, I see landscape visibility as indicative of the scale on which petroglyphs were intended to be viewed – be it regularly by a large audience, or only by a select few with knowledge of its location or the ability to find it. Petroglyph accessibility in a landscape, on the other hand, is a determinant for the identity of its creator. I view images created in low access contexts (such as on rock surfaces removed from known trails, or deep in remote rockshelters or caves) as being made and modified by only those positioned in the right network of cultural knowledge to have physical and social access them. Petroglyph creators play an important role in the manifestation of an image in a cultural landscape, thus, the idea that there may be a restriction on who had the power to create an image is an important aspect of its interpretation. This makes the analysis of landscape in addition to iconography a crucial part of petroglyph interpretation.

Assessing Petroglyph Publicity

To produce a relatively representative sample of petroglyph publicity and iconography at The Steps, I analyzed all petroglyph panels at the site that contain at least one example of repecking. Brinkerhoff (this volume) draws on the original 1990s documentation of The Steps to categorize the site's petroglyphs primarily into galleries, which divide the canyon's walls into forty sections (see Figure 3.3). I discuss the site's images in terms of "panels," or groups of petroglyphs clustered together in one landscape context, differentiated from other panels by distance or landscape features. The motivation for categorizing petroglyphs into panels comes from the idea that petroglyphs are placed together in ways that communicate an idea or create a narrative scene, much like motifs on objects of material culture.

For each panel sampled, I recorded the distribution of individual human-like anthropomorphic figures, animal-like zoomorphic figures, abstract geometric designs and all instances of repecking. To assess the publicity of the petroglyphs, I rated the panel in terms of its visibility and accessibility, or the ease with which it is physically accessed. Ratings were made on a relative 3-point scale as high (most easy to view/access), medium, or low (most difficult to view/access) in relation to other panels in the sample. Importantly, the degree to which petroglyphs are visible or accessible differs with one's physical location relative to each panel. My analysis of petroglyph audience and meaning accounts for these variances by describing publicity in terms of these differing locales.

THE STEPS AT ROCK ART RANCH

As previously mentioned (Brinkerhoff, Chapter 3), The Steps is an approximately 1,000 meter-long bend in Chevelon Canyon, so-named for the natural "steps" on the canyon's eastern wall. One of several canyons flowing into the Little Colorado River in the RAR research area, Chevelon Canyon once offered an abundance of important resources for the surrounding landscape. As a permanent source of standing water, the canyon sustains a variety of flora and fauna types in and around The Steps (K. Adams, Smith, and E.C. Adams, Chapter 2). These and other raw material procurement areas make the RAR area a "total landscape" capable of supporting human occupants for hundreds of years (Colwell and Ferguson 2014; Soza, Chapter 9).

While the relatively hidden quality of the entrance to The Steps positions the site as somewhat restricted in access, the extended timespan and magnitude of its petroglyph assemblage indicate that the site was accessed frequently. Projectile points from Clovis through late Paleoindian and early and middle Archaic periods evidence similarly diverse and prolonged use of the larger RAR area by preagricultural groups. The material origins of these points suggest that the earliest visitors to the area were both local groups and immigrant populations (Soza, Chapter 9). Architectural, ground stone, lithic, and ceramic evidence further show that the RAR area was continually visited, if not occupied, by Pueblo people until 1600 CE or later (Lange et al. 2017). Some Hopi people consider these archaeological remains to be "footprints" of their ancestors, which make the landscape an important mediator in the relationship between the past and the present (Kuwanwisiwma and Ferguson 2009). The petroglyphs that dot the walls of The Steps are indicative of a continued connection to the canyon by those who frequented the RAR area. Such a relationship makes the interpretation of the petroglyphs at The Steps all the more important to the study of the RAR area and the activities of its inhabitants.

THE HERD AT THE STEPS

With 212 petroglyphs, what I am designating as Panel 7 is the most densely populated panel at The Steps by nearly 40 petroglyphs. Panel 7 includes some (but not all) petroglyphs in galleries 7, 8, 9, and 10 (Brinkerhoff, Chapter 3).

Over the course of my analysis, I have chosen to call this panel "The Herd" based on the multiple rows of large quadrupeds that are prominently featured in its center. Other smaller zoomorphic figures, anthropomorphic figures, and geometric figures appear on the panel as well. The majority of these petroglyphs has been dated to the Archaic and early Basketmaker time periods using iconographic, stylistic analysis (Cole 1990; Kolber 2000; Schaafsma 1980). As Brinkerhoff (Chapter 3) has described, many of the petroglyphs of The Steps bear evidence of modification after their initial creation, including extensive grinding into portions of the images. Many of The Herd's petroglyphs have been "repecked" in this fashion (Figure 4.1).

Visibility

The majority of The Step's thousands of petroglyphs is placed along the canyon's walls, such that they can be easily viewed by anyone standing inside the canyon, at the base of the canyon wall. Based on their size and density, panels like The Herd are impossible not to notice by those who descend into the canyon. This is not necessarily true for those who do not enter the site but stand above it on the canyon's east or west sides. Because the canyon's walls slope downward and the entire landform bends inward to the east, views of the petroglyphs are obscured for those standing on its eastern side. Those standing on the western side of the canyon have a clearer view of the petroglyphs on the eastern walls, including The

Figure 4.1. Petroglyphs from The Herd at the Chevelon Steps, some with repecking and grinding indicated by solid fill (figures not to scale).

Herd. However, since the natural "steps" that provide access to the bottom of the canyon are located on its eastern side, those standing to the west without knowledge of their location may have been able to see the petroglyphs, but had no ability to take a closer look at them. Likewise, those standing to the east without prior knowledge of the "steps" theoretically could have found their way into the site, but were less likely to, given that they could not see the petroglyphs below.

Given the large size of many of its petroglyphs and their higher placement on the canyon's walls, The Herd is arguably one of the site's most prominently placed panels. Drawing on Wright's (2014) logic, I view the central placement of this panel as an intentional effort of its creators to assure its importance. While those who could enter the canyon were meant to view the petroglyphs, those who could not, no matter which side of the canyon they stood on, did not have the same detailed degree of visibility. Therefore, The Herd's high visibility and publicity was limited to those with cultural knowledge of the location and purpose of the gap in the canyon's walls that lead down into The Steps.

Accessibility

Though all those with the ability to enter the canyon may have been able to view The Herd, accessing the panel was a much more restricted task. Given its extraordinarily high placement on the canyon walls, I faced initial difficulty in determining how The Herd's creators (both those who made the petroglyphs, and those who repecked them) would have reached the panel. After careful examination of a large boulder to the left of the panel, I realized that it could be climbed by placing one's feet and hands in specific grooves along its edge. Once atop the boulder, I encountered an array of worn steps seemingly constructed through its frequent use as a staircase, in a similar fashion to the "steps" that lead into the site itself (Figure 4.2). The panel's steps, which are not visible from the ground, leads onto a flat surface directly in front of The Herd, from which the petroglyphs can easily be reached.

I view the relative inaccessibility of these petroglyphs as the product of another intentional choice made by the panel's creators. While the petroglyphs of The Herd were meant to be seen by many, they could only be physically reached, added to, or repecked by those with knowledge of how to find and use the steps that lead to it. The concealed nature of these steps lends itself to the interpretation of this group as a smaller, select group of individuals. After all, if the panel was meant to be accessed by all, why would it have been created in a place so difficult to reach?

Iconography and Publicity

Taken together, these observations can be used to form an understanding of the publicity of The Herd's petroglyphs. Given their placement in the landscape of the canyon—both in relation to its natural features and other petroglyphs at the site—the panel's petroglyphs boast high visibility, making the sight of them a largely public affair. However, the nature of the "steps" leading to it give the difficult-to-reach panel a low access rating, or a low publicity level of access. While seeing The Herd may have been meant for all those with access to The Steps, few among them could physically interact with the images.

Intriguingly, the ledge that provided a place to stand for The Herd's creators also served as an extension of its canvas. Atop the ledge is a small assemblage of petroglyphs. These images, along with a few others located in the crevices along the canyon's walls, are in close enough association with The Herd to be considered a part of the narrative but are not visible to those who admire the panel from the ground (Figures 4.3 and 4.4). They can only be viewed by those with the access to the panel that the ledge provides; in other words, the publicity of this group of petroglyphs is far more limited than that of the more visible group.

When compared, the visible assemblage of The Herd's petroglyphs and its more concealed images (which make up 17.5% of the panel's total assemblage) differ significantly in iconography, gender, and modification frequency. I review these differences below (Table 4.1).

Iconographic Type

Though zoomorphic figures represent the largest iconographic category of The Herd's petroglyphs, they represent a much smaller portion of the concealed assemblage than of the visible petroglyphs. This is a statistically significant deviance from expected frequencies (chi-square [df = 1, n = 75] = 16.042, p < 0.000). In a similar vein, geometric designs make up a significantly greater proportion of the concealed group than they do of the visible assemblage (chi-square [df = 1, n = 28] = 24.414, p < 0.000). These trends position the iconography and image meaning of The Herd as tied to petroglyph placement. While the panel's visible assemblage is characterized

Figure 4.2. Hidden access "steps" to the Herd panel at the Chevelon Steps; the panel is low on the cliff face to the left, see Figure 4.3..

4: Accessing the Audience—Panel Seven 75

Figure 4.3. The Herd panel at the Chevelon Steps, on the cliff face near the bottom of the photograph, just above the ledge with the diagonal bedding. The solid long arrow on left indicates the location of the hidden "steps" up to the panel, see Figure 4.2. Shorter arrows show the locations of the panel's concealed petroglyphs, ie, petroglyphs not visible from this perspective.

76 Doery

a. looking left, downstream.

b. left of center, on horizontal surface

c. looking right, upstream.

Figure 4.4. Concealed petroglyphs of The Herd.

4: Accessing the Audience—Panel Seven 77

Table 4.1. Statistical Trends Between the Visible and Concealed Groups of The Herd's Petroglyphs (statistically significant differences are shaded).

Publicity		Anthropomorphic Figures			Zoomorphic Figures	Geometric Designs	Modified		All Sampled Petroglyphs
		Sexed/ Gendered	Not Sexed/ Gendered	Total			Repecked	Total	
Visible	N	16	75	91	68	16	31	50	175
	%	17.6	82.4	52	38.9	9.1	17.7	28.6	82.5
Concealed	N	9	9	18	7	12	12	15	37
	%	50	50	48.6	18.9	32.4	32.4	40.5	17.5
TOTAL	N	25	84	109	75	28	43	65	212
	%	22.9	11.1	100	100	100	20.3	30.7	100

by zoomorphic figures, the concealed, less accessible assemblage employs more geometric designs. Such patterns indicates that those with the ability to reach the panel were meant to view different types of imagery than those without restricted access, an intention perhaps rooted in a difference between the significance of the concealed images and the more public, visible icons.

Anthropomorphic Sex/Gender

Approximately 13 percent of the site's anthropomorphic figures have sex or gender marked by anatomic (penises, vaginas, or breasts) or cultural features (hair whorls, a hairstyle worn by Hopi women). While The Herd's visible petroglyphs are sexed/gendered only somewhat more than expected (given site-wide proportions), the concealed assemblage includes a significantly high percentage of sexed/gendered anthropomorphic figures (chi-square [df = 1, n = 109] = 8.934, p = 0.003). Similar to the differences in iconographic type, this suggests that the role and meaning of The Herd's anthropomorphic petroglyphs may differ depending on the location of the images.

The idea that those with the heightened level of cultural knowledge needed to access the panel would be able to view more petroglyphs featuring sex/gender traits indicates the marking of sex/gender was an intentional choice made by petroglyph creators. It may be that sexed/gendered anthropomorphic figures play a role in a different type of cultural information, which, in this case, was only meant to be seen by a select few visitors to The Steps.

Modification Frequency

Based on field analysis targeting all instances of repecking at The Steps, I estimate that approximately 6.5 percent of the site's petroglyphs are repecked. In comparison,

17.7 percent of The Herd's visible assemblage and a whopping 32.4 percent of its concealed assemblage are modified in this way. The unexpectedly higher frequency of repecked petroglyphs in the more restricted concealed assemblage is a statistically significant deviance from regular patterns (chi-square [df = 1, n = 212] = 4.092, p = 0.043). This trend emphasizes once more the potential differences in the role of The Herd's visible and concealed iconographic images based on locational placement. Since the panel was only physically accessible to those with knowledge of the hidden "steps" that lead to it, a limited number of the panel's viewers would have had the ability to create and modify the panel. Furthermore, most of those modifications were not visible to those without such access. This positions petroglyph repecking as playing an important role in the landscape of the site, meant only to be accessed and seen by a select few with the power to do so.

Interpreting The Herd

This analysis illustrates the importance of considering iconographic design *and* landscape placement in the study of petroglyphs at The Steps. Publicity trends for the images of The Herd indicate that landscape visibility and accessibility factored into decisions about where to place the panel in the canyon. The size and identity of the groups meant to view, access, create, or modify the panel's individual images was also taken into consideration in the creation of the visible and concealed petroglyph assemblages. These choices, which can only be assessed by operationalizing landscape-based placement, are important to take into account when interpreting The Herd's role in The Steps and RAR landscapes, given that they reflect aspects of the intended meanings of the images.

In the following section, I incorporate Pueblo ontologies surrounding the use and importance of landscapes and petroglyphs into this analysis in order to form interpretations of the panel's images and roles. Given the ancestral connections documented between Chevelon Canyon, the RAR area, and the Hopi tribe, I primarily make use of Hopi ethnography in this section (E. C. Adams, Chapter 1; Fewkes 1898, 1904). It is important to note that the majority of the petroglyphs that make up The Herd was created in Archaic and early Basketmaker time periods, which precede the identification of a historically-defined Hopi culture. It has been established that the northeast Arizona landscape, which includes RAR, has been continuously occupied since at least the Basketmaker II era; the Hopi are said to have descended from these populations (Bernardini 2005).

Although forming direct links between this area's Basketmaker II residents and the modern Hopi tribe may not be possible archaeologically, Hopi tradition depicts an ineffable continuity between themselves, the landscape, the petroglyphs, and these early peoples. While empirical connections between Hopi and larger Pueblo ontologies cannot be precisely made with The Steps, their traditions remain a rich source for expanding possible explanations of the petroglyphs' meaning. They should not only be taken seriously but also as required considerations in the interpretation of this site.

Power

No discussion of landscape publicity and petroglyph audience would be complete without a consideration of power. Power is what divides those who can or are meant to view certain landscape features from those who are not. The group who knew of the entrance to The Steps could see more than 80 percent of The Herd's petroglyphs just by descending into the canyon. Those without this knowledge who traversed the east side of the canyon could stumble upon the "steps," but were unlikely to seek them out, given that they could only see very few of the site's images from above. Many more petroglyphs, including some from The Herd, were visible from the west side of the canyon, but those who found them would have difficulty getting a better view, given that The Steps' entrance is located on the opposite side.

These varying levels of petroglyph visibility indicate that The Herd's publicity level was determined by a tiered system of social and geographical knowledge. In order to get a good view of the panel, one would need to know how to access the site itself, as it is unlikely that those who travelled above the canyon that did not know of the expansive petroglyph site below would have found their way to it. The power to descend into The Steps and see the canyon's images may have come with membership to a specific social group, by aging into a specific societal role, or even through completing a certain societal rite of passage. Whatever the case, it would seem that all those with the power to enter the canyon also had the power to see the visible petroglyphs of The Herd, given the panel's central placement and general ease of viewing in the canyon.

Landscape accessibility similarly relates to individual power. Physical access to The Steps was restricted, but the ability to reach the petroglyphs of The Herd was even more restricted, limited to those who knew of the concealed "steps" leading to the panel. Possessing the power to come within touching distance of the panel was necessary to create or modify its images. It also came in tandem with visual and physical access to the panel's concealed assemblage of petroglyphs, which exhibited far different iconographic patterns than the visible group.

Once more, it is difficult to say exactly how and why certain visitors to Chevelon Canyon gained the power necessary to see and touch all of The Herd's petroglyphs, including those with the lowest publicity. Still, based on the panel's low level of accessibility, and the concealed petroglyphs' low level of visibility, it would seem that there was a significant power imbalance between those with full access to The Herd and those without. The group with heightened access was likely more elite, as they were privileged with abilities to see and interact with the images in ways that others were not. Given the panel's intentional placement in an area of high visibility, they also may have held a degree of power *over* those who could only view The Herd, to whom they may have communicated directed messages to through the panel (Bradley 2009; Wright 2014). Such a power imbalance between audiences of these Archaic and early Basketmaker petroglyphs may indicate the existence of long-held status differentiation within groups in the RAR area, where a select group was able or meant to view the imagery of The Herd, but only a few of them were able to directly interact with or modify the panel.

Tradition

Traditions allow individuals and communities to maintain connections with the past, whether it be through repeating a ritual throughout time or interacting with relics of the past with some regularity (Van Dyke and Alcock 2003). As with all Pueblo and non-Pueblo groups, Hopi view the continuation of traditions as an important aspect of modern life. For the Hopi in particular, maintaining a connection with the landscape through traditional activities sustains the wellbeing of the tribe and its relationship with the past, the future, and the most important resources of the Earth (Kuwanwisiwma and Ferguson 2009).

At The Steps, petroglyph traditions are

apparent in the revisitation of images after their initial creation, visible in the form of repecking. Pueblo people have long conceptualized petroglyphs as physical bridges between the landscape, ancestral creators, and modern community members (Bernardini 2005). Because of this, interacting with petroglyph-marked landscapes and the images themselves has been viewed as a proxy for connecting with Ancestral Puebloan ancestors (Colwell and Ferguson 2014; Schaafsma 1980; Young 1988). By grinding into the images created by those who came before them, visitors to The Steps made physical connections between themselves and their ancestors, reinforcing images into the landscape in the same place as before.

Repecked images appear quite commonly on The Herd in the panel's visible assemblage of petroglyphs and even more frequently in the concealed assemblage. Though it is difficult to date episodes of repecking, differing degrees of patina between modifications of the panel (including, in some cases, differences in repatination between modifications of a single image) indicate that repecking was practiced by many visitors to the canyon over a long period of time. Although Hopi tribal members continue to return to the canyon to this day (Lange et al. 2017), it is difficult to say whether the interactions they have with the canyon's petroglyphs mirror those of the site's ancestral visitors, or what sort of meaning those previous actions might have had. However, based on the evidence of historical revisitation and reengagement with the petroglyphs of The Herd, it is likely that The Steps resided in the social memory of descendant groups, influencing the canyon's ancestral populations to return to these images of the past. This positions The Herd as serving as a significant link between petroglyph creators and modifiers and their ancestral past, making the landscape one of historical importance for the site's most elite visitors throughout time.

Spirituality

In the Pueblo worldview, religion does not exist as a separate sphere of life, but is often indistinguishable from daily activities that would be viewed as secular in the Western world (E.C. Adams 1991; Fowles 2013). Because of this, attempts by Euro-American archaeologists to define the meaning of ancestral Native petroglyphs as conclusively linked to religious ideology are tautological at best. While the Hopi view religion and landscape as entirely connected (Kuwanwisiwma and Ferguson 2004) and the presence of petroglyphs mark the landscape of The Steps as a sacred place in the Pueblo tradition (Cole 1992; Schaafsma 1997), it is difficult to articulate an idea in Western thought that explains why. Though I cannot step fully into the Ancestral Pueblo worldview, nor describe it to an archaeological audience by making use of descendant voices, ethnographies, and syntheses of those who have done it prior, superficial categories of sacred iconography can be relied on to describe the spiritual content of The Herd's images.

For example, Kelley Hays-Gilpin and Jane Hill (1999) have asserted the existence of a linguistic and iconographic "Flower World" in early Southwestern and Mesoamerican culture. The Flower World is described as a spiritual domain, home to the souls of the deceased and evoked through images of flowers, birds, and rainbows. While Hays-Gilpin and Hill report a virtual absence of Flower World imagery in this region prior to 1300 CE, rayed, flower-like geometric figures, bird tracks, and rainbow images all appear in the petroglyph assemblage of The Herd. Squiggling, zig-zagging, and wavy lines, which are viewed as representative of the movement of wind and water between past and present worlds, also appear. So do spirals, which are judged as symbolic of Ancestral Puebloan movement in a migratory journey from their emergence place to their spiritual center (Schaafsma and Davis 1988). Hays-Gilpin (2003) has also connected the symbolization of sex/gender in anthropomorphic Pueblo figures to gender roles in religious ritual, arguing that petroglyph panels that include sexed/gendered anthropomorphic figures often articulate a narrative of spiritual content. Many of The Herd's anthropomorphic figures have clear sex/gender delineations, features which may distinguish them as spiritual representations.

It is notable that the concealed petroglyph assemblage of The Herd displays significantly greater amounts of spiritual iconography than is found in the panel's more visible areas. Geometric figures like those described above and sexed/gendered anthropomorphic figures are more common among the group of concealed assemblages—those that publicity analysis indicates required more power to view. It has long been established that landscapes containing watersheds, from which they first emerged, hold religious significance for the Hopi (Eggan 1994; Fewkes 1906). Given that a higher degree of geometric water signs and other forms of spiritual iconography are found in the concealed assemblage of this central panel, it is possible that The Herd plays a spiritual role in the lives of not only its canyon-wide audience, but its elite creators and modifiers.

The panel's concealed images are repecked more frequently than the visible petroglyphs. Studies of the panel's publicity indicate that this is an act that could only be participated in by those who possessed the level of access and knowledge necessary to physically reach the images. Recall that repecking petroglyphs is viewed by Pueblo people as a method for physically and mentally connecting with one's ancestors and the past. The idea that repecking The Herd was a traditional activity but was restricted to those with a high level of power, and its results were concealed from larger view, positions the action as all the more spiritually significant. Perhaps repecking the panel reinforced one's social status or place in the universe, or provided a particularly special connection to the Flower World through one's ancestors. Whatever the case may be, it stands to reason that the role and meaning of the imagery of The Herd, when considered in terms of both iconographic and locational data, may well have represented or reinforced the spiritual ideology of its creators and modifiers.

Conclusions and Future Directions

The interpretations described above are lacking in specificity and authority; this is entirely intentional. Due to large time gaps in history, the loss of traditional knowledge, and preservation deficiencies, the exact meanings of ancient petroglyph images and panels are frequently indefinable. By taking landscape and iconographic data into consideration, an understanding of petroglyph visibility, accessibility, and publicity can be achieved for The Herd at The Steps. When informed by ethnographic and ontological perspectives of Ancestral Pueblo knowledge, this information allows for the formulation of several possible interpretations of the panel's use by and meaning for the site's Archaic and Basketmaker visitors.

To gain a fuller understanding of the significance of this landscape and its petroglyphs, this study could be extended to include a site-wide analysis of the canyon's petroglyphs in terms of their publicity. There are also a number of locational factors that the current analysis has not taken into consideration. Acoustic studies of petroglyph landscapes target the degree to which certain sounds—including human and animal activity, and natural sounds like those of wind and water—can be heard at different locations.

Connecting auditory experiences to the publicity of the canyon's petroglyphs could provide nuanced information about the locational context of certain images. Viewshed analysis has also become an important part of landscape archaeology. Analyzing the types of landscape features and other images visible from each petroglyph panel produces new understandings of the visual connotations of each set of images. This too can lead to more detailed interpretations of the overall significance of the site's imagery.

Whatever their focus may be, further studies of the petroglyphs at The Steps must take into account the landscape context these images are found within. The importance of natural, cultural, and petroglyph landscapes to Pueblo peoples throughout time is well documented. Given that significance, understanding individual petroglyphs and panels in terms of their placement within a specific landscape adds salient detail to their interpretation that iconographic study alone cannot provide. Information gleamed from petroglyph study about the social activities of visitors to The Steps contributes to larger knowledge of the communities that occupied the RAR study area. Because of this, considering petroglyphs like those of The Herd in terms of their landscape context adds critical detail to the story of RAR.

Chapter 5
Archaeological Surveys and Testing In and Around Rock Art Ranch, Northeastern Arizona

Richard C. Lange, Samantha G. Fladd, and E. Charles Adams

SURVEY AND FIELD METHOD

Archaeological surveys were conducted each of the field seasons at Rock Art Ranch (RAR) from 2011-2016. Each summer, two to three survey crews operated daily, consisting of a supervisor and three to five students. Survey was designed to provide 100 percent coverage of the properties by using systematic transects with individuals at 10-meter intervals. Natural boundaries, such as fence lines, roads, and canyons, were used to define survey areas. Where physically possible, the edges and bottoms of canyons were included in the survey, which resulted in the identification of several previously unrecorded petroglyphs.

Experiments with the students showed that using the compass functions on the Global Positioning System (GPS) units to align transects was less than satisfactory. We used toilet-paper (TP) flags in bushes and grass clumps to mark edges of each transect to make it easier to follow the alignment on the return transect and ensure complete coverage. We tried to maintain spacing between crewmembers at ten meters—paced off and measured off with a tape. Regularly, with the GPS units, we found crews crossing over the TP lines, or major "bends" or "dog-legs" developing in the middle of the transects. However, with a simple magnetic compass (e.g., a Silva Ranger or Brunton), it was possible to keep the crew walking relatively straight lines in the transects. The simple magnetic compass also required far less time to "check" for orientation and direction. The GPS units were valuable, however, for recording coordinates for isolates, and for recording the datum and boundaries of sites and loci.

Each survey crew used a Garmin GPS unit to document isolates and sites encountered during transects. GPS units were set to either North American Datum (NAD) 27 or 83 with the setting carefully noted. Each site location was translated between the two settings to either plot onto existing USGS 7.5-minute topographic sheets (NAD 27) or import into ArcGIS software (NAD 83). Fortunately, it is possible to translate between the two coordinate systems easily. Unfortunately, they do give very different results in this area of the Colorado Plateau, so the translation from one projection to another is very important depending on what the data will be used for (in converting in the RAR area from NAD27 to NAD83, the NAD83 Easting is NAD27 + 64 m, the NAD83 Northing is NAD27 - 200 m).

All isolated material culture was recorded with a GPS point that listed the number and types of materials found at a given spot. Isolated artifacts were collected when deemed diagnostic (e.g., projectile points), rare (e.g., yellow ware ceramics, obsidian), or when in-field identification was not feasible (e.g., misfired ceramics).

Sites were defined based on observations of artifact density and diversity. Thus, a site would not be identified if it contained only several artifacts of the same type or a small number of different artifact types. When multiple discrete sites were identified in a similar setting and/or appeared to be contemporaneous based on the artifacts present, the same number was used with a letter appended to the end to designate separate loci (e.g., RAR-98A, RAR-98B, RAR-98C). Loci were also employed to designate definable temporal components of overlapping or congruous sites where possible. Ultimately, any field site within 100 m radius of another was grouped under one AZSITE number. For example, one site, AZ P:2:146(ASM), representing a massive Basketmaker II (BMII) lithic scatter, has 24 loci and includes 7 field sites. These concordances are detailed in Appendix I.

Collections or in field analyses were made at all sites and loci recorded by the survey teams. Small or low-density sites were collected from within the boundary with the goal of providing a representative sample of the materials. Rare or diagnostic materials were point located when encountered. Collections for larger sites or those of sufficient density involved the definition of collection units. Between one and ten units were defined at each site consisting of a five-meter diameter circle within which all materials were collected. The number of collection units varied as they were dependent upon the size and complexity of the site. For dense, more spatially extensive loci, five-by-five-meter grids were placed over identified midden areas with every other grid square collected by the survey crews. Each collection unit was numbered and labeled on site maps.

Site maps consisting of site limits, feature locations, collection units, and isolates were done in several ways. The technique used to produce site maps depended upon the density and expanse of each site. There were four methods used: 1) for very small scatters that were not collected with collection units, a center point was taken with the GPS unit and maximum expanses north-south and east-west measured with a tape; 2) a Brunton compass on a tripod and tape was employed to map sites that involved collection units and point located artifacts; 3) the GPS units were used to mark site boundaries and the location of collection units and point located artifacts for certain sites; or 4) highly complex or expansive sites were mapped using a total station. Site descriptions together with the map were recorded on special forms developed for the RAR Field School based on standard Arizona State Museum AZSITE site forms.

Ceramic types, projectile point types, and lithic technology were used to assign dates/developmental periods to each locus listed in Appendix I. Many loci were determined to be temporally multi-component due to mixtures of temporally diagnostic ceramic types and out-of-phase diagnostic projectile points. Temporal designations are abbreviated as follows: BMIII = Basketmaker III, PI = Pueblo I, PII = Pueblo II, PIII = Pueblo III, and PIV = Pueblo IV.

All collected artifacts were initially processed at an in-field laboratory. This included cleaning and initial documentation. Further detailed analyses of the collected materials were completed at the Homol'ovi Lab of the Arizona State Museum, University of Arizona, Tucson. Based on an agreement with the landowner, Brantley Baird, artifacts from RAR were on temporary loan to the Arizona State Museum (ASM) until the completion of the project. Excepting a representative sample donated by the Baird Family that are now a part of the permanent collection of the museum, the remainder of the artifacts collected from the ranch property have been returned to RAR. Under written agreement with Aztec Land

and Cattle (AZLAC), artifacts collected from AZLAC property by the RAR field school have been deeded to ASM and added to its permanent collections.

PROJECT RESULTS

A total of 247 loci representing 193 field sites and, ultimately, 147 sites entered into AZSITE, was identified and recorded by the combined surveys conducted by the RAR Field School from 2011 to 2016 (Table 1.2). This total includes full coverage survey of the RAR property and a portion of the adjacent property owned by AZLAC (AZLAC-Adjacent) totaling 5.65 square miles (3,616 acres) with 187 loci from 141 field sites reduced to 106 AZSITE sites (Figure 5.1). Additionally, a section (640 acres) 15 km south of RAR associated with Multi-Kiva Pueblo (AZ P:3:112[ASM]–FN-37) was 100 percent surveyed with 20 sites recorded. Three sites south of the survey section, two sites located along a major canyon east of Multi-Kiva (MK) Pueblo, and another three sites with seven loci near the Little Colorado River (LCR) 5 km north of the RAR-Core were also recorded but no additional survey was involved (designated AZLAC-Far North). These project areas are illustrated in Figure 1.4.

The Rock Art Ranch Area (RAR-Core)

Survey of the RAR-Core documented 88 sites whose locations and areas are entered into AZSITE from two townships and parts or all of eleven sections under ASM AAA permit 2011-029bl and ASM Accession AP-2012-0321 (Appendix I). The 88 sites in AZSITE represent 116 field sites and 158 loci originally recorded by the field school (Figure 5.1, Table 1.2). Total surveyed area in the RAR-Core was 4.65 sq. mi (12.04 sq km) or 2976 acres for a field site density of 19.1/sq mi and density of loci of 34.2/sq mi. Additionally, several thousand isolates—primarily sherds and lithics—were also documented and located using GPS (see Figures 5.2-5.8).

Site frequency (Table 1.1) is dominated by three periods: Preceramic (Late Archaic and early agriculture/BMII, 800 BCE-600 CE), BMIII/PI (600-1025 CE), and PII/III (1100-1255 CE). Additionally, three artifact scatters dating to the PIV period were recorded on sites dating to early periods. Distributions of the sites dating to these four time periods across the survey area are presented in Figures 5.9-5.12. Ceramic frequencies suggest a period of about 100 years (PII, 1000-1100 CE) when use of the study area dropped in intensity and may have been depopulated. Based only on site density, use of the area is the most extensive during the Late Archaic and BMII periods and concentrated along the edges of canyons. Evidence for habitation is in the form of pit houses during the BMIII/PI and PII/PIII periods with the addition of small pueblos in PIII. Population was low but comparable between the two periods.

Site density is very low until near Chimney, Bell Cow, and Chevelon Canyons (Figures 5.2-5.12). Between the canyons and the ranch were small (spatially), low-density scatters of sherds and flaked stone. Along the edges of the canyons are roughly 100-to-500-meter swaths of medium to high density nearly continuous artifact scatters of preceramic flaked and ground stone overlain by less continuous scatters of ceramic-period material. Density is highest along the lower half of Bell Cow Canyon and Chevelon Canyon towards the rock art site and is dominated by preceramic assemblages. Site numbers were assigned only to high density or diverse artifact clusters, often including metates, or where features were present (Appendix I).

Chevelon Canyon, differentiated from the others in the survey area by its depth and sharp drop-offs, was bordered by concentrations of

86 Lange, Fladd, and E.C. Adams

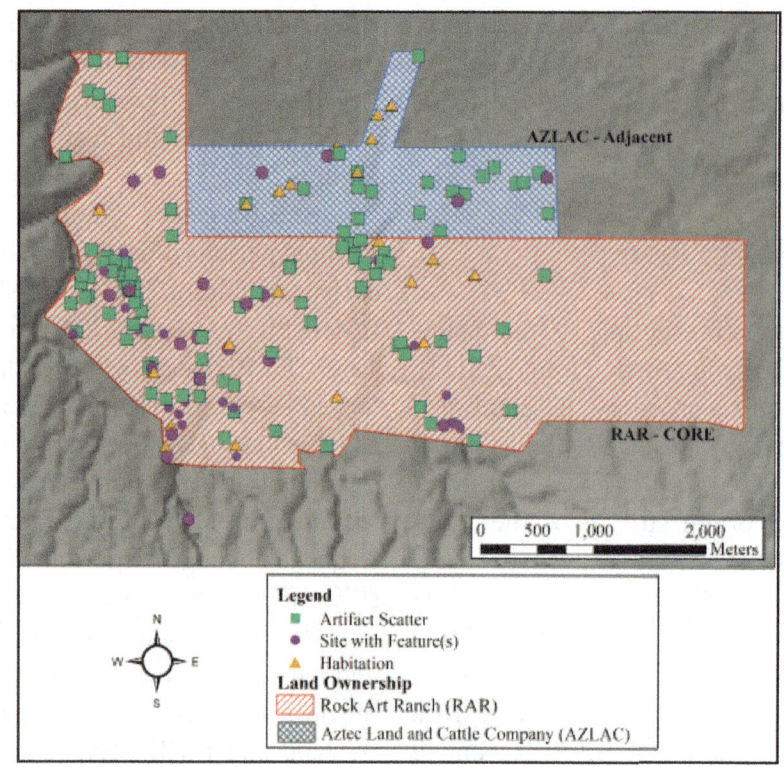

Figure 5.1. Sites identified in the Rock Art Ranch-Core and AZLAC-Adjacent areas; graphic prepared by Josh Conver.

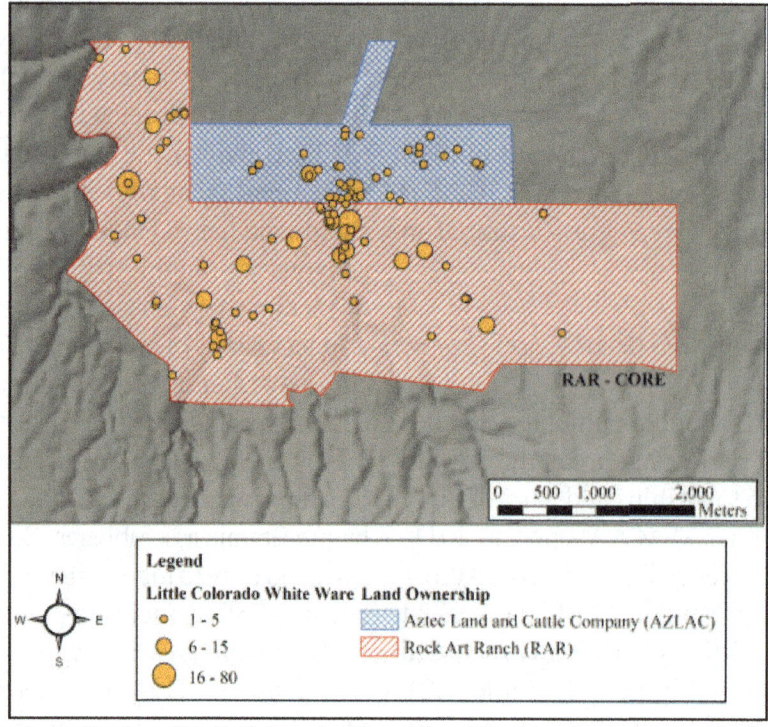

Figure 5.2. Distribution of isolated Little Colorado White Ware sherds in Rock Art Ranch-Core and AZLAC Adjacent areas; graphic prepared by Josh Conver.

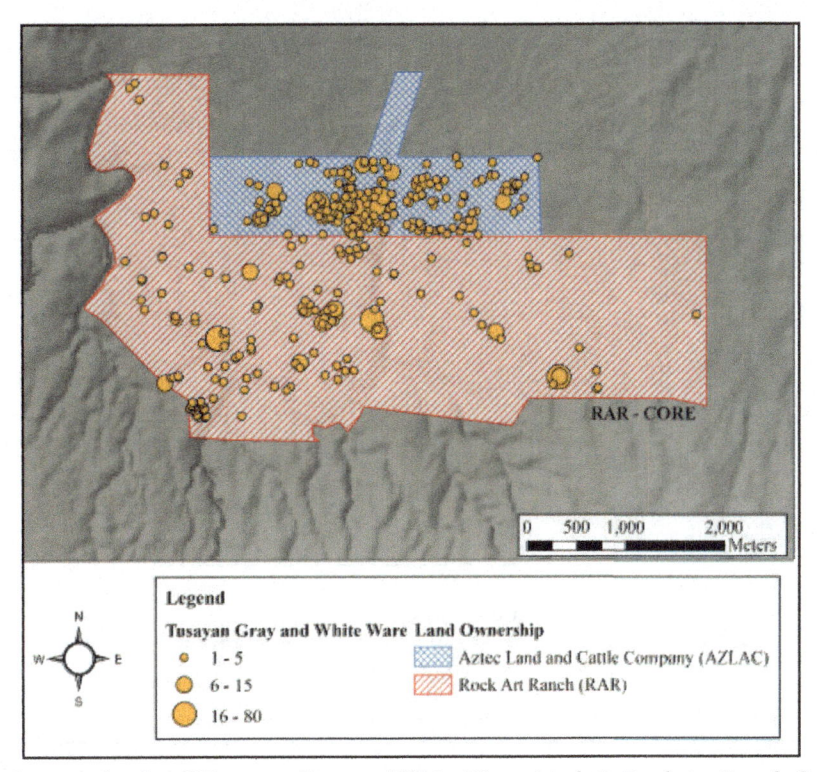

Figure 5.3. Distribution of isolated Tusayan Gray and White Ware sherds in Rock Art Ranch-Core and AZLAC-Adjacent areas; graphic prepared by Josh Conver.

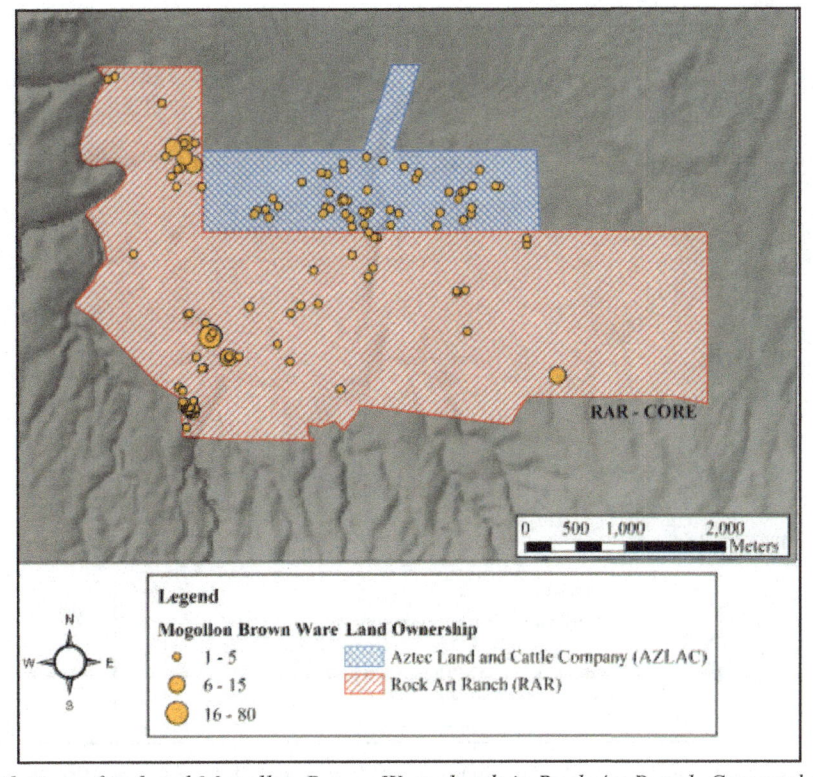

Figure 5.4. Distribution of isolated Mogollon Brown Ware sherds in Rock Art Ranch-Core and AZLAC-Adjaent areas, graphic prepared by Josh Conver.

88 Lange, Fladd, and E.C. Adams

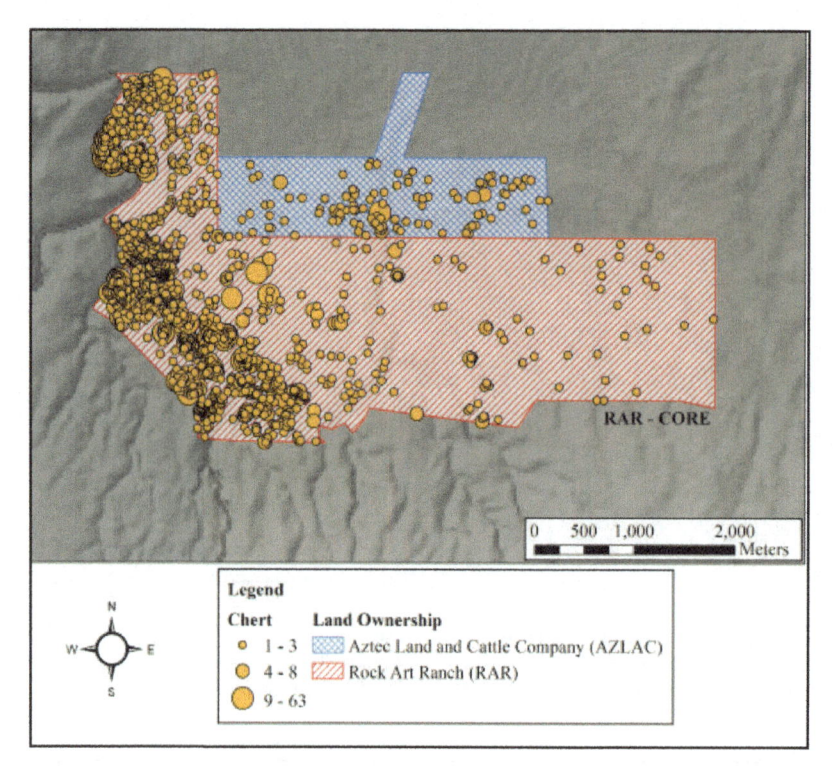

Figure 5.5. Distribution of isolated chert flakes in Rock Art Ranch-Core and AZLAC-Adjacent areas; graphic prepared by Josh Conver.

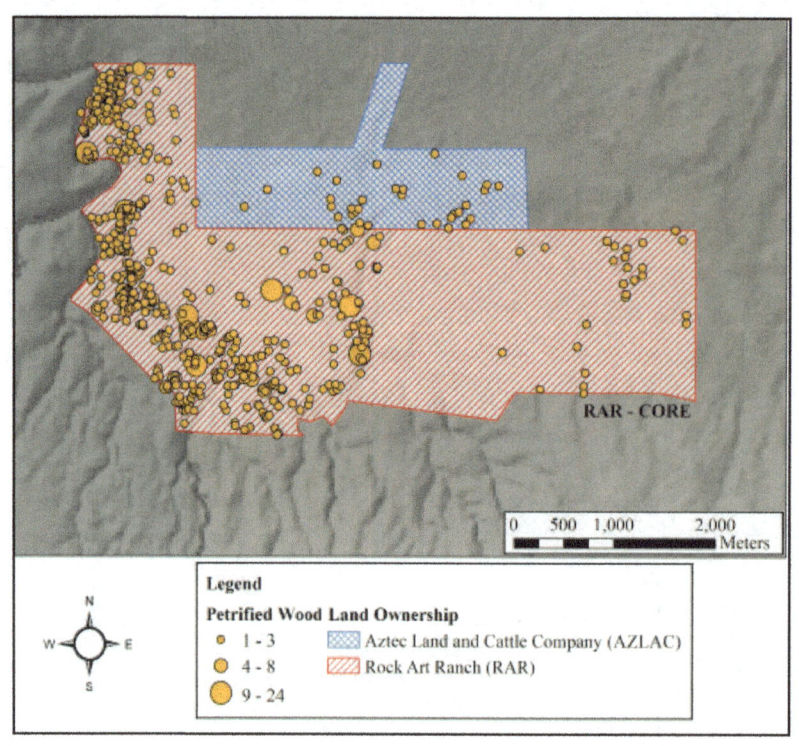

Figure 5.6. Distribution of isolated petrified wood flakes in Rock Art Ranch-Core and AZLAC-Adjacent areas; graphic prepared by Josh Conver.

5: Rock Art Ranch Area Surveys and Testing 89

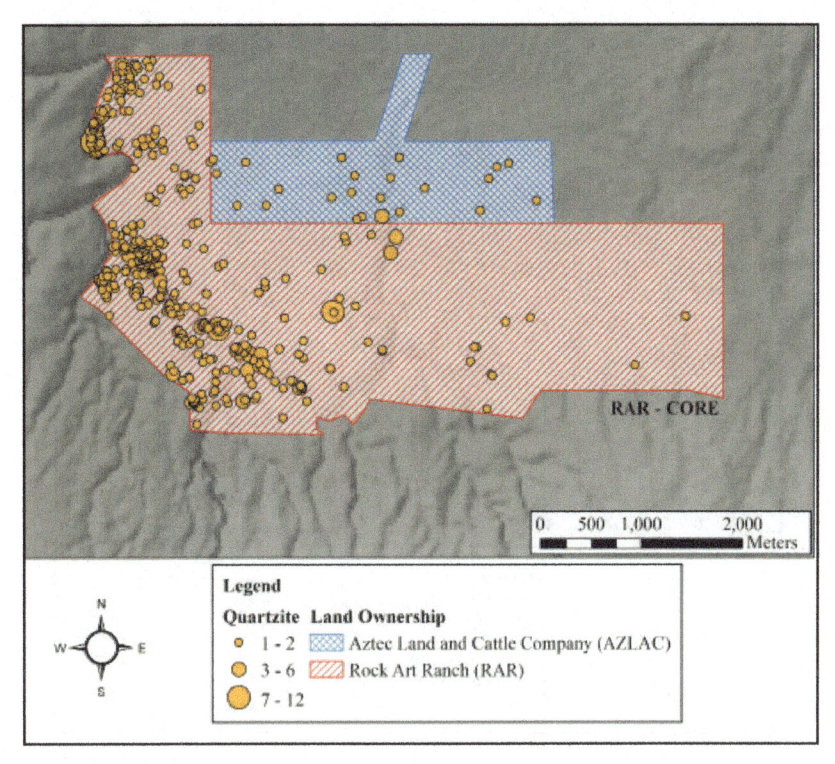

Figure 5.7. Distribution of isolated quartzite flakes in Rock Art Ranch-Core and AZLAC-Adjacent areas; graphic prepared by Josh Conver.

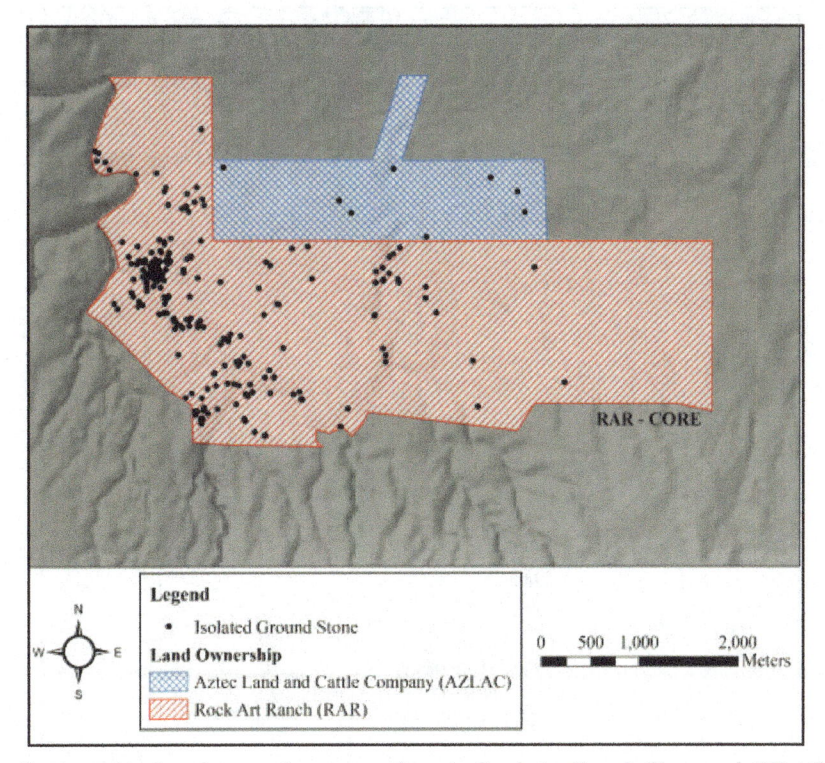

Figure 5.8. Distribution of isolated ground stone artifacts in Rock Art Ranch-Core and AZLAC-Adjacent areas; graphic prepared by Josh Conver.

90 Lange, Fladd, and E.C. Adams

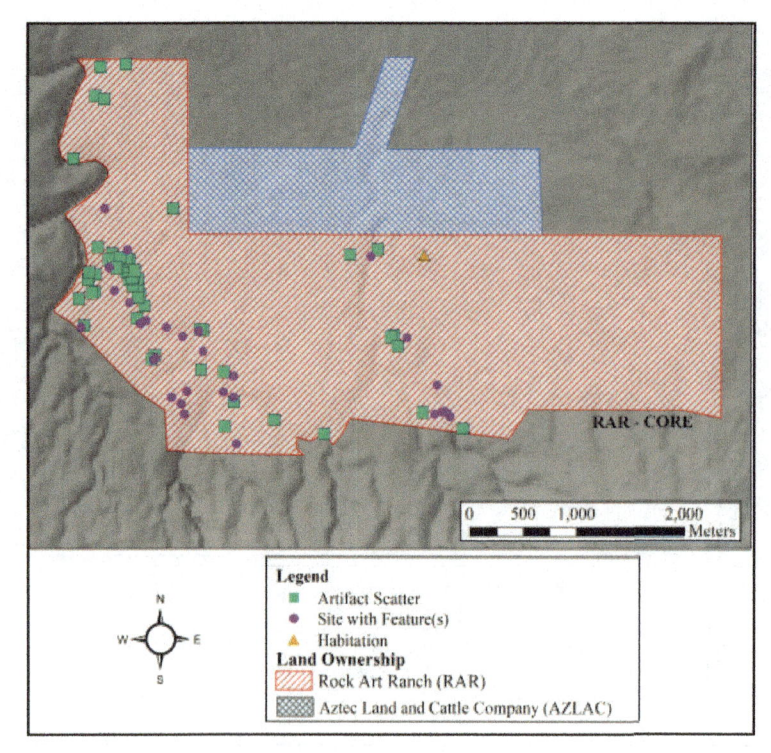

Figure 5.9. Distribution of preceramic sites in Rock Art Ranch-Core and AZLAC-Adjacent areas; graphic prepared by Josh Conver.

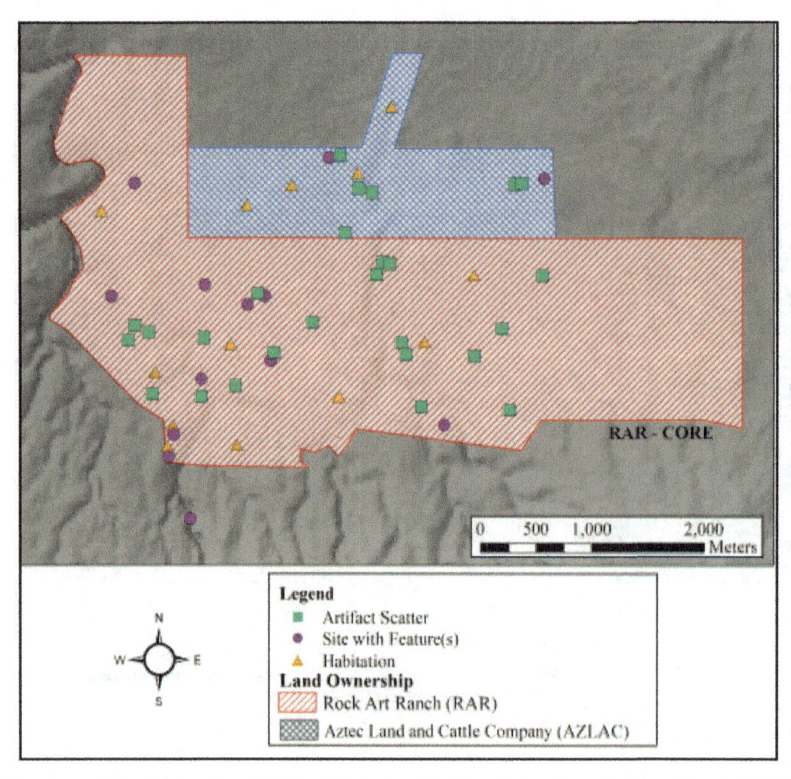

Figure 5.10. Distribution of Basketmaker III/Pueblo I sites in Rock Art Ranch-Core and AZLAC-Adjacent areas; graphic prepared by Josh Conver.

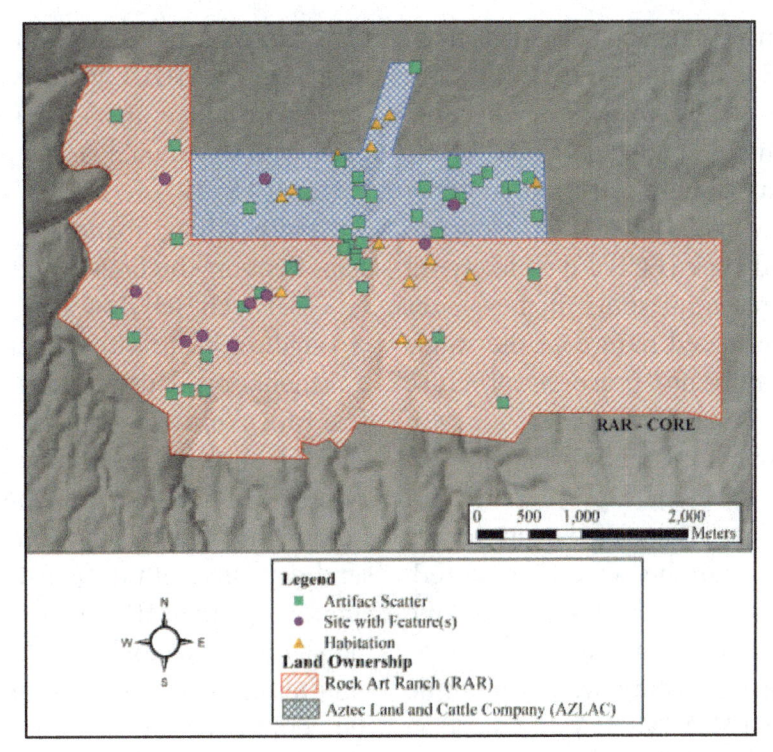

Figure 5.11. Distribution of Pueblo II/Pueblo III sites in Rock Art Ranch-Core and AZLAC-Adjacent areas; graphic prepared by Josh Conver.

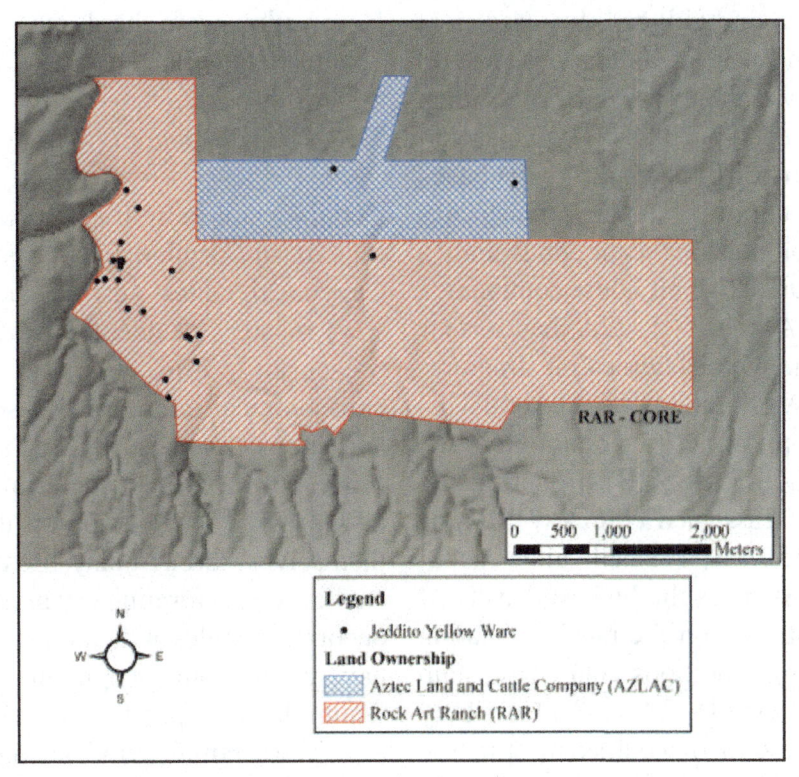

Figure 5.12. Distribution of Hopi Yellow Ware in Rock Art Ranch-Core and AZLAC-Adjacent areas; graphic prepared by Josh Conver.

early materials, many indicating Paleoindian use of the vicinity. For the numerous BMII sites, features were typically vertical or clustered burned or unburned sandstone slabs. These are interpreted as storage cists and cooking/roasting features with the latter often associated with fire-cracked rock (FCR). It is likely pit structures are present at some of these sites but the unconsolidated nature of the sands covering them may not preserve structure features without stone. During excavations of a 13th century pueblo, Brandy's Pueblo (AZ P:3:114[ASM]-RAR-2), a pre-ceramic pit structure and a dozen associated deep storage pits cut into the caliche were discovered, suggesting pit structures exist at pre-ceramic sites with features and dense artifact scatters. However, extensive testing around multiple features at AZ P:3:124(ASM)-RAR-12 found no traces of pit structures or intact stratigraphy beyond the features themselves.

Several habitation sites were recorded on small dunes and ridges, clustered near the canyons and near areas that appeared to be ideal for dry (rainfall-dependent) farming. These include small pueblos of 4-10 masonry rooms dating to PIII (1125-1255 CE) based on decorated ceramics located just north of the ranch boundary except for Brandy's Pueblo (BP). One large pit house community, AZ P:3:137A(ASM)-RAR-22A, has surface indications of numerous burned pit structures dating late BMIII into PI (700-1000 CE) and a smaller pit structure community (AZ P:3:137B[ASM]-RAR-22B) predating the small pueblos and assigned a PII/early PIII time range (1050-1150 CE). A small valley east of AZ P:3:137(ASM) has the highest density of sage and rabbitbrush on the ranch indicating ideal dry farming conditions. A large ash stain at AZ P:3:183(ASM)-RAR-68 also likely indicates the presence of a burned pit structure dating to BMIII/early PI. AZ P:2:104A-D(ASM)-RAR-4 located just south of Bell Cow Canyon, includes four loci belonging to a large BMIII/PI site with evidence of multiple midden areas, small above ground, jacal-wall style pueblos, and pit structures. AZ P:3:234(ASM)— RAR-123 is a small BMIII pit house village marked by several upright slabs denoting pit houses and storage features.

Between Bell Cow and Chimney Canyons is a shallow basin with higher outcrops capped by Moenkopi Sandstone to the north and south. The Moenkopi sandstone is also exposed as a low cliff above the Coconino Sandstone on the west side of Chimney Canyon forming the east side of the basin. The basin has deep, stable sand deposits with deeper dunes on the west supporting small BMIII/PI pit house sites and the shallower deposits on the east supporting long-term, small-scale, dry farming throughout the ceramic period (ca. 600-1255 CE) in the area. Sources of these populations appear to be the pit structure and pueblo habitation sites on high points surrounding the basin. Several Hopi yellow ware sherds recorded in the basin document continued use into the 1300s.

RAR-Core Ceramics Overview

Ceramics are more useful data for the many loci in and around RAR east of Chevelon Canyon; the sites west of Chevelon Canyon were mostly documented because they were pre-ceramic sites. Ceramics can provide chronological information based on ceramics and sites cross-dated by tree-ring dating and other chronometric techniques. Ceramics also provide information on the populations themselves, through clays, tempers, sourcing studies, vessel forming techniques, shapes, and decorative styles indicating where they may have come from (people and pots) and with whom the local population was trading.

The ceramic period pit house occupations begin in the general area along the LCR in BMIII times (after 600 CE; Lange 1998:43-

44, 148), and, somewhat different from other areas of the US Southwest, persist into the early 1200s. Stone-masonry pueblos generally begin later in this area (mid- to late-1200s) and quickly became the large late thirteenth and fourteenth century Homol'ovi villages that were the original focus of the Homol'ovi Research Program (HRP; E.C. Adams 2001, 2002, 2004, ed. 2016; Lange 1998, 2020). More evidence is being found, however, of overlapping pit house and pueblo occupations in the mid-1100s to early 1200s, such as at the late pit house villages and early puebloan Creswell Pueblo within the Homolovi State Park area, and especially in the RAR project areas documented in this report.

The ceramics from the RAR project area, and particularly from the ranch itself, can be better understood in the context of other ceramic assemblages. Table 5.1 notes the prevalence of wares shared among the project areas from Wupatki to the west, the Homolovi State Park (HSP) area to the northwest, the Hopi Buttes to the north, the RAR project area, and Zuni to the east (Figure 1.1). There are interesting similarities and differences in the proportions of wares in these various landscapes which appear to be related more to the phases of occupation and the trade/exchange networks operating at the time rather than pure proximity to the known or presumed sources. Homol'ovi has a strong presence of ceramics from the north during the latest period of prehistoric occupation (PIV) in the region. Such ceramics are largely missing from the Wupatki, Hopi Buttes, and RAR areas due to the general lack of occupation in those areas at that time. The dominant PIV ceramics in the Zuni area, however, are the White Mountain Red Ware (WMRW) types produced in closer proximity to Zuni.

The Wupatki, Homol'ovi, Hopi Buttes, and RAR project areas all have strong indications of Tusayan White Ware (TWW), Tusayan Gray Ware (TGW), Little Colorado White Ware (LCWW), and Little Colorado Gray Ware (LCGW; (Table 5.1); although LCGW does not occur as commonly in areas away from the Hopi Buttes. LCWW is more prevalent in the Hopi Buttes and at Wupatki than at Homol'ovi or RAR, but it is still strongly present there. Cibola White Ware (CWW) is distributed in decaying ratios from its production area to the southeast—lower percentages to the west at Wupatki and farther north in the Hopi Buttes, next lowest percentages at the HSP loci, and the highest percentages in the RAR loci, at over 30 percent of the loci in each of the RAR project areas detailed in Table 5.1. TGW is clearly an important commodity in all the project areas except for Zuni. Mogollon Brown Ware (MBW) is rare at Homol'ovi and in the Hopi Buttes, but is the most common ceramic type on RAR. As the closest other project area to RAR, the ceramics from HSP are presented in more detail in Table 5.2. TGW is clearly the dominant ware present there, with nearly equal percentages of Alameda Brown Ware (ABW), TWW, and LCWW. LCGW, Tsegi Orange Ware (TOW), CWW, MBW, and WMRW are present in much lower proportions. The most common ceramic types in HSP loci are indeterminate TGW and Tusayan Corrugated (Table 5.2b), following on the dominance of TGW in general. Little Colorado Corrugated is 8 percent of the types listed in Table 5.2b, no other type is greater than 5 percent of the HSP assemblage, with many types comprising 2 percent or less of the assemblage.

Ceramics in RAR-Core

Ceramics were analyzed from 80 survey sites and loci on RAR with the largest concentration from AZ P:2:104(ASM)–RAR-4 (Table 5.3). Counts from excavations at BP and AZ P:3:132[ASM]–RAR-17) are not included. MBW (30%), TGW (28%), and TWW (14%) are the most prevalent identified within the sample (Table 5.3), differing from ceramic isolates identified on the landscape summarized in Table 5.4. Combined percentages of TWW and TGW are similar between the RAR sites and RAR isolates (52% and 51%; Tables 5.3 and 5.4), but the differences are apparent in the percentages of Little Colorado wares (7% vs. 27%) and MBW (30% vs. 13%). Of the 80 loci with analyzed sherds, TWW occurs at 39 loci (49%; N = 862), TGW at 46 loci (58%; N = 1693), MBW at 39 loci (59%; N = 1789), and Puerco Valley Utility Ware (PVUW) at only 5 loci (6%; N = 295). Most sherds of TOW occur at a single locus (AZ P:3:153[ASM]–RAR-36) and at only five other loci (Table 5.3a and b).

The majority of Hopi yellow and Homol'ovi orange wares were from five loci: AZ P:2:105(ASM)–RAR-79, AZ P:2:150B(ASM)–RAR-113B, AZ P:2:169(ASM)–RAR-109, and AZ P:146T and U(ASM)–RAR-95B&C. Most of the yellow sherds that were found at loci or as isolates are located along Bell Cow and Chevelon Canyons and the density increases towards the rock art site (The Steps; Figure 5.12). Many of these appear to be pot drops. The conservation lab at ASM reconstructed one of these pot drops, an Awatovi Neckbanded jar with an interior design dating post-1400 (Figure 5.13). Almost all of the San Juan Red Ware (25 sherds) was found on AZ P:3:234(ASM)–RAR-123. No other BMIII/PI loci had more than a single San Juan Red Ware sherd. While the identified Tusayan sherds are more commonly gray ware (utility), the Little Colorado and Cibola sherds are more likely to be white ware (decorated).

Almost 1900 isolated sherds were documented, but not collected, during survey of RAR (Table 5.4). Tusayan wares account for 51 percent of the assemblage followed by large percentages of Little Colorado wares (27%) and MBW (13%; Figures 5.2-5.4). Combined, Alameda, Cibola, and Puerco wares account for only 13 percent of the total assemblage.

Ceramic types identified in the collections from the RAR sites are tabulated in Table 5.5. The MBW types (combined together N = 1662) are the most numerous (Plain = 863 and Corrugated = 799), followed by indeterminate TGW (N = 1403) and Tusayan Corrugated (N = 168; together = 1571). Two other utility ware types are present in only very low numbers (PVUW-Corrugated = 291; LCGW-Corrugated = 28). Among the principal decorated wares (TWW, LCWW, and CWW) TWW types are the most frequent (total N = 816, indeterminate TWW = 553, Lino B/g = 39, Kana-a B/w = 129, Black Mesa B/w = 86, Sosi B/w = 2, and Dogoszhi B/w = 7). LCWW types total 426, with counts of 307 for indeterminate LCWW, 21 for Holbrook-A B/w, 4 for Holbrook-B B/w, 13 for Padre B/w, and 81 for Walnut B/w. There are 270 CWW types, including indeterminate CWW = 178, Puerco B/w = 39, Escavada B/w = 16, Snowflake B/w = 21, and Reserve B/w = 16.

The ceramic assemblages from HSP loci, RAR, AZLAC-Adjacent, AZLAC-Far North, RAR-South, RAR-Southeast, and MK Site are summarized in Table 5.6. ABW is most strongly present in the HSP and AZLAC-Far North project areas, but is much less on RAR and other project areas. TWW is similar in proportions across all of the project areas in Table 5.6. However, among the other decorated wares, there are striking differences in the relative proportions of LCWW and CWW—the highest proportions of LCWW are in the RAR-South, RAR-Southeast, and MK Site project areas, while the highest proportions of CWW is in the RAR-South area. The proportions of utility wares also show the same sorts of differences. TGW is by far the dominant ware found at the HSP loci, and is strongly represented in the RAR and AZLAC-Adjacent project areas. It is somewhat less present in the AZLAC-Far North loci and much less frequent in RAR-South, RAR-Southeast, and at MK Site. The reverse is true for MBW, with very

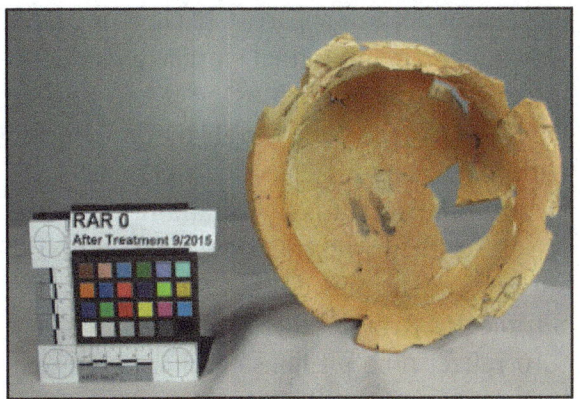

Figure 5.13. Reconstructed Awatovi Neck-banded jar with interior design dating post-1400 CE from Rock Art Ranch-Core area (photographs by Teresa Moreno, ASM Conservation Division).

low frequencies in the HSP loci, but prevalent at over 30 percent in the RAR project areas.

Different sources of population or changes in trade and exchange networks are suggested by the different proportions of wares—that themselves have different source areas—in the RAR project areas' collections. The different proportions of wares also suggest temporal changes in the area (Solometo 2004). A temporal component of these shifts in the RAR project areas is clearer when the ceramic types are more closely examined. A series of related tables explore these changes (Tables 5.7-5.10)—Table 5.7 compares decorated and utility types present at HSP and the various RAR project areas, and includes collections from all loci in these areas and sherds coded as "indeterminate" types; Table 5.8 compares decorated and utility types by habitation type (pit houses vs. pueblos) for the RAR project areas (sherds from general scatters or scatters with features are not included, but "indeterminate" types are counted); Table 5.9 compares only the decorated white wares (no "indeterminates" included) for HSP and the RAR project areas from all loci by time period; and Table 5.10 compares only the decorated white wares (no "indeterminates" included) for the different habitation types only (no scatters) in the RAR project areas by time period.

In Table 5.7, the RAR area is generally similar to the HSP and AZLAC-Adjacent loci while having less TGW, specifically a lot less Tusayan Corrugated, and a lot more MBW, specifically Brown Corrugated. Proportions of the BMIII type Lino B/g and PI Type Kana-a B/w vary between project areas—more Lino B/g relative to Kana-a B/w in the HSP and AZLAC-Far North areas; more Kana-a B/w relative to Lino B/g in the RAR, AZLAC-Adjacent, RAR-South areas (including at the MK Site—Tables 5.7-5.10). ABW types, as either Indeterminate ABW or Sunset Brown, are much more common at HSP loci. The next highest counts are in the AZLAC-Adjacent and AZLAC-Far North areas, although a variety of ABW types are present in all RAR project areas. Notably low frequencies of ABW (and only of Sunset Brown and Chavez Pass Brown) occur in the RAR-Southeast pueblos. Chavez Pass Brown is present in all project areas (HSP and RAR), and has the highest percentages of any ABW types except in the HSP and AZLAC-Far North areas where Sunset Brown (HSP) and Winona and Grapevine Brown (AZLAC-Far North) predominate (Table 5.7).

When the ceramic types are considered focusing on habitation type (Table 5.8), other differences become apparent. Except for BP, for which there are no formal surface collections, there are no other pueblos on RAR. For the RAR-South area, there is only the MK Pueblo with underlying pit house occupations; there are no other pit house communities in the RAR-South project area where intensive survey and formal collections were done. So, the RAR area tallies in Tables 5.8 and 5.10 reflect nine pit house loci from various early ceramic period occupations (Appendix I; Table 1.1): AZ P:2:140B&C[ASM]–RAR-4B&C; AZ P:2:176E[ASM]–RAR-119; AZ P:3:129[ASM]–RAR-14; AZ P:3:132[ASM]–RAR-17; AZ P:3:137A[ASM]–RAR-22A; AZ P:3:153[ASM]—RAR-36; AZ P:3:176A[ASM]–RAR-60; and AZ P:3:234[ASM]–RAR-123.

On RAR pit house loci are types reflecting BMIII occupations (Lino B/g) and even stronger PI and PII occupations, continuing on into PIII (Table 5.10). At the RAR pit house loci, Indeterminate TGW dominates the utility wares, with a small percentage (< 1%) of Tusayan Corrugated. ABW types are present in mostly low frequencies, but a higher percentage of Chavez Pass Brown that at any other RAR project area—by raw count or percentage. MBW is the second most frequent ware on RAR loci (after TGW), with a higher percentage of Brown Plain than Brown Corrugated (Table 5.8). In all other RAR project areas, Brown Corrugated occurs at higher percentages than Brown Plain (Table 5.8); this also includes the AZLAC-Adjacent area, where, although Brown Corrugated dominates the MBW types, there is a higher percentage of Brown Plain—trending toward the immediately adjacent RAR-Core.

Counts and percents from the excavations at BP are included in Table 5.10 for comparison. Compared to all other loci in the RAR-Core or just the pit house related loci there (Tables 5.9 and 5.10), there are no sherds suggesting a BMIII occupation, and only four sherds suggesting a PI occupation. There are also only a few sherds suggesting an early PII occupation from 1025-1100 CE, but many more sherds indicating occupation after 1100, including Escavada B/w, Puerco B/w, and Snowflake B/w—all CWW. BP shows a similar high percentage of PIII Walnut B/w when compared with other RAR project areas, however, the same or lower percentages of Walnut B/w occur at BP, at the RAR pit house loci, at the AZLAC-Adjacent pit house loci, and at the AZLAC-Far North pueblos, with much higher percentages of Walnut B/w at the AZLAC-Adjacent pueblos, the RAR-Southeast pueblos, and at MK Site.

Tables 5.9 and 5.10 have been noted in the preceding paragraphs, but several observations can be highlighted again. In Tables 5.9 and 5.11, the clear association of emphasis on BMIII occupations in the HSP and AZLAC-Far North and on PI occupations on RAR, AZLAC-Adjacent, RAR-South, and MK Site can be seen. As of PII times, CWW becomes more important in most RAR project areas (except for AZLAC-Far North), with percentages eclipsing the percentages of CWW at loci in HSP (Table 5.6). In Table 5.10, focusing on white ware sherds from different types of habitation loci, by both counts and percents, the BMIII and PI diagnostic types occur much less frequently in the MK Site in RAR-South—a temporally multi-component and mixed occupation of ceramic period pit houses and a pueblo. Walnut B/w, a LCWW, is clearly the dominant PIII decorated type in the HSP and RAR project areas.

Similar to the situation at HSP loci (Lange 1998), the PII and PIII occupations may be a mixture of different peoples with subtly different periods of occupations (even overlapping), different types of dwellings (pit houses vs. pueblos), and with different trade and exchange networks. Utility ware ceramics continue over time to come from the Hopi Mesas to the north (TGW), from the RAR-South and east (MBW), and from the Flagstaff area (ABW). In the RAR project areas, however, numbers of MBW sherds are equivalent to numbers of TGW sherds (RAR-Core) or far exceed those numbers (all other RAR project areas)—in stark contrast to HSP loci where TGW always predominates. Finally, in the RAR area, BP clearly stands out with less evidence of BMIII and PI occupations at that location (i.e., different from the MK Site) and strikingly higher percentages of CWW types in PIII times.

RAR-Core Flaked Stone

In the HSP area, 25 km downstream along the LCR from the RAR-Core, 91 lithic procurement loci were identified, that is, cobble exposures where raw materials were found and tested by the prehistoric inhabitants of the area (Lange 1998:16). Although the survey for the Park was four times larger than the RAR survey, the number of lithic procurement loci at Homol'ovi is far larger than the number at RAR (N = 91 vs. 3: AZ P:2:153A and B[ASM]–RAR-139A&B and AZ P:2:161[ASM]–RAR-57), reflecting the different geomorphological settings and histories of these two areas. The Homol'ovi area is downstream from RAR and is closer to the river—from right along the LCR to several kilometers back from the river. The RAR project areas (excepting the AZLAC-Far North subarea) are all many kilometers off the river. Although chert dominates the available raw materials (49%) as well as the flaked stone tools and debris at Homol'ovi (74%), quartzite is more prevalent at the loci closer to the LCR and chert is even more dominant in the uplands away from the LCR. There is little petrified wood or igneous material in the Homol'ovi loci (Lange 1998:65-69). Obsidian is rare in the Homol'ovi surface collections (N = 18, 0.07% of all lithic collections [Lange 1998:64]), but it is present in quantities in the PIV pueblos. At RAR, quartzite is the dominant raw material in the procurement loci (ranging from 57 to 60%) and igneous materials are present in greater proportions (Soza 2018:81-83).

There are low density scatters of cobbles on RAR, perhaps deflated from earlier surfaces. However, they do not appear to present the same opportunities for finding and testing cobbles present at the three true procurement loci at RAR or the many procurement loci in the HSP area.

Flaked Stone in RAR-Core

Over 6000 isolated lithics were documented, but not collected, during survey of RAR (Table 5.12). Almost three quarters (73%) of these were chert, with lower percentages of petrified wood (13%) and quartzite (8%; Figures 5.5-5.7). Other material types occur in much lower quantities. Differences in proportions of chert and quartzite were noted for the HSP loci (i.e., more quartzite in lower elevation exposures, more chert in higher elevation exposures; Lange 1998:69) and in a general sense this follows as well for the farther upstream quarries at RAR with even higher proportions of quartzite in the quarries. Chert, however, dominates in the RAR isolates and HSP loci showing it was more commonly selected for tasks out on the landscape. Very little petrified wood is present at HSP loci or exposures and is more evident in the isolates and cores in RAR area.

The chert, quartzite, and basalt/rhyolite/igneous materials are present to plentiful in the two lithic procurement sites located on the west side of the ranch—AZ P:2:153(ASM)–RAR-139 and AZ P:2:161(ASM)–RAR-57—and these are likely primary source areas for these materials on RAR (Soza 2018). Interestingly, nearly half of the projectile points are manufactured from nonlocal chert materials indicating the lithic isolates were not primarily for production of points but likely used for more expedient needs. The petrified wood/chalcedony/jasper likely was brought from what is today Petrified Forest National Park (PEFO) 40 km east.

The frequency of obsidian on RAR at 0.23 percent is extremely low when compared to frequencies at Homol'ovi pueblos (4%--Harry 1989; Lange 2020; Young 2001) and west of Chevelon Canyon (50%--Lyndon 2005). Obsidian occurs both on sites (BMII and BMIII) and as isolates and is concentrated along the edges of Bell Cow and Chevelon Canyons. The survey recovered only 14 flakes, almost all from AZ P:3:150[ASM]–RAR-33, AZ P:2:105[ASM]–RAR-79, AZ P:2:146T,U[ASM]–RAR-95, and AZ P:3:234[ASM]–RAR-123; Figure 5.14). Obsidian is usually associated with Jeddito Yellow Ware (JYW) or Awatovi Yellow Ware (AYW) on RAR and likely was brought by occupants of PIV villages at Homol'ovi or the Hopi Mesas postdating 1325 CE. More than 95 percent of Homol'ovi obsidian has been sourced to Government Mountain west of Flagstaff (Harry 1989; Lange 2020; Medeiros 2016; Shackley 2010; Young 2001) and is the likely source of the RAR flakes.

Over 250 lithic cores were found during survey of RAR (Figure 5.15). As with other lithic materials, chert is predominant within the sample at 58 percent. Quartzite cores account for 25 percent of the sample despite composing only 8 percent of the lithic assemblage, and only 6 percent of the cores are petrified wood despite being 13 percent of the lithic assemblage (Tables 5.12 and 5.13). These percentages are more in line with the frequencies of raw material recovered from intensive sampling of the two quarry sites where quartzite is most common followed by chert (Soza 2018).

Projectile points dating from the Paleoindian through Pueblo periods are found at RAR concentrated along Chimney and Bell Cow Canyons (Figures 5.16-5.20; Duke 2016). They were made primarily from non-local chert (some resembling padernal cherts and flints from eastern New Mexico or Texas; others are cherts from northern Arizona) and petrified wood from its source 40 km east across all time periods at RAR (Table 5.14).

RAR-Core Ground Stone

In the general middle LCR area, the local geology largely determines the raw materials available for ground stone tools—Shinarump and Moenkopi sandstones. Based on better cementing and coarser as well more variable granularity (Fratt and Biancaniello 1993), Shinarump is the preferred raw material. This is reflected in the percentages detailed in the analyses of the Homol'ovi survey manos and metates recovered and analyzed (66% Shinarump) and those from the PIV pueblo sites—59 percent at Homol'ovi IV, 60 percent at Homol'ovi II, 87 percent at Homol'ovi I, 95 percent at Homol'ovi III, and 96 percent at Chevelon Pueblo (Lange 2020:358). Almost none of Homol'ovi survey ground stone was basin manos or metates (less than 3% of the ground stone assemblage of nearly 600 artifacts).

Shinarump sandstone is not present in the geology of the RAR project areas, however cobbles from this formation are present as lag gravels. Also, there is another type of sandstone in the RAR-Core area, Coconino sandstone, that provided the necessary cementing and grain size for the needed grinding. Coconino sandstone slabs are very thin (usually only 2 - 4 cm thick) compared to the Shinarump and Moenkopi grinding tools. Coconino sandstone was used for the nether stone, as flat grinding slabs or shallow basin metates. The handstones (also called one-hand manos) in the RAR project areas used locally available materials and were often quartzite cobbles or shaped

5: Rock Art Ranch Area Surveys and Testing 99

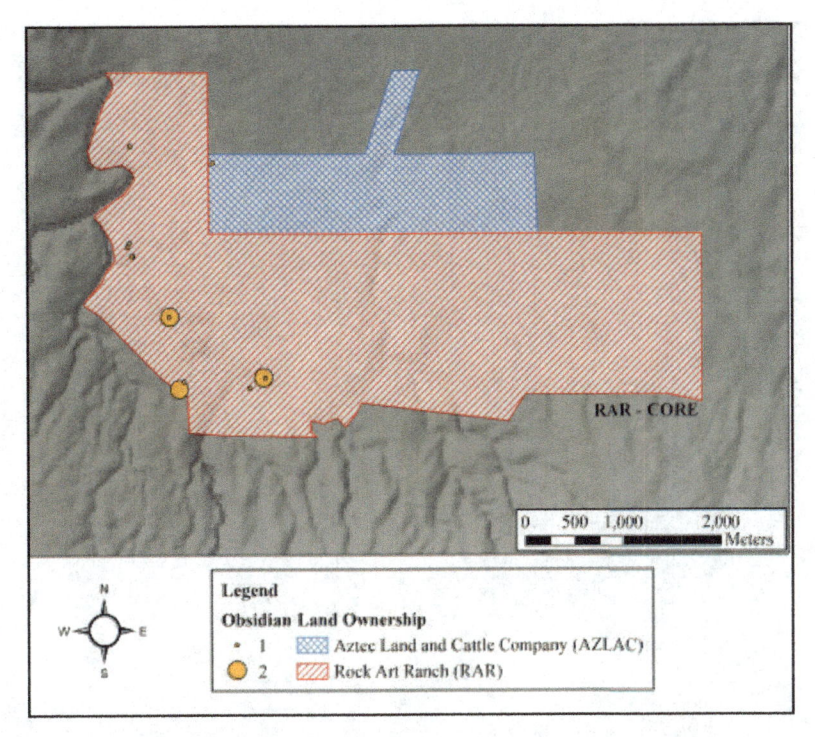

Figure 5.14. Distribution of obsidian artifacs in Rock Art Ranch-Core and AZLAC-Adjacent areas; graphic prepared by Josh Conver.

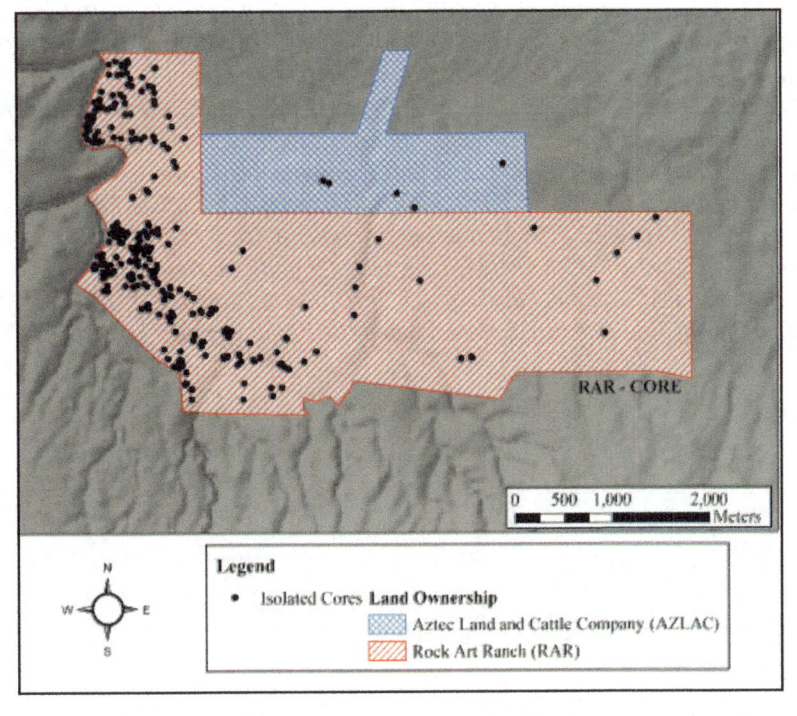

Figure 5.15. Distribution of cores in Rock Art Ranch-Core and AZLAC-Adjacent areas; graphic prepared by Josh Conver.

Figure 5.16. Spear and arrow points recovered from the ground surface during RAR survey 2011–2015: a. Clovis, isolate, Early Paleoindian; b. Clovis, AZ P:2:150B(ASM)–RAR-113B, Early Paleoindian; c. Plainview, AZ P:2:150B(ASM)–RAR-113B, Late Paeloindian; d. Midland, AZ P:2:150B(ASM)–RAR-113B, Late Paleoindian; e. Bajada, AZ P:2:152(ASM)–RAR-138, Early/Middle Archaic; f. Bajada, AZ P:2:167(ASM)–RAR-107, Early/Middle Archaic; g. Bajada, AZ P:2:150C(ASM)–RAR-113C, Early/Middle Archaic; h. Pinto, AZ P:3:237(ASM)–RAR-129, Early/Middle Archaic; i. San Jose, AZ P:3:234(ASM)–RAR-123, Middle/Late Archaic; j. San Jose, AZ P:3:234(ASM)–RAR-123, Middle/Late Archaic; k. San Jose, AZ P:3:117A(ASM)–RAR-5A, Middle/Late Archaic; l. San Jose, AZ P:2:176E(ASM)–RAR-119, Middle/Late Archaic; m. Northern Side-Notched, AZ P:3:234(ASM)–RAR-123, Middle/Late Archaic; n. Datil, AZ P:2:152(ASM)–RAR-138, Late Archaic; o. Gypsum, AZ P:2:152(ASM)–RAR-138, Late Archaic; p. Black Mesa, AZ P:3:234(ASM)–RAR-123, Basketmaker II; q. San Pedro, isolate, Basketmaker II/III; r. San Pedro, AZ P:2:152(ASM)–RAR-138, Basketmaker II/III; s. Pueblo Side-Notched, isolate, Pueblo III/IV; (photograph by Richard C. Lange).

5: Rock Art Ranch Area Surveys and Testing 101

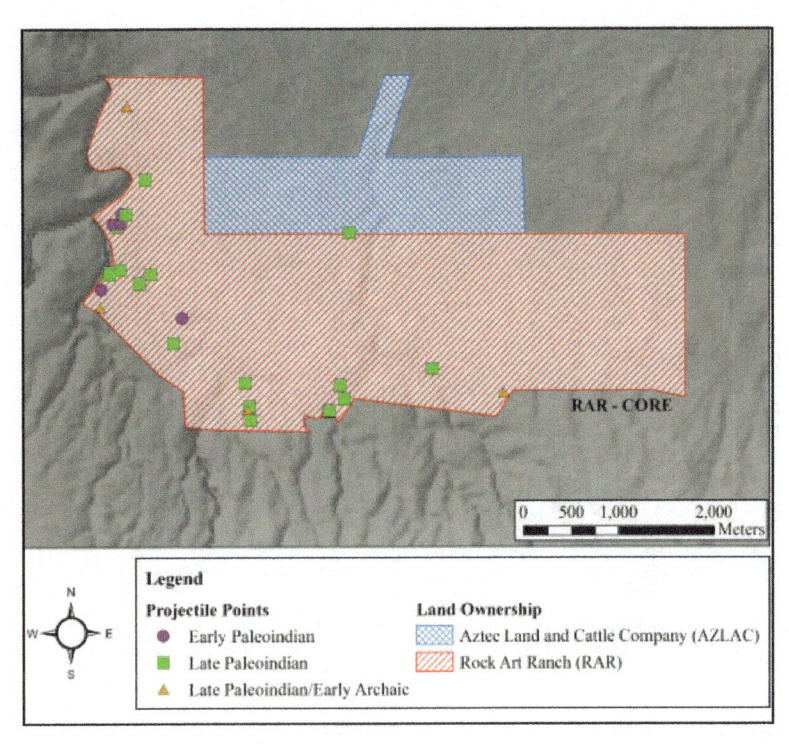

Figure 5.17. Distribution of Paleoindian and Paleoarchaic period projectile points in Rock Art Ranch-Core and AZLAC-Adjacent areas; graphic prepared by Josh Conver.

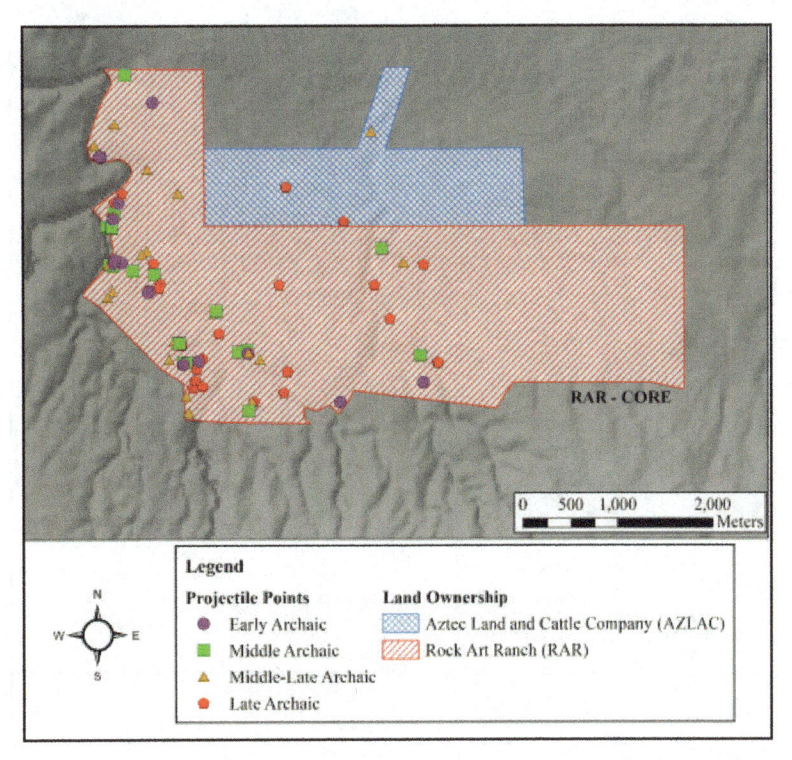

Figure 5.18. Distribution of Archaic period projectile points in Rock Art Ranch-Core and AZLAC-Adjacent areas; graphic prepared by Josh Conver.

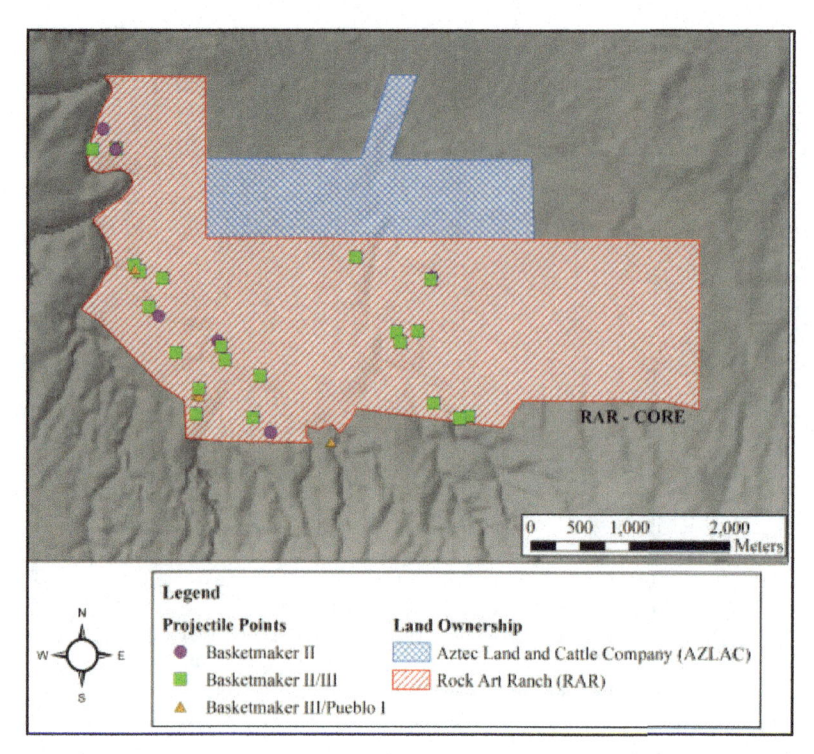

Figure 5.19. Distribution of Basketmaker period projectile points in Rock Art Ranch-Core and AZLAC-Adjacent areas; graphic prepared by Josh Conver.

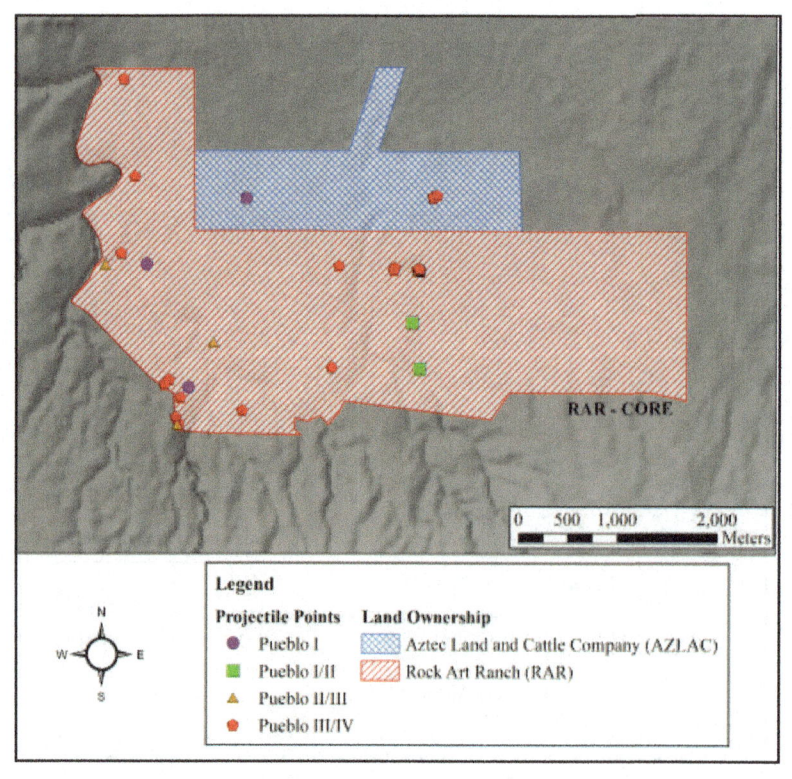

Figure 5.20. Distribution of Pueblo period projectile points in Rock Art Ranch-Core and AZLAC-Adjacent areas; graphic prepared by Josh Conver.

and worn nodules of various sandstones and igneous cobbles.

Over 1000 pieces of ground stone were recorded during survey of RAR (Figure 5.21). The nearly 250 analyzed ground stone objects were largely composed of basin and flat metates of Coconino sandstone and manos from lag gravels (Pitroff 2014; Table 5.15). Most of the metates were broken fragments, and most likely date to the pre-ceramic period. Typically these are concentrated along the canyons, mirroring the locations of the preceramic loci (Figures 5.17 and 5.18). Additionally, two caches of paired, two-handed manos were found during survey of the area. The paired manos (one Shinarump and one Moenkopi sandstone) in each cache have different coarseness and are likely grinding sets.

Bedrock grinding features were identified at RAR in both Chimney and Bell Cow Canyons. There are also "grinding slicks" at The Steps in Chevelon Canyon on a steeply inclined surface on a large boulder in the canyon bottom that may not be in its original position. There is a grouping of grinding slicks in Chimney Canyon with another one or two slicks a bit farther upstream—these are all on flat lying bedrock surfaces in the bottom of the canyon. Over 50 bedrock grinding features occur along Bell Cow Canyon (Figures 5.22 and 5.23), and some of these are also on vertical or inclined surfaces. They occur in groups of five to ten features, and range from pecked areas prepared for grinding to basin-shaped grooves.

Rock Art at RAR

The 40 galleries recorded in Chevelon Canyon document more than 3000 petroglyphs largely dating to the Archaic and early agricultural (BMII) periods (3000 BCE–600 CE). Their documentation is a result of the volunteer efforts of the Arizona Archaeological Society under the direction of Donald E. Weaver, Jr., over five years during the late 1990s (Brinkerhoff, Chapter 3; Kolber 2000; Malotki 2007; Weaver et al. 2000). During the six field seasons of the RAR survey, an additional 11 petroglyph panels were identified and recorded (Figure 5.24). Six of these are located on the walls of upper Bell Cow Canyon, while two appear on rock faces downslope near the convergence of Bell Cow with Chevelon Canyon. One is on an unnamed drainage on the east side of Chevelon Canyon one kilometer north of the primary petroglyph site at The Steps. One anthropomorphic figure was documented, along with several zoomorphic and geometric designs (Figure 5.25). The last panel is at AZ P:3:117C(ASM)–RAR-3A on a boulder at the bottom of Bell Cow Canyon. It appears to be a map of the canyon with numerous zoomorphic and anthropomorphic symbols associated with the geometric line depicting the canyon (Figure 1.2). Stylistically, it likely dates PIII/PIV.

Testing at RAR

Rather than relying only on projectile point typology to build the chronology for the preceramic sites on RAR, testing of burned features discovered during survey on these sites to collect samples for radiocarbon dating seemed necessary to provide absolute dates that could strengthen the typologically-based chronology. Evidence of charcoal in several of the burned features that had been disturbed by wind or livestock trampling along with the early BMII radiocarbon date from maize collected at nearby AZ P:2:56(ASM) made the project optimistic that useful dates could be obtained as well as observing whether or not maize was present in any features on RAR. In the end burned features from seven preceramic or aceramic sites were tested by excavating half of the feature to create a cross-section that was mapped along with a plan map for the feature

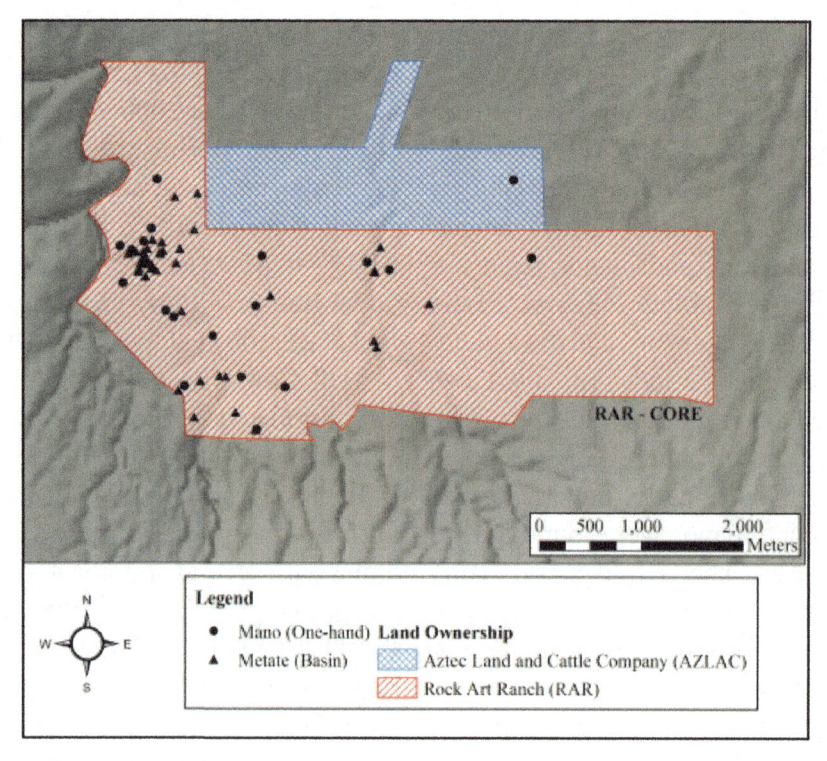

Figure 5.21. Distribution of isolated basin manos and metates in Rock Art Ranch-Core and AZLAC-Adjacent areas; graphic by Josh Conver.

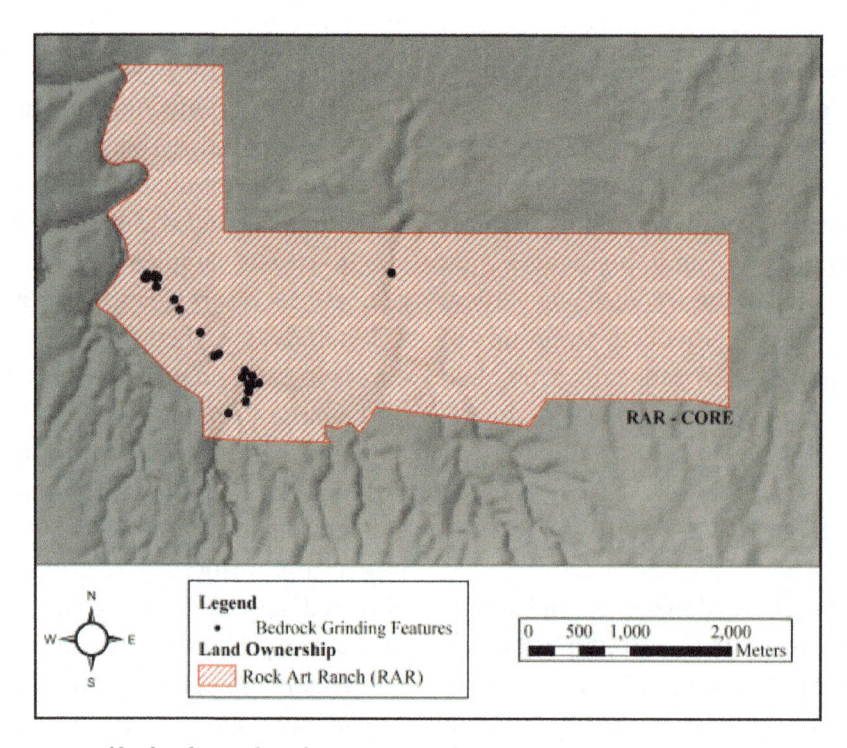

Figure 5.22. Locations of bedrock grinding features in Rock Art Ranch-Core area; graphc prepared by Josh Conver.

5: Rock Art Ranch Area Surveys and Testing 105

Figure 5.23. Photograph of bedrock grinding feature at AZ P:2:148(ASM)—RAR-106 in Rock Art Ranch-Core; photograph by E. Charles Adams.

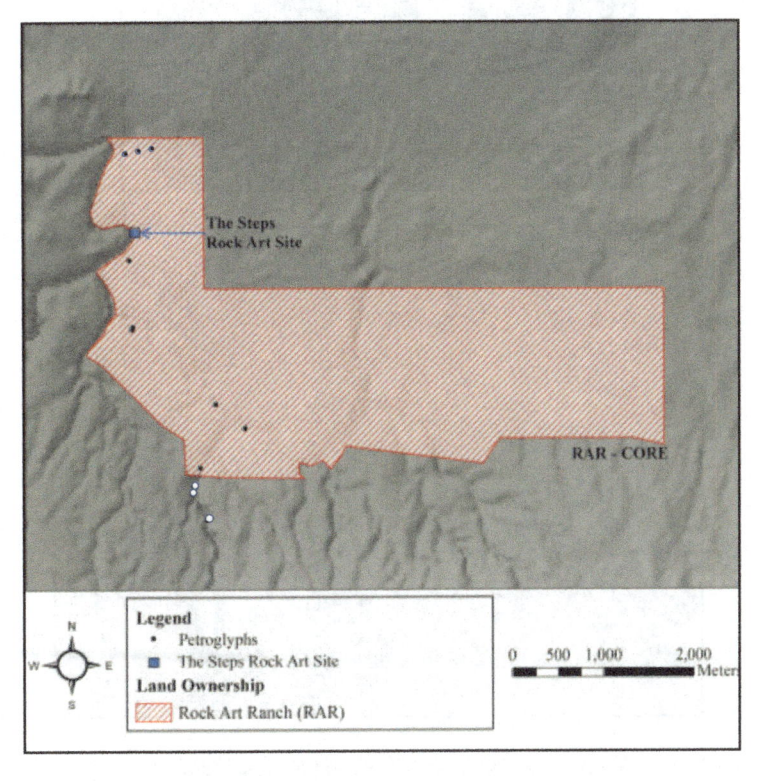

Figure 5.24. Locations of petroglyphs in Rock Art Ranch-Core area; graphic prepared by Josh Conver.

Figure 5.25. Examples of petroglyphs recorded by the Rock Art Ranch Field School (a: AZ P:2:170[ASM]—RAR-110; b: AZ P:2:181[ASM]—RAR-134; c: AZ P:2:171[ASM]—RAR-111; photographs by Samantha Fladd.

whose location was marked through GPS (Figure 5.26). Fill from the features was floated and burned annuals were selected and sent to the University of Arizona Radiocarbon Lab. Results for the samples are given in Table 5.16. Six of the seven dates fall within the established chronology for BMII while the seventh dates to early PII.

Excavation at BP uncovered a preceramic pit house and a dozen deep storage features. However, no intact stratigraphy dating to BMII remained at the site with only rare BMII artifacts recovered from the deep features. Details are described in Chapter 7. The absence of intact BMII deposits at BP seemed to characterize the 33 sites having features on RAR. To test this assumption, 1m x 2m excavation units were excavated adjacent to and near a cluster of BMII features in AZ P:3:124(ASM)–RAR-12. Excavations were done in 10 cm increments below loose sand to the caliche layer. Profiles of trench sides were made; however, no discernible stratigraphy, let alone BMII period strata, were identified. As at BP all deposition postdates human use. Although disappointing, especially adjacent to intact storage cists and thermal features, the results were not surprising. It is highly likely the other BMII sites with features have the same subsurface conditions.

Summary of Rock Art Ranch

The RAR-Core is distinctive when compared to the occupation in the general RAR Research Area. There is more evidence of Paleoindian and Archaic uses of the landscape than is evident in the other project subareas, particularly along the shallow canyons and in the vicinity of The Steps and Chevelon Canyon—the extensive petroglyph site from which the ranch takes its name. Ceramic period occupations re-used many of the same locations over the centuries, but in response to greater interests in farming also move out across the landscape into the dune areas between the drainages. It is in

Figure 5.26. Ash and charcoal in burned feature at AZ P:3:137C(ASM)--RAR-22C; photograph by E. Charles Adams.

the RAR area that some of the best evidence exists for contemporary occupations of both pit house and stone-masonry villages. These contemporary occupations are believed to result from the coexistence of peoples from different areas with different ceramic and architectural traditions and connections during the 1100s and early 1200s CE. It is also in the RAR-Core (and in the petroglyphs at The Steps) that there are scatters of Hopi Yellow Ware pottery indicating continued visits to the RAR area even after the general closure of the large HSC pueblos around 1400 CE.

Surveys and Collections on Aztec Land and Cattle Company Properties

Early in the surveys at RAR, we discovered that some of the sites we had initially been shown were not on RAR property. The Baird Family leased some grazing acreage from AZLAC. Arrangements were made between ASM and the RAR Field School and AZLAC and its chief executive officer, Mr. Stephen Brophy, for permission to survey on their land and make surface collections. These collections have been donated to ASM (AP-2012-0321).

Intensive (100% coverage) survey on AZLAC lands occurred in the south halves of two sections just north of RAR-Core (AZLAC-Adjacent), and included the sites we had been first shown by Mr. Baird in 2010. Survey of the two half-sections resulted in the documentation of 18 sites and 29 loci.

Three other sites (7 loci) are in the AZLAC-Far North section north of RAR and Territorial Road and east of Chevelon Canyon: AZ P:3:215(ASM) and AZ P:3:216(ASM) are pueblos with four and two roomblocks, respectively. AZ P:3:228(ASM) is an artifact scatter contemporary with the pueblos. Also, on AZLAC lands, a stone-masonry pueblo was documented and collected in the RAR-Southeast project area (AZ P:3:240[ASM]), near another small pueblo on State Trust land (AZ P:3:239[ASM]). The final sites on AZLAC lands are in the RAR-South project area, one (AZ P:3:164[ASM]) just north of the State Trust land section that was surveyed intensively in the RAR-South project area and another three loci south of that State land section. In all, 25 sites with 41 loci were documented on AZLAC lands (Table 1.2).

For comparisons of the human occupations at and around RAR, one fact stands out—in contrast to the RAR-Core area immediately to the south, there is a lack of pre-ceramic loci on the AZLAC-Adjacent property. The ceramic period AZLAC loci can be subdivided into pit house villages, pueblos comprised of stone masonry, and general artifact scatters (some with features such as remains of slab-lined storage pits). The pueblos in the AZLAC-Far North parcel are approximately 7 km from the RAR-Core and BP, 17 km from the pueblo in the RAR-Southeast parcel, and 17 km from the MK Site in the RAR-South area (see Figure 1.4). The pueblo in RAR-Southeast is only about 6 km from the MK Site.

The ceramic analyses, flaked stone analyses, and general chronology of occupation will be discussed by these subsets for the AZLAC sites and loci.

AZLAC Sites – Ceramics

The several loci on AZLAC lands considered likely to have pit house occupations (AZ P:3:119[ASM], AZ P:3:121A[ASM], AZ P:3:176B[ASM], and AZ P:3:223[ASM]) are all in the AZLAC-Adjacent subarea. Their ceramic assemblages are dominated by TWW among the white wares, and TGW and MBW for the utility wares (Tables 5.17 and 5.18). Only one of these loci (AZ P:3:223[ASM]) has much in the way of ABW; otherwise, most ABW occurs at the pueblos while MBW occurs at both pit houses and pueblos (Table

5.18). TGW occurs in higher percentages at the pit house sites and in the AZLAC-Adjacent loci in general. The pueblo southeast of RAR (AZ P:3:240[ASM]) is like the pueblo site AZ P:3:227A(ASM) in AZLAC-Adjacent in having the lowest percentages of TGW among all of the AZLAC habitation loci, and similar percentages of MBW. However, AZ P:3:240(ASM) has the highest percentage of PVUW; one other pueblo in the AZLAC-Far North has a similar percentage. Only two of six pit house loci have PVUW present, while the ware is present at seven of the nine pueblo loci. The differences in wares present likely represent differences in social origins and connections as well as possible subtle differences in the timing of occupations.

In comparing ceramic types across the AZLAC loci, only 3 pit house loci (AZ P:3:119A, AZ P:3:176B, and AZ P:3:223(ASM) have the most typical BMIII type for the area—Lino Black/gray (B/g; Tables 5.19-5.21); Table 5.22 presents the same data, only focused exclusively on habitation loci on AZLAC lands). The Lino B/g type is present at only 2 others of the 29 loci in the AZLAC-Adjacent subarea. When typical TWW PI and PII types (Kana-a B/w and Black Mesa B/w) occur together at a locus, Kana-a B/w is the more dominant in five cases, Black Mesa B/w is the more dominant in four cases. Lino B/g occurs at 5 of the AZLAC-Adjacent loci, Kana-a B/w at 14 loci, and Black Mesa B/w at 17 loci. Although Indeterminate TWW is present at almost all of the AZLAC-Adjacent loci (only absent in 7 loci), the later PII diagnostic types Sosi B/w and Dogoszhi B/w occur at only 5 and 7 loci, respectively. Flagstaff B/w occurs at only 3 of these loci.

There is a little more LCWW than TWW at the AZLAC loci (Table 19a). The PII and PIII LCWW types of Holbrook-A B/w, Holbrook-B B/w, Padre B/w, and Walnut B/w are present at 7, 8, 7, and 15 loci, respectively, in the AZLAC-Adjacent subarea. Indeterminate CWW is present at 15 loci, but is only 13 percent of the quantity of Indeterminate LCWW. The most common types of CWW are Puerco B/w and Snowflake B/w. Reserve B/w is present in the AZLAC-Adjacent subarea, but only at 9 of the loci.

Two of the pueblos in the AZLAC-Far North subarea have Lino B/g (BMIII) with 12 of the 13 sherds at one pueblo—indicating an heirloom or more substantive early occupation there. PI diagnostics are also rare in the AZLAC-Far North, one locus at one pueblo has one sherd of Kana-a B/w. Three of the six AZLAC-Far North loci have Black Mesa B/w, two have Sosi B/w, and Dogoszhi B/w is present at five loci. Flagstaff B/w is only present in low frequencies at two of the AZLAC-Far North pueblos.

The AZLAC-Far North pueblos and the one in the RAR-Southeast all have Indeterminate LCWW. Holbrook-A B/w, Holbrook-B B/w, and Padre B/w are present at two, three, and four of the seven loci, respectively, and in low frequencies. However, Walnut B/w is present at six of the seven loci, with the absence at AZ P:3:215A(ASM) indicating a likely temporal difference between the room blocks in AZ P:3:215A and B(ASM). Indeterminate CWW and other formal CWW types are present at four of the AZLAC-Far North and RAR-Southeast loci in low frequencies, with a notable emphasis on Reserve B/w at four of the loci.

Two of the nine pueblo loci have ceramic indications of PI and PII occupations, also going into a bit later PII occupation due to the presence of Sosi and Dogoszhi Black-on-whites. All but one of the pueblo loci have percentages of the PIII hallmark Walnut Black-on-white. The AZLAC-Adjacent property of the various RAR project subareas has the strongest indications of PI and PII occupations compared to the other RAR subareas and the Homol'ovi survey (Tables 5.19 and 21).

The presence of these ranges of types, from BMIII to PIII for the AZLAC pit house and pueblo sites, give further evidence to a mixed occupation period in the late PII through PIII times in the RAR area that has both pit house and pueblo occupations. And, the general increase in percentages of MBW at the pueblo sites suggests not only a re-orientation of trade networks in PII times but population from the southeast moving into the middle LCR (HSP area) and RAR areas based on ceramics and architecture.

AZLAC Sites – Flaked Stone

Flaked stone data for AZLAC sites come from those loci just north of RAR, as well as from the AZLAC-Far North and one locus to the RAR-South (Table 5.23). The comparisons of pit house to pueblo sites are limited in that only two pit house loci were analyzed vs. seven of the pueblo loci. Natural flaked stone sources in the form of lag gravels along the ancient terraces of the LCR would all be equally accessible to each of the loci and also be the same sources available to loci in the RAR-Core.

Two pit house loci, ceramically dated earlier as well as somewhat coeval with the pueblo loci, show a dominance of chert, followed by petrified wood and quartzite (Table 5.24). Similar proportions are evident for five of the seven pueblo loci. One other locus has very few flaked stone artifacts documented (AZ P:3:215A[ASM]; N = 3); the other has a slightly higher proportion of petrified wood artifacts. The latter locus also has one obsidian artifact, only two other pieces of obsidian were documented at all of the other AZLAC loci. The loci show that the same sources were used throughout time and materials were equally available via the trade networks through the same time periods.

As habitation loci, be they pit houses or pueblos, similar sorts of activities and needs for flaked stone tools can be posited. As noted above, material types chosen or acquired were similar for the different site types. Proportions of debitage types are similar, with roughly 20 to 30 percent complete flakes and usually above 30 percent debris (Table 5.25). For both pit house loci and one pueblo locus, they have 13 percent or higher proportions of broken flakes. Hammerstones and hammerstone spalls are more common at the habitation loci than at general artifact scatters, as are cores. Edge-damaged and retouched pieces also occur more frequently on the habitation loci. Both the manufacturing tools and flaked stone tools indicate a more wide-ranging and concentrated set activities related to making tools and to skinning, cutting, and shaping occurring at the habitation sites. Numbers of bifaces and projectile points are low, making it impossible to see any clear patterns of association by habitation or non-habitation loci.

The proportions of raw materials in general (above, Table 5.24) follow through into the various debitage and tool categories (Table 5.26), that is, there is no specific preference or restriction of a particular debitage or tool type for a particular material type. As noted in the general HRP collections (Lange 1998:69), there is a preference for the heavier manufacturing tools (hammerstones and peckingstones) to be made from the heavier and less brittle material—quartzite. In the RAR area assemblages, however, chert is used almost as frequently for such tools—curious in that quartzite is readily available in the RAR quarries near the AZLAC-Adjacent loci (Table 5.12).

Preferences for the finer-grained materials (chert, chalcedony, petrified wood, and obsidian) for creating and re-sharpening cutting and scraping tools is seen in the proportions of the various sizes of flaked stone materials (Table 5.27). There are small quartzite flakes, but only chert and quartzite have the largest flakes, spalls, and tools. Most of the AZLAC flaked-stone material (for all loci) comes from general lithic reduction, after initial testing or flaking of a cobble (Tables 5.28 and 5.29). The majority of flaked stone artifacts from the AZLAC loci have no or only some cortex present, particularly for the finer-grained materials. Only quartzite has a larger proportion of flaked stone artifacts with cortex present.

Locus type also appears to have no effect on the size of flaked stone materials. All sizes, including the smallest flake sizes, occur in roughly equal proportions at all locus types (Table 5.30). And finally, in manipulating the data in a slightly different manner to reinforce observations made above, the finer-grained materials were worked and reworked into smaller artifacts. The distribution of artifact sizes trends noticeably toward larger for quartzite when compared to the other materials (Table 5.31).

Summary of Loci on AZLAC Properties

The AZLAC-Adjacent property, just north of the RAR-Core, is the most similar of the various RAR subareas to the RAR-Core. As in the RAR-Core, there is evidence of contemporaneous pit house and pueblo occupations, with even greater indications of the movement downstream, out into the dunes and ridges between drainages, and the move into small, stone-masonry pueblos. The small pueblos on AZLAC properties in the AZLAC-Far North, RAR-Southeast, and RAR-South are further evidence of the changeover in social contacts (seen in the ceramic assemblages) and principal mode of living (stone-masonry pueblos) in PIII times (early 1100s to early 1200s CE). This is, however, also one of the principal differences with the RAR-Core, where there is just one instance of a stone-masonry pueblo. Also different, from opposite ends of the general regional chronology, are no instances of the earliest Paleoindian and Archaic (pre-ceramic period) occupations and no instances of the PIV and later uses of the landscape as do occur in the RAR-Core.

ARCHAEOLOGICAL WORK WEST OF ROCK ART RANCH (RAR-WEST)

Archaeological work west of RAR and west of Chevelon Canyon was done by the HRP and by Bruce and Lisa Huckell of the University of New Mexico under ASM/HRP permits (Figure 1.4). The initial survey work (1989; ASM AAA permit 1989-45ps) was part of the general HRP Survey (Lange 1998) which focused in this area on AZ P:2:56(ASM)-HP-349, a site in a hanging canyon tributary of Chevelon Canyon located southwest of RAR. In 1989 the site and visible features were mapped, and artifacts were collected. Work by the Huckells involved survey and documentation of sites west and north of AZ P:2:56(ASM) in 1994, 1995, and 1997, as well as testing of the site itself in 1992, 1998, and 1999. The Huckells' survey work was done under several project specific (ps) permits: 1994-70ps, and 1995-70ps; the testing at AZ P:2:56(ASM) and other survey work were done under several other permits: 1992-50ps, 1998-70ps, and 1999-83ps. Materials from the various surveys and testing projects have been included in two ASM accessions: AP-1994-3 for the original documentation at AZ P:2:56(ASM) and AP-2012-321 for the other materials and records.

Surveys West of Chevelon Canyon

To provide context for the work at AZ P:2:56(ASM) as well as exploring for other potential research opportunities, the Huckells did informal surveys in 1994 and 1995 and a more formal survey in 1997. These were opportunistic surveys to examine likely locations for early sites, not systematic 100-percent surveys as done for the RAR surveys in the RAR-Core area and in the State Trust land section to the RAR-South. Nine loci (AZ P:2:106 through P:2:114[ASM]) were documented in 1995 in the area west, northwest, and north of AZ P:2:56(ASM), scattered across seven sections of land (with mixed ownership and jurisdictions; Figure 5.27; Table 5.32). Another eight loci were recorded in 1997 (AZ P:2:184 through P:2:187[ASM]), north of AZ P:2:56(ASM) and mostly occurring in a single section of State Trust land.

Ceramic period loci were less common and had diagnostic ceramic types indicating BMIII/PI and PII/III periods of occupation. Of the 17 loci recorded apart from AZ P:2:56(ASM) west of Chevelon Canyon, 8 had purely Archaic occupations, while 5 had purely ceramic period occupations, and only 3 had both (Table 5.32)—showing that, as on RAR project areas east of Chevelon Canyon, different occupations had different preferences for locations on the landscape. These preferences reflect different emphases on resource procurement, habitation sites and features, and activities such as farming (Figure 5.27). The only formal collections from RAR-West came from the original documentation and later testing at AZ P:2:56(ASM). Artifact collections from AZ P:2:56(ASM) include ceramics, flaked stone, and ground stone. Collections that are reported on here involve those made during the initial survey and documentation in 1989 (Lange 1998), flaked stone from the 1998 work defining the pit house and adjacent processing area (Fogle and Arias 1998), and flaked stone from the 1999 work analyzed by Lange.

Ceramics West of Chevelon Canyon

The only formal collections of ceramics were made during the original mapping and documentation of AZ P:2:56(ASM) in 1989. Wares and types collected and analyzed are summarized in Tables 5.33 and 5.34. Although these are only a few over four dozen sherds, the proportions are generally reminiscent of RAR-Core and AZLAC-Adjacent project areas. There are several PIV JYW sherds that seem to coincide with the occupation of the late, large HSC pueblos and indicate use of this topographic feature during that time. Interestingly, the most numerous sherds are of locally produced Homolovi Orange Ware (HOW)—plain and corrugated, suggesting some use of the side canyon in the late thirteenth and early fourteenth centuries. This ware and these types are missing from the RAR project areas east of Chevelon Canyon. The next most abundant wares are ABW (of mostly indeterminate types) and TGW (non-corrugated plain ware). The very small numbers of TWW and LCWW sherds (of only indeterminate types) suggest ephemeral visitations of the side canyon during the centuries-long ceramic period, mirroring the even longer-term use evident over the millennia in the flaked and ground stone assemblages from there.

The ceramics identified from other loci west of Chevelon Canyon during the 1990s surveys come from the notes and site forms. The types and wares noted again suggest similarities to the PI, PII, PIII, and PIV occupations east of Chevelon Canyon in the RAR-Core area: Kana-a B/w, AYW, TGW, miscellaneous brown ware, Holbrook-B B/w, LCWW, and ABW.

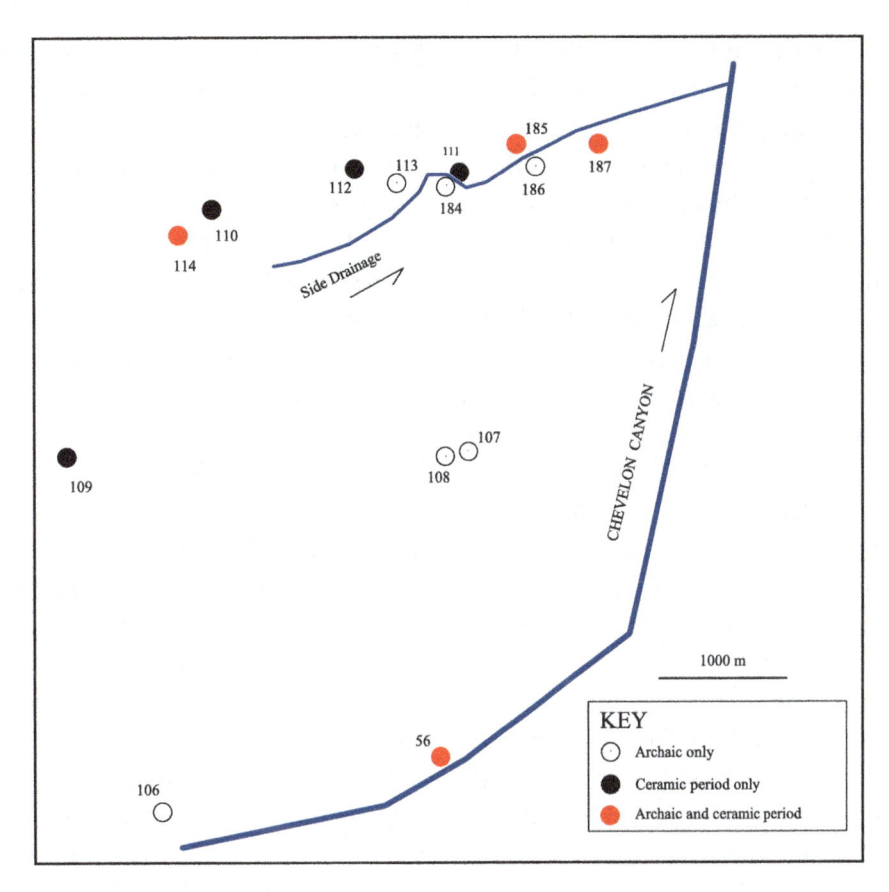

Figure 5.27. Sites in RAR-West, west of Chevelon Canyon; (all sites are AZ P:2:xxx[ASM]; graphic prepared by Richard C. Lange).

Flaked Stone West of Chevelon Canyon

Flaked stone debris, debitage, and tools are clearly the most numerous artifacts at AZ P:2:56(ASM) west of Chevelon Canyon. Tables 5.35-5.37 show flaked stone artifacts by provenience for material type and artifact type, and material type by artifact type for the 1989 surface collections and the 1999 testing collections. The majority of flaked stone (60%) from surface collections at AZ P:2:56(ASM) is chert, and lower percentages of quartzite (24%) and petrified wood (11%). The greatest number of flaked stone artifacts are debris, followed by complete flakes and flake fragments.

One contrast between the 1989 and 1999 collections discussed here is that the 1989 artifacts were collected from formal surface collection units, the 1999 artifacts came mostly from the 1/8-in screening done in excavation units. The AZ P:2:56 (ASM) assemblage is overwhelmingly chert (Table 5.35) with over half of the quartzite coming from one collection unit, and just less than a third of the petrified wood coming from the same unit. Interestingly, the majority of artifacts from the surface collections could be classified into one of the formal flake categories (Tables 5.36 and 5.37), but most artifacts from the test units were classified as debris because of the difficulties in dealing with the very small artifacts.

The size of the flaked stone artifacts is best reported for the test units: over 65 percent of the artifacts are less than 1 sq cm in size (Table 5.38), and over 70 percent of these are chert (Table 5.39; see also Fogle and Arias 1998). There are peckingstones and hammerstones present at AZ P:2:56 (ASM), but these were not formally included in the data tables. Their presence, along with the abundant small flakes, indicates that creating and sharpening flaked-stone tools was being done here. Most of these small flakes are what have been referred to as "bifacial thinning flakes" and are typical of preceramic period assemblages—the clear period of most activities at AZ P:2:56(ASM).

The loci recorded during the various surveys were similar in that many showed point types and flaking debris indicative of Archaic period use (Figure 5.28; Table 5.40)—primarily Middle-Late Archaic (Elko-, San Jose-, and Northern Side-Notched-style points—N = 1, 3, and 4, respectively), Late Archaic (Cortaro- and Datil-style points—N = 1 and 1), and BM II (San Pedro-style points—N = 3). Several points or point fragments were not collected and included additional examples of Elko (AZ P:2:186[ASM]), San Jose (AZ P:2:185 and 187[ASM]), corner-notched (AZ P:2:187[ASM]), and BMII (AZ P:2:185[ASM]) points. Additional projectile points from AZ P:2:56(ASM) and west of Chevelon Canyon are shown in Figures 5.28–5.29 (Table 5.41), and include additional examples of the San Jose, San Pedro, San Rafael, Datil, and Pueblo Side-Notched styles.

Ground Stone from West of Chevelon Canyon

Ground stone was collected from AZ P:2:56(ASM) during the original survey and mapping in 1989. The majority of artifact types for the over 20 examples of manos and metates is related to the basin ground stone form (Table 5.42), with only two flat mano forms documented. The raw materials attributed for these artifacts from AZ P:2:56(ASM) are unclear—one variable codes 23 of the 26 artifacts as Shinarump vs. "limestone;" another variable codes many as "unknown" or "indeterminate" or assigns the artifacts to Coconino, Shinarump, or Kaibab sandstones.

Like the ground stone artifacts east of Chevelon Canyon, these artifacts from AZ P:2:56(ASM) are likely Coconino sandstone.

Some of the manos were illustrated in the general Homol'ovi survey report (Lange 1998:106). One of the basin metates recovered in 1989 was large, deep, and had been broken into pieces, and is clearly evidence of long-term and periodically intensive use of this side canyon area.

Testing at AZ P:2:56(ASM)

In 1992, the Huckells did initial testing at AZ P:2:56(ASM), which spurred informal surveys in 1994 and 1995 and a more formal survey in 1997 of nearby drainages. Concerned about increasing vandalism at the site and features, additional excavations were done at AZ P:2:56(ASM) in 1998 (Huckell and Huckell 1999) and again in 1999. The testing done in 1992, 1998, and 1999 is summarized here.

AZ P:2:56(ASM) is in a small side canyon that traps moisture in a "C"-shaped catchment in the Coconino Sandstone. Sand is relatively deep in the upper portion of the catchment and is shallower as it turns toward Chevelon Canyon. It is a hanging canyon that would hold water effectively in the sand matrix and in four tinajas (natural tanks) before reaching the pour-off point that drops straight down to the floor of Chevelon Canyon, some 45 m below. The water retention capacity of the little canyon was exploited by pre-ceramic as well as ceramic period populations, making use of the water available in the tinajas as well as an ideal location for farming and gathering due to the moisture levels in the sand. Artifact concentrations have been disturbed as well as created by erosion—both wind and water. Some areas of the site show accumulated sediments (mostly sand), other areas have been deflated and scoured.

The 1992 work, done over two weeks in

Figure 5.28. Projectile points from sites and isolates in RAR-West (key to types and materials in Table 5.40; photograph by Richard C. Lange).

116 Lange, Fladd, and E.C. Adams

Figure 5.29. Projectile points from AZ P:2:56(ASM)–HP-349 and other sites in RAR-West (key to types and materials in Table 5.41; photograph by Richard C. Lange)/

late June and early July, defined two spatially distinct temporal components—Areas 1 and 2 (Figure 5.30). Area 1 was interpreted as primarily a Middle Archaic/BMII component, and Area 2 as more associated with the ceramic period occupation (PII through PIV). The testing sought to define these occupations more clearly, particularly through the dating of archaeobotanical remains. It was hoped that such dating could narrow down the use of AZ P:2:56(ASM) during the 6000- to 8000-year Archaic period on the southern Colorado Plateau.

Excavations in 1992 involved four test pits (2 – 1 x 1 m; 1 – 1 x 2 m; and 1 – 2 x 2m) and two features in Area 1 and three test pits (all 1 x 1 m) and three features in Area 2. The features excavated in Area 2 included two slab-lined roasting pits and a rectangular firebox. The test units and features in Area 2 indicated this was primarily a PII/III period locus of activities, while Area 1 was more Middle Archaic/BMII—and thus received the greater emphasis to address the research goals (Huckell and Huckell 1999:2).

Feature 1 (Area 1, Test 2) was a deeply

5: Rock Art Ranch Area Surveys and Testing 117

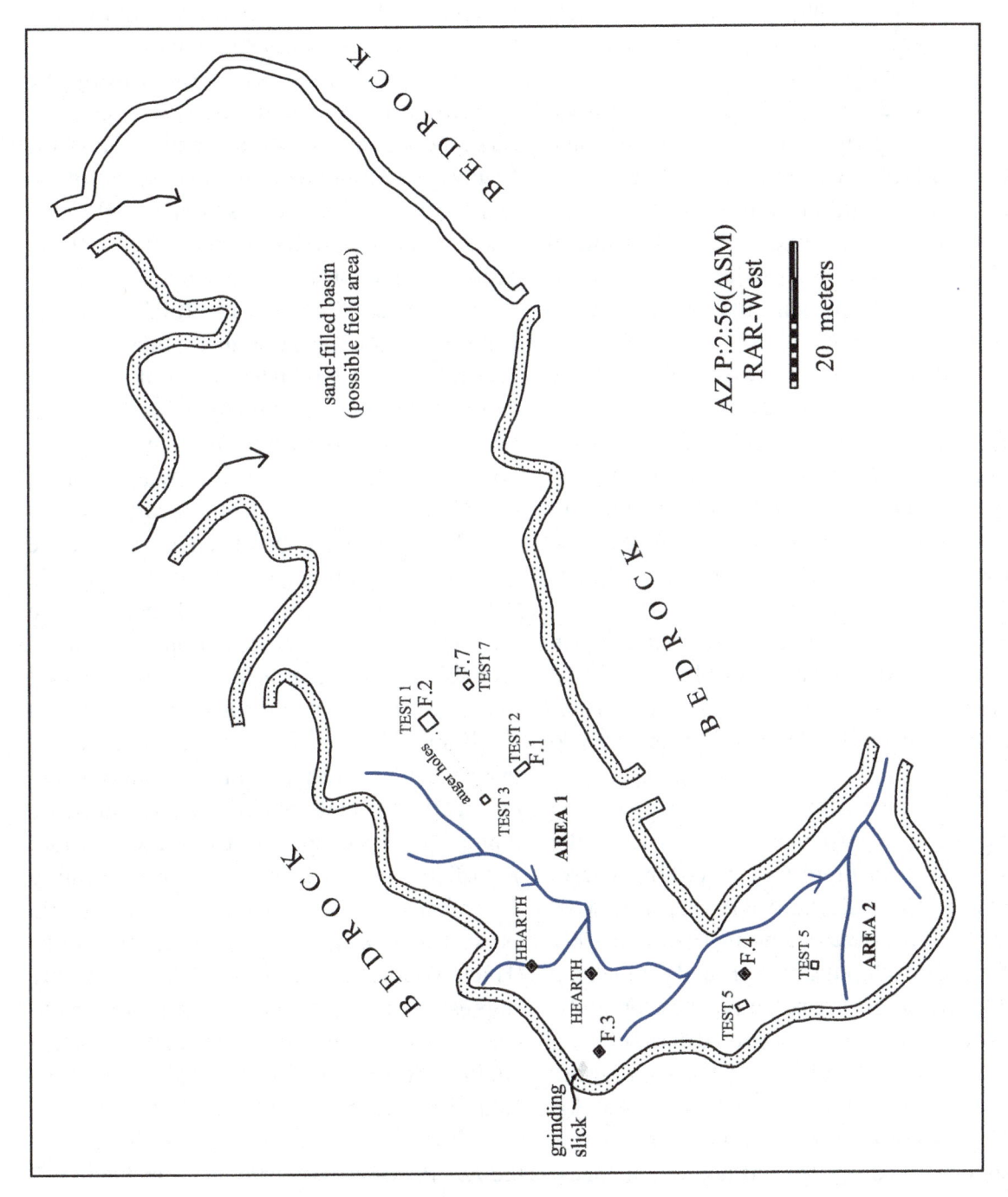

Figure 5.30. Plan map of features and test units at AZ P:2:56(ASM); CAD map by Richard C. Lange.

buried (0.8 m) shallow pit (0.8m diameter, 0.06 m deep) containing seven sandstone slabs. One of the sandstone slabs was nearly half of a shallow slab metate. Although suspected of being Middle Archaic in age, no carbonized material was recovered from a flotation sample taken from this feature.

Feature 2 (Area 1, Test 1) was an oval (0.7 m x 0.5 m), 0.20 m deep hearth associated with a surface concentration of lithic debris, fire-cracked rock, and burned small animal bones. The surface above the feature contained a Middle Archaic San Rafael Side-notched style point, but this point may not have been in its original context.

Feature 7 (Area 1, Test 7) discovered a portion of a large pit feature, possibly a pit house, whose floor was quite shallow, only about 0.3 m below present ground surface (Figure 5.31). A flotation sample from the fill contained a maize cupule that was radiocarbon dated to 2555±55 BP (calibrated at 2-sigmas to 815-500 BCE; Sample AA-10172)—suggesting a BMII age for this feature. An additional BMII point (probable) was found several meters south of Feature 7, further suggesting the BMII dating of this feature and area of the site.

With the promising results from the initial testing, particularly from Area 1, the possibility of a more intensive, longer-term study of the AZ P:2:56(ASM) area was raised. Surveys were done in 1995 and 1997 to further develop the background for the area and to identify other potential sites for study. However, the surveys discovered that, although there were sites and loci of the appropriate age, sites with intact deposits (such as at AZ P:2:56(ASM)) were rare. The other sites, despite the appropriate artifact assemblages, were eroded and deflated, and between 1995 and 1997 were being subjected to increased vandalism. Thus, priorities shifted to doing additional work at AZ P:2:56(ASM) in 1998.

Another two-week field session was done at AZ P:2:56(ASM) in 1998, again in the late June to early July time frame. Additional tests were done around Features 1 and 2 to try to find information about the time, duration, and nature of the occupations in Area 1.

The emphasis was continuing the definition and understanding of Feature 7. First, the area around the original test unit was stripped to define the shape and extent of the feature, then the feature was excavated. Feature 7 was found to be a shallow basin (0.2 to 0.3 m deep), circular pit structure (approximately 2.5 m in diameter). The only identifiable internal feature (Feature 7.01) was an irregular informal hearth (0.75 x 0.5 m) in the center of Feature 7, defined by a concentration of ash and charcoal flecks. The floor of Feature 7 was not formally prepared or plastered and was heavily disturbed by rodent runs and roots from a nearby juniper tree. A complete, one-handed mano was on the floor at the south edge of the central hearth. Otherwise artifacts in the fill of Feature 7 were rare. A broken and re-worked projectile point of probably BMII style was found in the upper fill of the hearth, along with burned and unburned small animal bones. The maize cupule dated from the initial test of Feature 7 came from the hearth as well, establishing a solid date range for the occupation and use of Feature 7. Pollen samples from the floor of Feature 7 confirmed individual maize pollen grains as well as one aggregate of multiple grains (Huckell and Huckell 1999:10). This certainly suggests that green maize was brought into the structure for processing or that the pollen got into the structure by other cultural or even natural processes.

The postulated field area "upstream" in the AZ P:2:56(ASM) canyon from Feature 7 did not pan out, at least in terms of confirming an area of maize production. A biface fragment from some 0.3 m down in one test unit in the field area appears to be of BM II style—

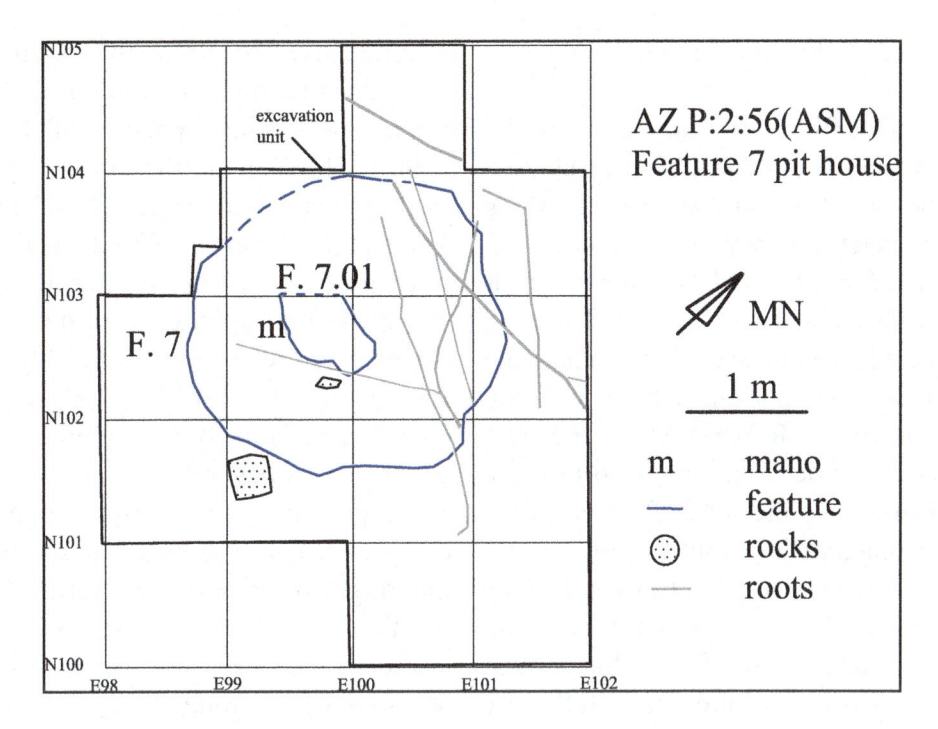

Figure 5.31. Plan map of Feature 7 (pit house and hearth) at AZ P:2:56(ASM): CAD map by Richard C. Lange.

indicating similarity or use of this area along with the structure, Feature 7. A pollen sample from this same depth, however, failed to find maize or other cultigen pollen grains, but did find abundant cheno-am and Asteraceae pollen (S. Smith 1999). Thus, the field area could have been an area of maize production, but the farming would have also occurred in other nearby areas.

The Huckells and a small crew returned to AZ P:2:56(ASM) for a week in early summer of 1999. The goals were to further define the pit house and nearby processing area, to search for other features, and to try to recover additional pollen samples that would confirm an early field nearby. Systematic testing with a soil auger was done south and west of the pit house to try to identify other features, however, none were found. Two test pits were excavated in the field area, but discovered evidence of heavy rodent activity and other bioturbation processes, so no additional pollen samples were taken.

Six 1 m-x-1 m units were excavated to sterile during the 1999 work. Two units were in the processing area near the pit house and found a deep, circular pit (Feature 9). The pit contained several large fire-cracked rocks and a metate (also burned) that had been used as a deflector in the southeast portion of the pit. Two other units along the eastern perimeter of the pit house discovered part of a basin-shaped pit (Feature 8). The contents of Features 8 and 9 were quite different. Feature 8 (near the pit house) had generally low artifact and animal bone densities; Feature 9 in the processing area had high artifact and animal bone densities. The faunal remains have not been formally analyzed, but observations in the field indicate that rabbits and other rodents were common food resources. Despite numerous projectile points, evidence and remains of larger mammals were rare.

Summary of Loci West of Chevelon Canyon

The loci west of Chevelon Canyon are similar to the sites recorded in the RAR project areas east of Chevelon Canyon that clustered along the canyons in terms of point types represented, the presence of features, and the general periods of occupation. There are some differences, however: evidence of earlier Paleoindian and Early Archaic occupations were not found at these loci in RAR-West which are also more eroded and deflated compared to those in RAR-Core. Like the RAR-Core, sites are clustered along a major tributary flowing into Chevelon Canyon. Chevelon Canyon is deep and inaccessible through most of this area, and like the side drainages east of Chevelon Canyon in the RAR-Core, Chimney and Bell Cow Canyons, this main tributary west of Chevelon Canyon is shallow and would have been easily accessible for subsurface water and has the soil and water conditions for suitable for small-scale farming and other natural resources. This is because bedrock is at or very close to the surface in much of the area west of Chevelon Canyon, resulting in shallow soils generally not suitable for farming.

Sites and Survey in RAR-South and RAR-Southeast

The formal survey near the MK Site looked at approximately a square mile in an upland area 600 ft higher than the elevation of BP and RAR-Core. The area is similarly open grassland, but with denser juniper trees and closer proximity to the pine forest. The survey methods described above for doing the survey and documenting sites and loci were followed for the area around the pueblo. A total of 35 loci was recorded (Table 5.43), and the sites and loci recorded and artifacts collected are described below.

The upland area is a southwest to northeast oriented oval of about three-square miles. Elevations range from around 5700 ft (1737 m) in the southern portion of the basin to 5600 ft (1707 m) in the northern portion, as the topography slopes gently to the northeast. The upland basin is mixed open grassland with moderately dense stands of juniper along the tops of the low ridges. Much of the area is covered by a thin layer of sand (ranging usually from 20-to-50 cm). Bedrock, consisting of mostly Coconino Sandstone, is exposed or is never deep throughout the area. Some portions of the basin are geologically complex because the Coconino Sandstone is interfingered with a shoreline of an old Permian Sea that formed the Kaibab Limestone. Some erosion in the basin has also exposed the higher Moenkopi Sandstone. All of these geological units supplied stone for construction of the pueblos and features recorded in this area. The combination of nearby pinyon and juniper due to higher elevation than the RAR-Core area, good water, good drainage, and good soils seem to be what attracted prehistoric populations to occupy this area for hunting, gathering, and farming.

Several ranch roads occur in the area, and otherwise modern disturbances are related to cattle-grazing throughout the area—bladed-up water tanks and fence-lines. Although several of the sites show evidence of pothunting/vandalism, those sorts of impacts are relatively minimal on the prehistoric remains documented in the basin.

Sites – RAR-South and RAR-Southeast

Most sites recorded by the survey in the area south and southeast of the RAR-Core are non-habitation sites (Table 5.44); meaning that they are artifact scatters of ceramics, flaked stone, and ground stone indicating many types of activities, but are lacking in features or structures that would indicate more permanent residence at these locations. The loci are mostly on State Trust land, with several also on AZLAC property. Analyzed artifacts indicate that the most intensive use of the area occurred during PII and PIII times (roughly 1050-1225 CE) with periods before and after this time being only sparsely represented (Table 5.44).

The sites recorded are mostly along the western edge or in the southern two-thirds of the of the section that was the primary survey area south of RAR (Figure 5.32). The two earliest loci (Archaic/BMII; AZ P:3:191A[ASM] and AZ P:3:194[ASM]) occur near the southern edge of the section and along the major drainage in the eastern portion of the basin. The PII/III sites are along drainages as well, but also in the more open areas and ridges away from the drainages suggesting locations for dry-farming in the dunes.

RAR-South and RAR-Southeast – Ceramics

Table 5.45 has counts from surface collections on three RAR project area parcels, mostly from State Trust lands—AZ P:2:56(ASM) west of Chevelon Canyon, RAR-South, and RAR-Southeast (with two later [PIII] pueblos). The RAR-Southeast parcel is southeast of the RAR-Core area, but northeast of the State land section (Figure 1.4). AZ P:2:56(ASM) is nominally a BMII site with a radiocarbon date on maize of 815-500 BCE. However, there is a later ceramic period use of the topographic feature (PIV) made evident by the JYW and HOW ceramics there that are contemporary with the occupation of the fourteenth century Homol'ovi Settlement Cluster (HSC; E.C. Adams 2002) pueblos. The wares present at the RAR-South and RAR-Southeast sites are

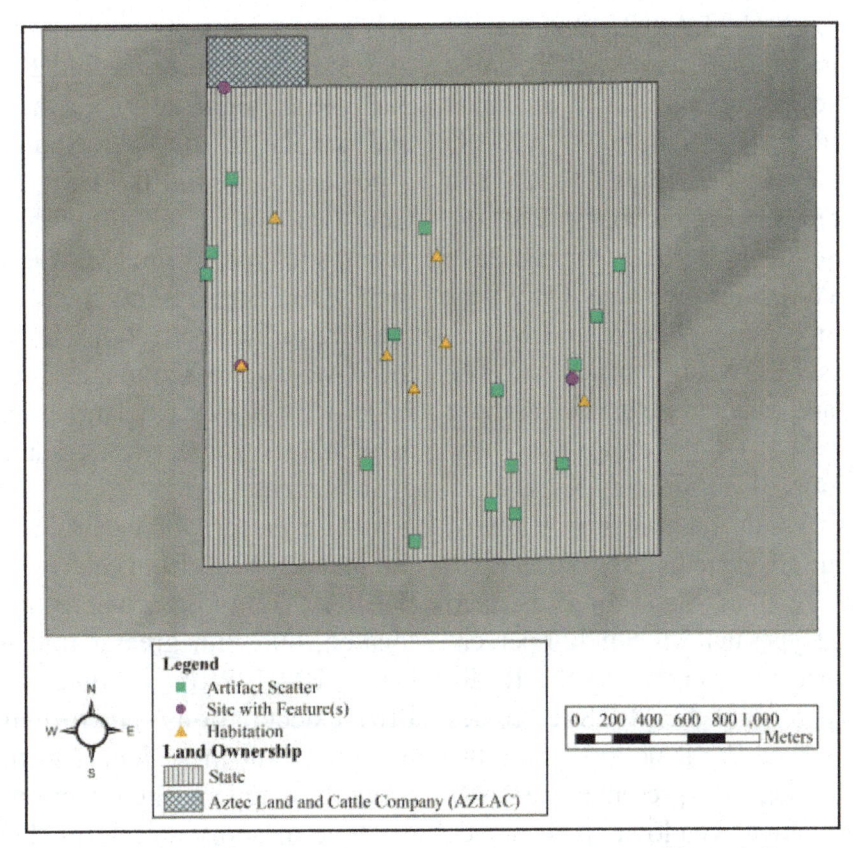

Figure 5.32. Distribution of sites in RAR-South project area; graphic prepared by Josh Conver.

similar, dominated by MBW and LCWW. ABW and TGW are present in small quantities, with slightly higher proportions of TWW, CWW, and possible PVUW.

The MK Site is in the RAR-South project area and, although it is primarily a locus of a large PIII stone-masonry pueblo, surface collections at the site and adjacent ridge and slope area (Loci B and C), soil auger testing, and excavations in the pueblo and midden areas confirm the presence of pit houses and other features that are temporally earlier. Thus, from the MK Site are ceramic types diagnostic of BMIII, PI, PII, and PIII occupations. These are multiple, short-term occupations, however, not a single, long-term, multi-century occupation of the pueblo and ridge top.

The percentages of ABW, TWW, LCGW, TOW, CWW, MBW, and WMRW are similar between the RAR-Core, RAR-South, and RAR-Southeast project areas. There are differences as well: the RAR-South loci have higher percentages of PVUW (and possible PVUW) and the proportions of TGW are much lower in the sites to the south (2% in RAR-South and 7% in RAR-Southeast vs. 28% in the RAR-Core). Compared to loci in HSP, the loci in RAR-South and RAR-Southeast have much less ABW; about the same TWW; far less TGW; much more LCWW and MBW; similar, but less, LCGW; similar TOW, CWW, and WMRW; and as could be expected, more PVUW.

Proportions of ceramic types are, of course, reflective of the relative proportions of their wares, but are nonetheless informative. Indeterminate TWW accounts for 17 percent of the decorated types in RAR-South, 7 percent in RAR-Southeast, 9 percent in the RAR-Core, and 17 percent at the MK Site (Tables 5.46 and 5.47). Lino B/g is not present in the RAR-Southeast loci, but is present in the RAR-Core loci (1%) and at even lower percentages in the RAR-South loci and at MK Site (0.2 and 0.3%, respectively). Lino B/g sherds are 2 percent of the ceramic assemblages in the HSP loci. Kana-a B/w is also absent in the RAR-Southeast loci, but again is present in the RAR-Core loci, in RAR-South loci, and at MK Site (all at 2%). Kana-a B/w makes up only one percent of the assemblages at HSP loci. Comparing these two types, the RAR-South loci have the second lowest Lino B/g to Kana-a B/w ratio (Table 5.11), suggesting, as in the RAR-Core area, more intensive occupation during PI times.

Temporally diagnostic ceramic types for the PII and PIII periods can also be compared between the various RAR project areas and HSP loci. Black Mesa B/w is at 8 percent in the RAR-South collections vs. 7 percent at the RAR-Southeast pueblos, 1 percent in the RAR-Core, and only 2 percent at the HSP loci. Black Mesa B/w is also 7 percent of the MK Site surface collections. Sosi and Dogoszhi B/w are present at 1 percent or less in the RAR-South loci, at 6 and 1 percent of the RAR-Southeast pueblos (the highest of any of the project areas), and, similar to the RAR-South numbers, at 1 percent or less in the HSP loci, the RAR-Core loci, and at MK Site. The primary PIII diagnostic type, Walnut B/w, is 12 percent of the RAR-South assemblages, 14 percent of the MK surface collections, only 1 percent of the RAR-Core assemblages, 3 percent of the HSP loci, but a clearly large proportion of the assemblages from the RAR-Southeast pueblos at 36 percent.

The pattern of early ceramic sites in the uplands back from the river continues in the RAR-South area where the MK Site is located, but with greater indications of the earlier BMIII/PI occupations and less of the PII/III occupations. No formal collections were made at these loci, and they were not formally mapped. There were no indications of stone-masonry structures; however, there were extensive ash stains suggesting likely pit houses. Also present were some slab-lined features typical of Archaic as well as the early ceramic period. From notes made during documentation of the sites, ceramic types present include Lino B/g, Kana-a B/w, and Dogoszhi B/w, and ceramic wares ABW, LCWW, TGW, and TWW.

During the surface collecting and testing at the MK Site and documenting sites in the RAR-South area, a notable ceramic artifact was frequently encountered—ceramic disks (often referred to as "gaming pieces") that are 5-to-7 cm in diameter. These artifacts are very different from relatively abundant worked sherds found at Homol'ovi II (AZ J:14:15[ASM]; Lange 2020:186-191, 215-218). The worked sherds from Homol'ovi II were much smaller, were usually sub-rectangular or trapezoidal, and were usually made from JYW. The worked sherds from the section RAR-South of RAR and the MK Site are mostly made on PII and PIII types of LCWW and TWW (Holbrook-A, Walnut, Black Mesa, and Sosi B/w; Figures 5.33-5.35; and Tables 5.48-49).

RAR-South and RAR-Southeast – Flaked Stone

Relatively few lithics were found as isolates and collected during the survey of this upland basin (N = 144; Table 5.50). Chert predominates the raw material types (36%), but is less dominant than the proportions at AZ P:2:56(ASM) (over 60%; Table 5.35) and at the AZLAC-Adjacent or AZLAC-Far North loci (Table 5.24). Obsidian is extremely rare or entirely absent at these sites (Tables 5.24, 5.35, 5.50, and 5.51).

These upland sites are dominated by flaked stone debris, particularly at the MK Site, followed by the various flake categories. Notable at the MK Site are larger numbers of hammerstones and hammerstone spalls, including many that are chert (Tables 5.52 and 5.53). These artifact types were not noted at AZ P:2:56(ASM) (Table 5.36), but the proportions are similar from the habitation sites on the AZLAC-Adjacent or AZLAC-Far North properties (Tables 5.25 and 5.26).

Artifact size and material are compared in Table 5.54. The percentage of very small artifacts are made nearly equally of fine-grained materials, either chert or petrified wood, and those less than 1 sq cm in size comprise about 10 percent of the upland collection. This percentage is similar to the AZLAC-Adjacent and AZLAC-Far North loci, but the relative proportions of chert and petrified wood are not the same (Table 5.27).

Cortex is absent on a much higher percentage (73%) if the artifacts from the upland area (Tables 5.55 and 5.56) are compared to the artifacts from the AZLAC lands (41%; Tables 5.28 and 5.29), perhaps indicating more intensive reduction of lithic materials in the upland area farther from actual sources. Another comparison of artifact size, this time by site (Tables 5.57 and 5.30), shows that the smallest artifact sizes are more common at the habitation sites and loci. The AZLAC and upland sites are more similar with higher proportions of the 4-to-9 sq cm artifact sizes. These differences and similarities apply regardless of the raw materials involved (Tables 5.58 and 5.31).

Projectile Points and Other Flaked Stone Tools – RAR-South and RAR-Southeast

Projectile points from Paleoindian through the Pueblo periods (N = 32) are present in this upland basin area (Table 5.59). However, the earlier point styles are nowhere nearly as prevalent as they are along the principal canyons and drainages in the RAR-Core (Chapter 9). Slightly over 40 percent of all projectile points from the survey area were found at MK Pueblo. The points at the pueblo

124 *Lange, Fladd, and E.C. Adams*

Figure 5.33. Isolated worked sherds from Rock Art Ranch-South (key to types and wares in Table 5.48; photograph by Richard C. Lange).

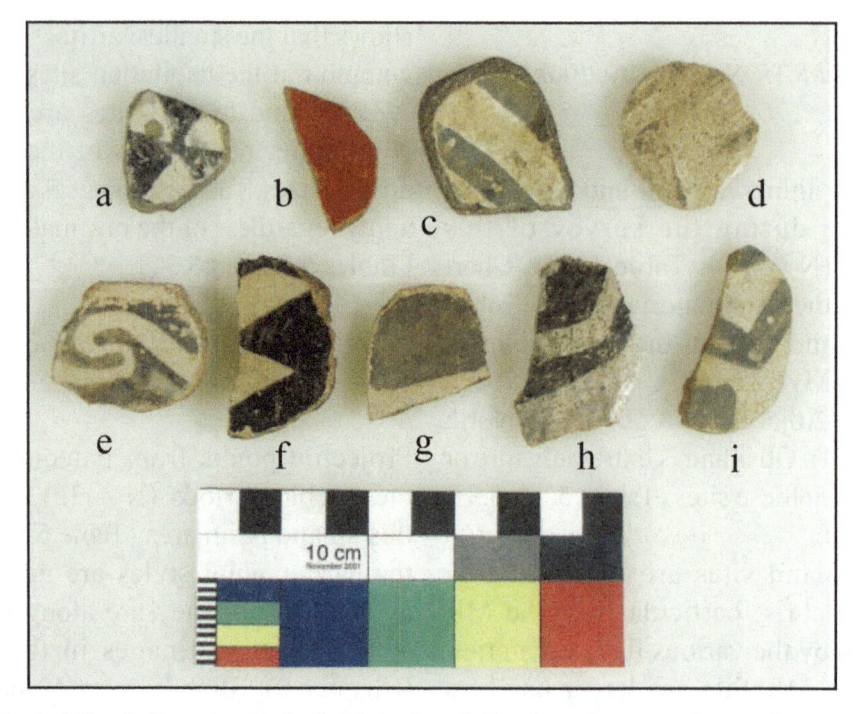

Figure 5.34. Worked sherds from sites in the Rock Art Ranch-South project area (key to sites, types, and wares in Table 5.48; photograph by Richard C. Lange).

Figure 5.35. Worked sherds from surface collections at Multi-Kiva Site (AZ P:3:112[ASM]–FN-37) in RAR-South (key to types and wares in Table 4.49; photograph by Richard C. Lange).

are certainly indicative of earlier hunting activities at that location, as well as collection, curation, and possible special ritual uses of these earlier points (Medeiros and Vonarx 2016; Soza 2018).

The overwhelming material type for projectile points found in this survey area is chert with only a few from petrified wood or igneous materials, and just one projectile point made on obsidian (Table 5.59). The majority of point styles come from the general area, that is, from no particular direction (Table 5.60). The next most frequent source direction is for styles from the east/northeast (over 20% for both points from the general survey and points from the pueblo). Point styles from either the north/northwest or west/southwest are the next most common, and point styles from the south/southeast are represented by a single San Pedro-style point.

Isolated projectile points found in the upland RAR-South area closely mirror those from the isolated points and sites west of Chevelon Canyon. Most are made on chert and similarly date from the Archaic to the BMII/III periods (Figure 5.36; Table 5.61). Points collected from sites in the RAR-South area are more frequently made of petrified wood and involved Late Archaic and Middle-Late Archaic as well as PI and later ceramic period styles (Figure 5.37; Table 5.62).

Some other flaked stone tools are illustrated in the figures cited above, including bifaces, burins, drills, and scrapers in addition to the projectile points (Figure 5.38; also in Table 5.63). One curious artifact type was collected from several different sites in the upland area, and especially from AZ P:3:165(ASM)— serrated flakes made mostly on petrified wood (Figure 5.39; Table 5.64). The function of these quite distinctive tools is unknown and they do not seem to occur in the RAR-Core area or other project areas.

126 *Lange, Fladd, and E.C. Adams*

Figure 5.36. Isolated projectile points from Rock Art Ranch-South (key to types and materials in Table 5.61; photograph by Richard C. Lange).

Figure 5.37. Projectile points from sites in Rock Art Ranch-South (key to types and materials in Table 5.62; photograph by Richard C. Lange).

5: *Rock Art Ranch Area Surveys and Testing* 127

Figure 5.38. Examples of flaked stone tools from Multi-Kiva Site (AZ P:3:112[ASM]) in Rock Art Ranch-South (key to types and materials in Table 5.63).

Figure 5.39. Serrated petrified wood and chert tools from Rock Art Ranch-South (key to proveniences and materials in Table 5.64; photograph by Richard C. Lange).

RAR-South and RAR-Southeast Ground Stone

Compared to the RAR-Core area to the north, very few pieces of ground stone were found in this upland survey area or at MK Pueblo. Of the 15 pieces found from the general survey area, about half were manos and half were metates (Table 5.65). The few pieces of ground stone could reflect the fact that these were valuable implements and were taken along when the inhabitants of this area moved on to other locations. Flat, two-hand manos and metates are the dominant types of ground stone found.

Summary of RAR-South and RAR-Southeast Areas

The RAR-South and RAR-Southeast project areas are reflective themselves of many of the subtle differences in settlement locations over the centuries of the general ceramic period. The later-in-time masonry pueblos that are the main archaeological features of these areas are all near shallow drainages and upland basins like the habitation sites in the RAR-Core and AZLAC-Adjacent areas. However, there is evidence of earlier occupations under the MK pueblo and along the same ridge top, and the sites even farther south also have indications of the earlier BMIII and PI occupations. The MK Site and the two pueblos in the RAR-Southeast area all date solidly to PIII, with the MK Site being perhaps slightly earlier than the RAR-Southeast pueblos, BP in the RAR-Core, and most of the pueblos in the AZLAC-Adjacent and AZLAC-Far North areas. This is interesting because the MK Site is by far the largest pueblo in the RAR research areas and, along with other nearby scatters, has artifacts not present or rare in the other project areas: steatite objects, serrated petrified wood tools, argillite, and worked sherds in the form of relatively large, circular disks (see Chapter 6).

SUMMARY OF SITE AND SCATTER DISTRIBUTIONS

The vicinity of middle Chevelon Canyon with RAR and Bell Cow Canyon on the east side and the drainages and hanging canyons of RAR-West on the west side are where all of the more than 100 loci dating Late Archaic through BMII are located with 36, 33 east of Chevelon, having features. Many sites have material indications of use and/or occupation during more than one time period (Table 1.1). Seven of these sites had thermal features from which burned annuals or corn were extracted with all dating in the span of 815 BCE to 567 CE. East of Chevelon Canyon in the RAR-Core is also where nearly all pre-Late Archaic points were recovered. While no sites definitively date to the Paleoindian or Early/Middle Archaic periods, a quarry site in the area with numerous Paleoindian, Early, and Middle Archaic artifacts and technology suggests use dating to the earlier periods. BMII covers a broader range of years than the later periods; thus, the larger number of sites may reflect the greater length of time rather than a greater intensity of use of the landscape. Interestingly, 18 (10%) of the loci exhibit surface evidence of occupation during multiple time periods, suggesting reuse of resource-rich areas east and west of Chevelon Canyon.

As shown in Table 1.1, the majority of the documented sites was artifact scatters consisting largely of lithics and ceramics as well as some ground stone. Sites with features, such as ash stains or vertical slabs, totaled 51, with 30 habitation structures representing the rarest site form, as would be expected. Evidence for sedentary habitation of the area begins during the BMIII/PI period with the appearance of both gray and brown utility ware. Large sites with features occur in the RAR-Core area with at least four large PI pit house villages. Ceramics also indicate a small

BMIII presence beneath or near the AZLAC-Far North pueblos and small surface scatters along the southern boundary of the RAR-South survey area and alongside drainages west of Chevelon Canyon.

Pueblo II/III period scatters and occupation sites consisted originally of pit houses in the RAR-Core area during the 1100s that were replaced between 1175-1200 CE by masonry pueblos in all areas—RAR-Core, AZLAC-Far North, RAR-Southeast, and RAR-South. At least 14 loci have room blocks. Although PIII pit house villages have a mix of gray and brown utility pottery, pueblos nearly always have a majority of Obliterated Corrugated Brown Utility Ware suggesting their occupants originated south or east of the study area. The larger number of artifact scatters dating to the PII/III period and higher number of sites in general suggest a higher density occupation. Only five scatters date to the PIV period representing visitation rather than occupation, possibly by groups living at one or more of the seven villages comprising the nearby HSC. The appearance of historic yellow ware sherds confirms later visitation to the area possibly for collecting flora and fauna for ritual activities as documented in 1896 by Fewkes (1898, 1900, 1904).

Temporal Trends in the Rock Art Ranch Research Areas

Paleoindian and Early/Middle Archaic (11,500 – 2,000 BCE)

The abundance of projectile points from Clovis through Late Paleoindian, Early Archaic, and Middle or Middle/Late Archaic periods (Figures 5.8 and 5.9) makes it clear that the nonagricultural resources of the study area were long important in the seasonal rounds of local populations (Duke 2016); 79 of the typed points, representing 32 percent of the assemblage, date to these time periods (Table 5.14). The earlier survey west of Chevelon Canyon, however, failed to document use represented by projectile points until the Middle Archaic period (Huckell and Huckell 2004). Additionally, a unique blade core likely dating to Clovis, or minimally, Paleoindian was located near a later site in the area, suggesting the residents may have curated this rare artifact (Figure 5.40). The concentrations of these points near the canyon edges suggests a focus on hunting, a seasonal practice continued by early agriculturalists. The presence of permanent water in Chevelon Canyon and easily accessible water with shallow wells in Chimney and Bell Cow Canyons must have been important factors in continuous use of the study area for over 13,000 years.

Projectile points are made principally on non-local cherts and petrified wood, with some use of local cherts and other materials from local gravels concentrated in two localities (AZ P:2:162[ASM] and AZ P:2:153[ASM]), termed quarries (Table 5.14). Numerous Paleoindian and Archaic projectile points, tools, and flakes were observed close to and downslope from AZ P:2:161(ASM). Given the density and concentration of artifacts and the presence of multiple material types for lithic tool production, it is likely that this quarry was used extensively during the Paleoindian and Early/Middle Archaic periods. At the very least, it was a significant location on the local landscape utilized repeatedly throughout the occupation of the area.

Petrified wood sources may have been tied to groups who migrated to the study area from areas east along the LCR where petrified wood is abundant. These routes are ancient as exhibited by two Clovis points made from petrified wood. Non-local cherts resemble outcrops in northern Arizona and the Great Basin as well as pedernal cherts and flints

Figure 5.40. Formal chert blade core from AZ P:2:174(ASM)–RAR-116; photograph by ASM Photo Collections).

in north-central New Mexico. The San Juan style petroglyph tradition likely came from the north beginning in the Middle to Early Archaic either through the movement of the populations themselves or the transfer o the style during interactions between mobile groups (McNeil and Shaul 2018). How these groups interacted with existing populations is unclear. Possibly, local groups were forced west of RAR-South into more mountainous areas where Middle and Late Archaic sites and points are common (Herr 2014; Sliva 2018).

Late Archaic (2000-800 BCE) and Basketmaker II (BMII) (800 BCE –600 CE)

As noted in Table 1.1, 91 sites, 63 percent of which are artifact scatters, date to these time periods in the RAR-Core survey area with another 11 in the area surveyed west of Chevelon Canyon. They are concentrated along Chevelon, Chimney, and Bell Cow Canyons (Figure 5.9); in particular, Bell Cow Canyon and its confluence with Chevelon Canyon exhibit significant use during this period. The majority of sites (85%) dating to these periods are located within 250 m of the canyons with 66 percent near Bell Cow Canyon. The two quarries and many of the Paleoindian and Early/Middle Archaic projectile points are found along Chevelon Canyon or its confluence with Bell Cow Canyon. In contrast, Late Archaic/BMII sites are concentrated farther upstream along Bell Cow as well as along upper Chimney Canyon suggesting a subtle shift in use of the landscape. The 11 Late Archaic/BMII lithic scatters in th RAR-West area are concentrated along major tributaries in Chevelon Canyon, which resemble the drainages east of Chevelon in the RAR-Core area. For either side of the Chevelon Canyon, the permanent water source available in Chevelon Canyon likely continued to attract large game that would be appealing to hunter-gatherer populations throughout the preceramic use of the area. Generally, Late Archaic and BMII sites are located in shallow, sandy eolian deposits ranging from 10 cm to 2 m deep, often thinning as slope wash onto bedrock at the edge of the canyons. Few sites are more than 10 m above the bottoms of these side canyons. All sites are within 4 km and most are within 2 km of The Steps, the only access to the canyon floor from the east side in this section of Chevelon Canyon and the location of the petroglyphs. Site density on the west side of Chimney Canyon compared to the east side is much sparser and site size is considerably smaller although four sites do have features. Sites along Bell Cow and Chevelon Canyons tend to be rather large scatters that can be considered continuous in many places.

Thirty-six Late Archaic and BMII sites have at least one feature; these features are roughly evenly divided between storage (indicated by alignments of vertical slabs) and thermal uses indicated by ash stains and, rarely, fire-altered rock. Projectile points dating to this time period were also common (see Figures 5.9 and 5.16; Table 5.14).

One BMII pit house and numerous bell-shaped and straight-sided storage cists were discovered during excavations at BP. These are described in detail in Chapter 7. The pit house is 2.7 meters in diameter and 20 cm deep with a single central storage pit 60 cm in diameter and 40 cm deep. Bruce and Lisa Huckell excavated a similar small pit house at AZ P:2:56(ASM)]) located 6.5 km southwest of the RAR-Core survey area (Huckell 1999, 2004). This pit house was 2.8 meters in diameter and 15–20 cm deep with a central thermal feature containing burned corn that yielded a ^{14}C calibrated age of 815–500 BCE.

Calibrated ^{14}C ages from burned annuals found in thermal features at six other BMII sites, a Pueblo II site, and AZ P:2:56(ASM) are shown in Figure 5.41. Although seven dates are a small sample, they cluster into three time periods, all within the early agricultural phase or BMII period: 815 –500 BCE, 200 BCE – 250 CE, and 320 – 575 CE. Only the feature from AZ P:2:56(ASM) had maize, suggesting it was not widely grown in the region at this time. These dates match the estimated age of about 75 percent of the petroglyphs at The Steps (Brinkerhoff, Chapter 3; Kolber 2000). The strong association of BMII sites with the canyons is expected as they hold the greatest variety of natural resources, including plants, a habitat for large ungulates, a reliable stone source for metates, and permanent water accessible by shallow wells. Surrounding the canyons are diverse species of grasses, including Indian rice grass (*Oryzopsis* sp.*)*. Edible plants are most abundant in spring and late summer, while game is most abundant in fall and winter (see K. Adams, Smith, and Adams, Chapter 2).

So, what were these early agriculturalists doing in the area? The best indicator is the abundant ground stone. More than 350 fragments of ground stone have been documented in the RAR-Core including basin and flat metate forms strongly associated with BMII sites and features on those sites (Pitroff 2014). In addition to the metates, over 50 bedrock grinding features were encountered, largely located along the length of Bell Cow Canyon (Figure 5.22). These features were often found in clusters of five to ten and ranged from pecked areas prepared for grinding to basin shaped grooves clearly heavily used (Figure 5.23). This suggests the predominant activity during BMII times was processing plant remains. The complete absence of maize from burned features on RAR suggests food processing was focused on the abundant and diverse grasses and other edible plants, even though the bottoms of both canyons seem well suited to garden plots for maize. Given the

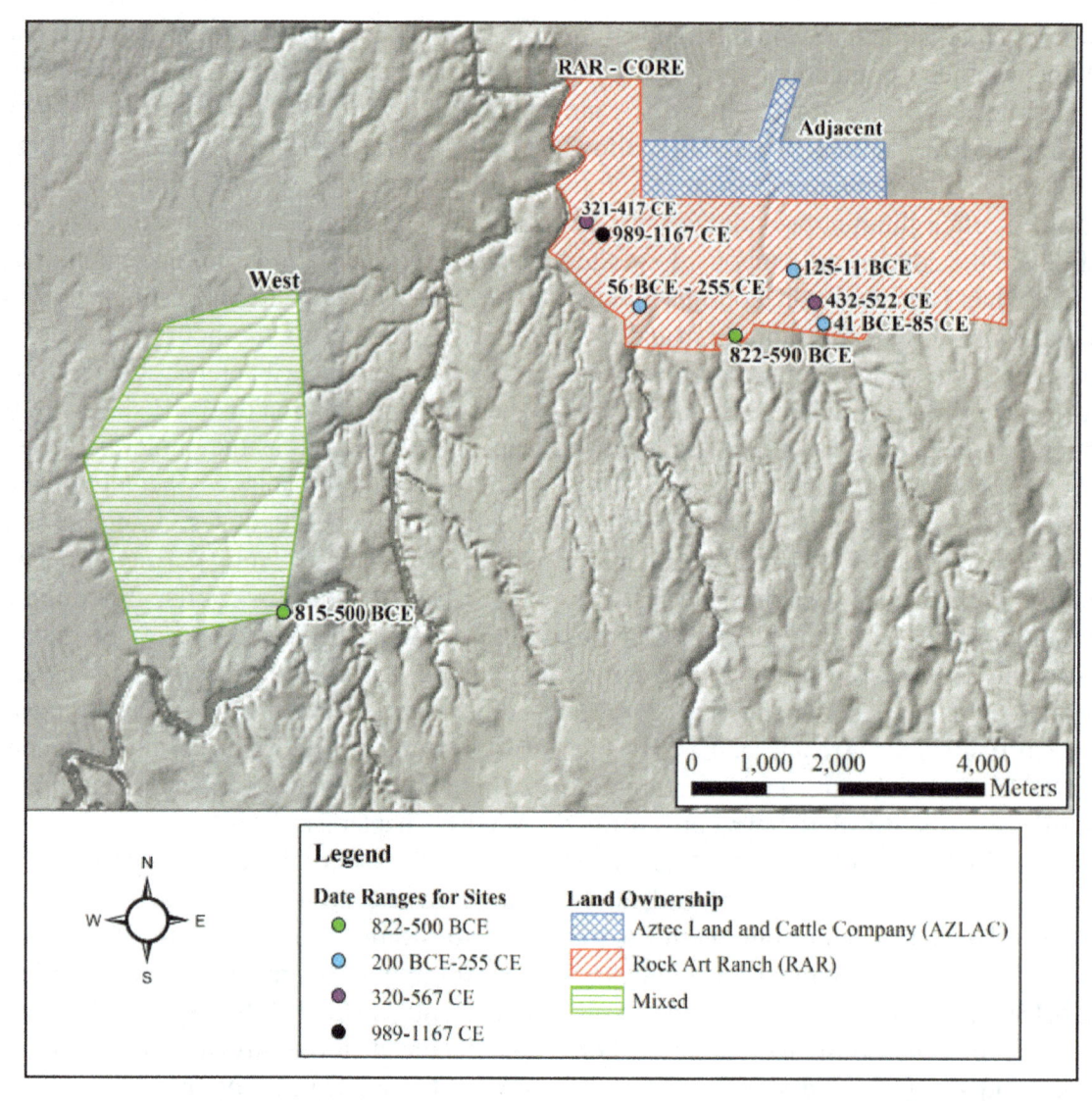

Figure 5.41. Radiocarbon dates from tested and excavated features in the Rock Art Ranch research area (graphic prepared by Josh Conver).

small sample size of flotation samples from thermal features, it certainly is possible maize is present and some farming was practiced.

Late Archaic/BMII projectile points are abundant with 53 represented by 9 types including 21 San Pedro in the RAR-Core area (Table 5.14). All 13 of the preceramic points west of Chevelon date Middle/Late Archaic or BMII. These occur on sites and as isolates suggesting hunting was an important dietary supplement (see Soza, Chapter 9, for other possible uses of points). This is reinforced by the predominance of bifaces, retouch and other fine manufacturing flakes on BMII sites with features in the RAR-Core (see Soza, Chapter 9 for a detailed analysis of bifaces recovered during survey of RAR property). Flaked stone is dominated by local cherts. The two local quarry sources (AZ P:2:161[ASM] and AZ P:2:153[ASM]), which are formed from eroded Shinarump Formation gravels near Bell Cow and Chevelon canyons, contained cobbles of chert as well as quartzite and rare instances of igneous and petrified wood. However, the diversity of petrified wood in color and quality as points and flakes from sites dating to these periods indicates the majority is not from these local sources and likely originates from as far away as the Petrified Forest 55 km to the east (Table 5.66). Notable is the continued scarcity of obsidian. Its absence suggests a social boundary with groups west of Clear Creek, where 57.4 percent of projectile points are obsidian (Lyndon 2005:156) and petroglyphs are of a local style quite different from the San Juan/Palavayu style at Chevelon Canyon (Malotki 2007; McNeil and Shaul 2018; Pilles 1975).

The evidence so far suggests the RAR-Core/AZ P:2:56(ASM) areas were important seasonal components of BMII subsistence. There are few pit houses, which should be visible on at least some of the highly deflated BMII sites in the RAR-Core, suggesting winter homes may have been elsewhere. Given that groups using the area during this period were mobile, the presence of petrified wood as points and flaked stone along with 33 percent of the points typed as San Pedro hints at their potential range or interactions being to the east and south. Recent work at and below the Mogollon Rim suggests this area may have provided the resources for winter homes (Herr 2017; Sliva 2017),

Basketmaker III and Pueblo I (600–1025 CE)

The distribution of sites created by the first ceramic users in the region associated with BMIII and PI groups is the broadest of any time period occurring in the RAR-Core, AZLAC-Far North, RAR-South, and West regions. This is likely due to the additional focus on farming as a subsistence strategy (Figure 5.10). Only in the RAR-Core area are there obvious habitation sites with one to multiple pit houses; however, four sites in RAR-West (AZ P:2:109[ASM], AZ P:2:110A&B[ASM], AZ P:2:111[ASM], and AZ P:2:112 [ASM]) may have contained pit houses based on artifact density and ash stains with uncertainty caused by their being highly disturbed and eroded. All are associated with major side drainages to Chevelon Canyon. Sherd scatters dating BMIII are present in the AZLAC-Far North and RAR-South with no indication of habitation sites in either area. There is no BMIII in the RAR-Southeast. In the RAR-Core area sites shifted farther away from the canyon edges compared to BMII with only half (51%) located within 250 m of these landscape features. Slightly more of these are found along Bell Cow Canyon (28%) compared to Chimney Canyon (21%) with only one site dating to this period located near Chevelon Canyon. Smaller sites with 1–3 pit houses, storage features, and middens are scattered between the canyons. Ceramics indicate these sites were created by BMIII groups (600-825 CE) of 1–3 households who may have been present only seasonally (Young and Gilman 2012; Young 1996). Multiple artifact scatters in the grasslands between the two canyons suggest the area was preferred for farming. Sources of population for these small groups may have been the numerous larger villages along the LCR located 5–10 km north (E.C. Adams 2002; Lange 1998; Young 1996).

Settlement changed substantially during PI when most of the population in the RAR-Core area occupied large pit house villages while PI sites in the RAR-West are smaller, if pit houses are present. In the AZLAC-Far North and RAR-Southeast PI is nearly to completely absent; whereas, in the RAR-South are ceramic scatters with possible pit houses. In the RAR-Core area, two large PI sites are located 2.5 km apart, one on the east side of Chimney Canyon (AZ P:3:137A[ASM]–RAR-22A) and the other (AZ P:2:104A-D[ASM]–RAR-4) on the west and south side of Bell Cow Canyon. Each of these sites has more than 10 pit houses and extensive middens. The predominance of Kana'a B/w pottery in these settlements suggests they were occupied sometime between 825–1025 CE. Burning of most structures indicates there was no expectation of return when these communities were depopulated and suggests possible ritual decommissioning of the structures (E.C. Adams and Fladd 2017; Roth and Schriever 2015).

Two additional sizable PI pit house communities with similar ceramic assemblages are located on AZLAC property adjacent to the north boundary of RAR. AZ P:3:176B(ASM)—RAR-160 and AZ P:3:223(ASM)—RAR-164 each contained several pit house depressions associated with dense ash and artifact scatters suggesting these pit houses too were burned when occupants left. A third PI site on AZLAC property, AZ P:3:119B(ASM)–FN-8 and FN-147, had extensive PI period MBW and TGW assemblages. Communities similar in size to the PI sites in the study area occur along the LCR but ceramic assemblages (lower frequencies of Kana'a B/w than on RAR) suggest they predate those in the RAR-Core area (Young 1996; Young and Gilpin 2012). Pit house sites in RAR-West seem more similar to those in HSP but absence of detailed surface collections means these are mostly impressions.

Details of house form and size are not known, but 56 percent of ceramics from RAR-Core sites are part of the Tusayan Tradition from the north, similar to the 53 percent in those excavated by Young (1996) in HSP. Interestingly, at HSP the next highest frequency of ceramics was ABW from the mountainous regions to west (Barker and Young 2017), a trait it shares with AZ P:2:104(ASM) in upper Bell Cow Canyon where 17 percent of ceramics are ABW. Nevertheless, there are important differences between the two areas. MBW makes up 26 percent of total ceramics from AZ P:3:137A(ASM) and 37 percent from AZ P:2:104(ASM) (Estes, Chapter 10), much higher than the 6 percent from the pit house village in HSP. More than 300 MBW sherds from AZ P:2:104(ASM) are either Plain or Polished consistent with BMIII/PI occupation; whereas, AZ P:3:137A(ASM) has over 100 Plain or Polished brown ware sherds. Notably, AZ P:3:176B(ASM) had the largest MBW Polished assemblage of any site found during survey of the RAR areas. These numbers suggest either robust exchange or, most likely, co-residency of groups originating from the north and south during the early occupation of villages in the RAR-Core.

The presence of several sizable PI sites (825–1025 CE) indicates the RAR-Core was a locus of immigration from surrounding areas similar to the Hopi Mesas and Puerco Valley of the West, both areas where larger settlements are known (Bernardini et al. 2021; Roberts 1939, 1940; Schachner et al. 2021; Throgmorton 2012; Wilshusen et al. 2012). In the case of the RAR-Core, ceramic evidence points to co-residence of RAR-Southern and northern groups with their distinctive brown ware and gray ware traditions. These may have set the stage for later immigration during PIII when pueblos were established. Petroglyphs from this period, ca. 600–1000 CE, are present at The Steps, but miniscule in number compared to the BMII glyphs. The continuous use and occupation of the RAR-Core throughout this time period demonstrates changing relationships with the landscape.

Pueblo II (1025–1130 CE)

Occupation during PII is most prominently represented by the ubiquitous Black Mesa B/w (1025-1125 CE) with much lower frequencies of Dogozshi and Sosi B/w (1050–1075 CE); however, only 11 sites have pure PII ceramic assemblages. Ten are in the RAR-Core area with three along Bell Cow Canyon just north of the large pit house village, AZ P:2:104(ASM) and seven along northern Chimney Canyon.

There is also one pure PII site west of Chevelon Canyon (AZ P:2:187A [ASM]). The sites in the RAR-Core are artifact scatters with the exception of AZ P:3:217(ASM), which has features, and appear to be farming locales for residents of pit house villages that are situated on or adjacent to the large PI pit house villages. The PII use is shorter and less intensive than PI with ceramics suggesting later PII (1100–1150 CE) while PII occupation appears less intensive from the end of the PI to the early PII period, ca. 1025–1100 CE (Figure 5.11). This pattern is similar to the one identified by Lange (1998) in his survey of HSP. AZ P:2:187A(ASM) west of Chevelon Canyon is unique in being the only site with possible pit houses that is purely PII.

Use of the landscape continues to change with far fewer sites located within 250 m of the canyon edges (32%). For the first time, more sites are found near Chimney Canyon (21%) as opposed to Bell Cow Canyon (12%). As noted in the section above, settlements in the region to the east during this period are abundant involving large, complex communities (Burton 1993; Theuer 2012). These coalescent communities are similar to ones in southwest Colorado and the Zuni area and seem connected to the Chaco system that expanded out of the Canyon about 950 CE (e.g., Cameron and Duff 2008; Lekson 2006, 2019; Throgmorton 2012). Clearly, the entire survey area is marginal to these events likely due to a lack of resources able to support communities of sufficient size (Dean et al. 1985; Herr 2001; Van West 1996a).

Ceramics and architecture suggest increased settlement of the study area resumed around 1100 CE, which is best exemplified by the ceramic patterns at AZ P:2:104(ASM) that included Black Mesa B/w, a few sherds of Dogoszhi B/w, and one sherd each of Holbrook-A, Holbrook-B, and Padre B/w. Padre B/w is from the LCWW tradition and comprises 2.5 percent of the AZ P:2:104(ASM) assemblage. LCWW developed in the Hopi Buttes in the mid-1000s and supplanted TWW in the study area and surrounding region by 1100 CE (Lange 1998; Mills et al. 1999). Also significant is an extensive and diverse assemblage of ABW totaling 260 sherds recovered from AZ P:2:104(ASM), which is consistent with a late PII village and suggestive of possible co-residence by Sinagua from the west (Estes, Chapter 10). In addition to extensive middens with late PII ceramics, AZ P:2:104(ASM) has a small amount of surface (jacal-style) architecture; several pit houses are also likely present. The middens associated with this site suggests either a large short-term occupation or a smaller, long-lived one.

Additionally, Black Mesa B/w appears at AZ P:3:137A&B(ASM), indicating a PII component to the large PI village on the terrace east of Chimney Canyon. This pattern mimics the one in HSP where pit house communities with external storage continue into the early 1200s (Estes, Chapter 10; Lange 1998; Young 2008); however, in the RAR-Core, pit house settlements end soon after the appearance of Walnut B/w (1130–1230 CE), as it is not present on AZ P:2:104(ASM) and the pit house village at AZ P:3:137A&B(ASM) only has traces of Walnut B/w.

AZ P:3:137A&B(ASM) ceramics are the earliest to include numerous CWW sherds, which are dominated by Snowflake B/w (1100–1275 CE), suggesting the site was occupied the first half of the 1100s. Otherwise, MBW (33.0%) and TGW (51.6%) dominate the site assemblage. Obliterated Corrugated Brown Ware, comprising 10 percent of the AZ P:3:137A&B(ASM) assemblages along with CWW anticipate movement of pueblo-building groups from the south or east into the area around 1200 CE. The ceramic assemblage also may reflect a continuation of co-residency between northern and southern groups first encountered on the large PI sites (Estes, Chapter 10).

Numerous artifact scatters having LCWW west of Chimney Canyon and north and east of Bell Cow Canyon are likely loci of garden farming by occupants of pit house and later pueblo settlements who would also have used Chimney Canyon itself. The subsurface water available in the canyon would have provided drinking water and was likely used to hand-water crops.

Pueblo III (1130-1255 CE)

The next significant settlement change in the RAR area occurred in the late 1100s or early 1200s CE when four or five small pueblos (BP, AZ P:3:114[ASM]–RAR-2; AZ P:3:118[ASM]–RAR-6; AZ P:3:121[ASM]–RAR-10; and AZ P:3:227[ASM]–RAR-169) settled just north of AZ P:3:137(ASM) along Chimney Canyon (Figure 5.11). Notably, whereas Bell Cow Canyon was a focus of settlement throughout BMII to PII, there was not a permanent occupation there dating after 1125 CE. Three of the sites are 1-2 km north of the excavated sites (AZ P:3:114[ASM] and AZ P:3:132[ASM]), together named Brandy's Pueblo, where the walls of Chimney Canyon are completely eroded away, and for the next 2 km, whatever water flows in the canyon spreads over a wide, flat floodplain approximately 1 km wide. Today, this floodplain is filled with driftwood and deep sandy soils at its mouth. It is around this area that the remainder of the pueblos are concentrated.

Excavations to complement survey data focused on BP (AZ P:3:114[ASM] and AZ P:3:132[ASM]) with five calibrated radiocarbon dates on maize from AZ P:3:114(ASM) and one on burned closing material to the pit structure roof of AZ P:3:132(ASM) combined to date occupation of the sites to 1225-1254 CE (LaMotta [2013] from UA AMS Radiocarbon Lab, samples AS101448-101453).

Walnut B/w (1130–1230 CE) is either the most common or second most common decorated type in assemblages of these pueblos placing them solidly in PIII. Similarly, Mogollon Brown Obliterated Corrugated is greater than 50 percent of the assemblages of all except AZ P:3:227(ASM), which is 35 percent, likely because it has 63 percent of its assemblage decorated versus 25-30 percent in the other pueblos. In contrast TGW ranges from 4.5-20 percent in the pueblos. Dominance of MBW is also typical of pueblos documented in the RAR-South area, including MK Pueblo, indicating the likely source of the groups building these pueblos came from the south. In Chapter 8, Krystal Britt also documents local production of most brown wares further indicating population sources are southern/eastern.

CWW, the dominant decorated tradition recovered from excavations at BP at over 56 percent, is only 23 percent at AZ P:3:227(ASM) with similar most common types of Puerco B/w, Reserve B/w, and Snowflake B/w, suggesting the pueblos are contemporary. In contrast, CWW is present at less than 2 percent of decorated wares at AZ P:3:118(ASM) with Reserve B/w and Tularosa B/w (1200–1325 CE) represented, and completely absent from AZ P:3:121(ASM). All pueblo sites have low percentages of TWW, which is nearly absent at BP (E.C. Adams and LaMotta, Chapter 7; Estes, Chapter 10). The white wares are complemented by Tsegi Orange Ware (TOW), including Tusayan B/r (1050-1225 CE) and Tsegi B/o (1225-1300 CE), the latter also at AZ P:3:118(ASM). These differences are usually chronological suggesting AZ P:118(ASM) and AZ P:3:121(ASM) were established earlier than BP but may have been depopulated about the same time.

Seven kilometers north of the RAR-Core are another two small pueblos, one with four room blocks (AZ P:3:215A-D [ASM]—RAR-151A-D) and another with two blocks of rooms

(RAR-152A&B, AZ P:3:216A&B [ASM]). Ceramics from these sites vary from the RAR-Core area in the nearly complete absence of CWW and similar percentages of LCWW to TWW at AZ P:3:215(ASM) but much higher TWW at AZ P:3:216(ASM) suggesting it may be slightly earlier (ca. 1150 CE) or have a slightly different source population. AZ P:3:215B-D(ASM) loci have far and away the highest percentages (20-25%) of ABW of any pueblo on RAR or AZ P:3:216(ASM), suggesting some of its occupants were from the mountainous regions to the west.

With Walnut B/w the most common white ware type followed by Black Mesa B/w and Dogoszhi B/w and just as many Tsegi OW as white ware, including the same types as pueblos in the RAR-Core area, as white wares, these AZLAC-Far North pueblos likely overlap in their occupation with the early end of the pueblos in the RAR-Core (1175-1225 CE). The rarity of CWW is either chronological or the much higher frequencies of TWW, ABW, and TGW could point to assemblage differences due to migration sources or exchange partners to these pueblo occupants. Britt (Chapter 8) determined local manufacture of Brown Obliterated Corrugated similar to other pueblo occupants in the region indicating possible social connections between the RAR-Core and the AZLAC-Far North pueblos.

Excavations at BP uncovered a badly damaged, four-room long, linear arrangement of masonry rooms with a ramada that abutted the entire northeast side of the pueblo. Room size averages 8 sq m, more similar in size to mountain (Mogollon) groups than Pueblo groups occupying Hopi Mesas pueblos. The most common ceramic, comprising 57.4 percent of the assemblage, is Brown Obliterated Corrugated manufactured by groups living south and east of BP, as well as at the pueblo itself (Britt, Chapter 8; Ownby 2016, 2017).

There is no ceramic evidence of populations occupying these pueblos or any portion of the region within the surveyed RAR project areas after 1255 when radiocarbon dating suggests BP occupants left. There is a complete absence of any type whose manufacture began after 1250 CE including later White Mountain Red Ware types (Pinedale Polychrome and later), Roosevelt Red wares, or even white wares. Absence of red wares and polychromes whose manufacture began after 1250 suggests depopulation of the RAR-Core and AZLAC-Far North areas near the LCR preceded the circulation of these types and wares, confirming the radiocarbon dates.

Petroglyphs dating to the PII/PIII period represent about 10 percent of the glyphs at The Steps. Quite likely occupants of the PIII villages along Chimney Canyon carved at least some of these. No such settlements occur west of Chevelon Canyon. At less than 10 km away, the AZLAC-Far North pueblos (AZ P:3:215[ASM] and AZ P:3:216[ASM]) could easily have visited The Steps at Chevelon Canyon as well. The question, as posed by Doery in Chapter 4, did they have access or could access have been restricted by pueblo groups living closer?

Pueblo IV and Historic (1275–1700 CE)

There is no ceramic evidence of populations occupying any portion of the region within the surveyed area after 1275 CE. Indeed, one of the most interesting phenomena in the RAR-Core area is the relative paucity of JYW and WOW ceramics that would indicate use of the area by the populations living at Chevelon Pueblo or other Homol'ovi villages after 1300. Chevelon Pueblo with 500 rooms and as many as 300 occupants is only 7 km north of the RAR-Core along the LCR (E.C. Adams, ed. 2016). Frequent visitation of the RAR-Core area by residents of Chevelon and other Homol'ovi villages was expected given its unique ecology and the concentration of millennia of petroglyphs at The Steps. Instead, there is only limited evidence of visitation by individuals or groups possessing WOW manufactured at HSC villages and JYW and AYW manufactured at Hopi Mesas communities used heavily at the Homol'ovi/ Chevelon villages after 1330 CE.

Relatively few yellow ware sherds were encountered during survey until near the juncture of Bell Cow and Chevelon Canyons (Figure 5.12). Many of these clusters of yellow ware represent pot drops (Figure 5.13) and the majority is located on BMII sites, particularly AZ P:3:105 (ASM)—RAR-79 and AZ P:2:146T&U(ASM)—RAR-95B&C. The presence of these later ceramics along with flakes of obsidian on early sites suggests deliberate actions to signal visitation of ancestral locations on trips to and from The Steps (Kuwanwisiwma and Ferguson 2009). Additionally, the majority of the JYW and AYW sherds postdate 1400, after HSC villages were depopulated.

Two Cibecue Polychrome (1300-1325 CE) sherds of the MBW tradition were recovered from extramural fill during BP excavations. Additionally, one Kechipawan Polychrome (1375-1475 CE) sherd of the Zuni Glaze Ware tradition was recovered from the surface. Another sherd from the Zuni area, Matsaki Polychrome (1375-1680 CE), was recovered from survey of RAR suggesting visitation by Zuni individuals or groups during late prehispanic to Mission Period times comparable to Hopi visitation. These ceramics suggest sustained, but limited, visitation of the area from 1275 to as late as 1700 despite the cessation of local occupation. Fewkes (1898, 1900, 1904) documented oral traditions of Hopi visitation to Chevelon Canyon in the 1890s to collect water, birds, and turtles for ceremonial uses, and the ceramics and obsidian are likely related to practices similar to those described by Fewkes.

DISCUSSION AND CONCLUSIONS

The survey of the RAR-Core revealed material culture spanning almost 13,000 years of use and occupation. As illustrated in Figures 5.9, 5.10, 5.11, and 5.17, use of the landscape changed through the history of occupation in the RAR-Core and surrounding areas. This evidence ranges from isolated finds and small scatters of temporally diagnostic artifacts to large pit house villages and small pueblo sites. Initial utilization of the area began with Paleoindian hunters and gatherers who were likely drawn to the permanent water source located in Chevelon Canyon and standing water in the lower reaches of Bell Cow Canyon, the game animals this water would attract, and the available sources of lithic materials located in two nearby quarries (see Soza, Chapter 9). Recent research on this period has discovered the importance of gathering wild plants to the lifestyle of peoples formerly understood mainly as big game hunters (Ballenger et al. 2017). Thus, the diversity of plant life available along the canyons may have been an initial draw at this time as well.

Use continued throughout the Archaic and into the BMII period with a greater emphasis on and potential seasonal occupation of areas along the edges of the shallow side drainages to Chevelon Canyon. During this time, a dense concentration of ground stone and bedrock grinding features the length of Bell Cow Canyon indicate the growing prominence of plant resources to local subsistence practices (Figure 5.22). While corn has not been found in the samples from excavated features at these sites, it is known to have been available in the broader region by BMII (Huckell and Huckell 2004; Smiley 2002a, 2002b). Its absence may signal specialized use of the RAR-Core for its reliable, seasonal non-agricultural resources to supplement the diet for mobile BMII populations dependent on a broader resource area (Smiley 2002b; Young and Gilpin 2012)

While pulses in intensity of use are indicated beginning with Clovis, the most expansive prehispanic habitation appears to have occurred between the BMIII, PI, and late PII/early PIII periods, as evidenced by the presence of several large sites. Just as with preceramic sites, the earliest ceramic sites dating 600-1025 CE are concentrated in the RAR-Core. Initially, BMIII occupation consisted of habitation sites of one to three pit houses and numerous artifact scatters that are farther away from the canyon edges in areas that were more suitable for agriculture and construction of deeper pit houses. Population density remained low. This changed with consolidation of settlement during PI into as few as four villages each having more than 10 pit houses. Nearly equal mixtures of Pueblo and Mogollon ceramics characterize especially the PI sites suggesting co-residence (Estes, Chapter 10). These large PI sites are also characterized by pit house burning suggesting depopulation in the early 1000s CE. Outside the RAR-Core area only limited artifact scatters dating BMIII/PI are present in the RAR-South and AZLAC-Far North areas.

Use and occupation appear much reduced from ca. 1000-1100 CE with only ten purely PII sites in the RAR-Core (7 of these in lower Chimney Canyon) and another in RAR-West. All but the RAR-West site are sherd or artifact scatters, which are likely locales for sand dune farming. If there are any habitation sites dating to the 1000s CE they are using the same locales as the large PI pit house villages and obscured by heavier use after 1130 CE pit house dwellers.

Thus, the rebound in regional occupation during the late PII/early PIII period is driven by resettlement in the same locations as the largest PI sites in the RAR-Core area with continued construction of pit houses that likely look similar to those at AZ J:14:36(ASM) in HSP (Young 1996). Even more so than in HSP, sites in the RAR-Core have mixing of Pueblo and Mogollon ceramics. Sinagua ceramics are also present suggesting possible co-residency of three groups with enduring differences in ceramic production and pit house style. In contrast, in the AZLAC-Far North, RAR-Southeast, and RAR-South areas pueblos are constructed with gray ware dominant in the AZLAC-Far North but Brown Ware dominant in the RAR-South and RAR-Southeast. Ceramics suggest construction of these pueblos as early as 1150 CE and certainly before 1175 CE. Contemporary sherd and artifact scatters dot the landscape in the RAR-South near MK Pueblo and this is no doubt the case in the AZLAC-Far North where one sherd scatter was recorded but no official survey was conducted and the RAR-Southeast where no survey was conducted. Ceramically, the late PII/PIII sites have Black Mesa B/w with low counts of Dogoszhi and Sosi B/w and Walnut B/w with much lower counts of other LCWW. These combinations coalesce in the 1100-1175 CE timeframe. CWW is low in the RAR-Core and AZLAC-Far North but present in reduced numbers in the RAR-South and RAR-Southeast pueblos.

Late PIII (post-1200 CE) consists of a settlement shift in the RAR-Core and continuity elsewhere represented by dominance in decorated and undecorated ceramics by brown ware-producing (Mogollon) populations who also established a new architectural tradition in the RAR-Core through construction of several small masonry pueblos. These are concentrated slightly upslope east and west from Chimney Canyon around the most abundant arable land in the RAR-Core. Construction on pueblos north of BP could predate 1200 CE. Their location on the landscape heavily used from BMIII to PIII make it difficult to pinpoint.

Population was likely no more and possibly less than that of the PI maximum. BP is dominated by CWW and secondarily by Walnut B/w suggesting CWW, as elsewhere, marks the latest occupation of pueblos in the region. Their virtual absence in AZLAC-Far North pueblos and some RAR-Core pueblos suggests their depopulation before 1225 CE. MK and RAR-Southeast pueblos are also likely no longer inhabited after 1225 CE leaving the RAR-Core area as the only area in the broad study area occupied after 1225 CE.

When occupation of the immediate area ends ca. 1250s CE marking the end of PIII, PIV occupation shifts to the large pueblos of the HSC by the 1280s, including nearby Chevelon Pueblo where increased population aggregation required agricultural intensification focused on the LCR floodplain and away from upland areas, such as the RAR-Core (E.C. Adams 2002, ed. 2016). The continued importance of the RAR-Core, particularly the rock art at The Steps, is noted by the appearance of orange and yellow wares nearby (Figures 5.12 and 5.13). Together, the survey record tells the story of changing relationships with the landscape over time that coincide with shifts in subsistence practices, community size, and material culture.

Survey data have several important connotations for our understanding of the links between local populations and more distant areas. The sparse occurrence of obsidian, for example, suggests ties to the west were weak at least until Pueblo II with the appearance of ABW at larger pit house villages established in late PI. Furthermore, the ceramic evidence supports strong links to the north, east, and south as demonstrated by the presence of Tusayan/Little Colorado, Cibola, and Mogollon decorated and undecorated wares. Taken together, these materials suggest extensive involvement in exchange and possibly settlement by groups to the north, east, and south with only minimal ties to materials coming from the west.

Although northern Tusayan (Pueblo) ceramic traditions are the earliest in the RAR-Core survey area appearing during BMIII (ca. 600 CE), southern/eastern groups producing brown wares are nearly as common on large PI sites as are Tusayan Gray wares. Late PII witnessed the addition of western ABW manufacturers to the region along with LCWW manufactured in the Hopi Buttes 80-100 km north (Douglass 1987, 1990). Thus, while decorated wares suggest exchange between areas, utility wares suggest settlement by these groups as utility wares are seldom exchanged long distances (Barker 2017; Britt, Chapter 8). The LCWW tradition is different in that it is not accompanied by comparable LCGW ceramics. Thus, there is no suggestion groups from the Hopi Buttes migrated to the study area.

After 1200 CE, CWW decorated ceramics replace LCWW and seemingly signify replacement of Pueblo or Sinagua groups occupying the entire study area by groups affiliated with the Mogollon Tradition originating from the south or southeast. In addition to the complete dominance of brown utility wares at BP (E.C. Adams and LaMotta, Chapter 7), and complemented by the white wares, the regional architectural tradition south of the RAR-Core also changes. These changes are well represented by MK Pueblo in RAR-South [Lange, Chapter 6]) and include thick-walled, large-roomed pueblos that appear and replace pit house architecture. Thus, utility pottery provides excellent measures of identity of groups occupying the all the survey areas while decorated pottery is not a reliable indicator. Britt explores the nature of the identity of groups occupying the small, PIII pueblos, their relationship to each other, and to more distant groups in Chapter 8.

Many of the large sites and scatters indicate use during multiple periods suggesting people returned to an area over several centuries, if not longer. While possibly explained by the environmental and physical conditions of the location, these sites may also illustrate the importance of materializing ties to the past by these groups especially in the context of the expansive petroglyph tradition in nearby Chevelon Canyon (Brinkerhoff, Chapter 3). This is further evidenced through the curation of early projectile points at later sites (Soza, Chapter 9). Likewise, the deposition of yellow ware pottery on early sites in the area and the continual addition or modification of petroglyphs to The Steps supports revisitation of ancestral areas through time (Doery, Chapter 4). Combined, the importance of the area to local populations spanning from mobile hunter and gatherer groups to settled agricultural villagers is clearly demonstrated. Moreover, the significance of the area continued through periods of increasing aggregation when this region ceased to be used for habitation. The long memory materialized by the places, artifacts, and rock art found at RAR maintained a prominent place in the lives of descendent communities, particularly Hopi (e.g., Mills and Walker 2008). As such, it is clear the RAR-Core area is marked as an important "footprint" of the past (Hedquist et al. 2014; Kuwanwisiwma and Ferguson 2009; Whiteley 2011).

The long history of archaeological work in the US Southwest often leaves the impression that there may be little more to learn about the region. However, the survey of RAR and adjacent AZLAC properties highlights a largely untapped and crucial resource in our reconstructions of the region's past: documentation of the cultural history record on private property. Arguably, it will be collaboration with local landowners to assess the cultural resources found on private lands that has the most potential to reshape our understandings of the prehispanic US Southwest in the coming decades. The survey of RAR and AZLAC properties merged with more traditional work on State and Federal managed lands demonstrates the potential data waiting to be documented and incorporated into reconstructions of the past.

Table 5.1. Comparison of Ceramic Ware Distributions by Sites and Loci from Project Areas in Northern Arizona.

Site Group	WUPATKI *N	WUPATKI %	HOMOL'OVI N	HOMOL'OVI %	HOPI BUTTES N	HOPI BUTTES %	RAR** N	RAR** %	FAR NORTH N	FAR NORTH %	SOUTH N	SOUTH %	ZUNI N	ZUNI %
WARE														
Hopi White	4	6	3	1										
Jeddito Yellow			180	48	3	2	14	13	1	17			8	18
Awatovi Yellow	1	2	56	15			10	9			1	4		
Winslow Orange			106	28					1	17				
Homolovi Orange			24	6										
Alameda Brown	60	95	178	47	3	2	40	37	6	100	10	43		
White Mountain Red	1	2	50	13	18	9	7	7	2	33			44	98
Tusayan White	61	97	206	55	91	45	65	61	6	100	21	91		
Tusayan Gray	62	98	288	76	182	90	71	66	6	100	16	70		
Little Colorado White	62	98	179	48	192	96	65	61	6	100	18	78		
Little Colorado Gray	5	8	119	32	125	62	26	24	5	83	10	43		
Tsegi Orange	56	89	76	20	24	12	23	21	5	83	5	22		
Cibola White	3	5	110	29	23	11	38	36	4	67	14	61	44	98
Roosevelt Red	0	0	5		0		4	4					9	20
Mogollon Brown			56	15	37	18	75	70	6	100	15	65		
San Francisco Gray	45	72	6	2	63		4	4						
San Juan Red			6	2			4	4						
Zuni			2	0.5									37	82
Prescott Gray	35	56												
Number of Loci/Sites	63		^377		201		^107		^6		^23		45	

*Note: N = number of sites or loci with a particular ware; based on Table 3.12 (Lange 1998:49).
**Note: Rock Art Ranch Core Area + Aztec Land & Cattle Adjacent loci.
^Note: number of loci with ceramics.

Table 5.2. Ceramic Wares and Types from Homolovi State Park Surface Collections.

a. Ceramic Wares.

Ware*	Count	Percent
Alameda Brown	2485	11
Tusayan White	2795	13
Tusayan Gray	11305	52
Little Colorado White	2514	12
Little Colorado Gray	1238	6
Tsegi Orange	301	1
Cibola White	453	2
Mogollon Brown	413	2
White Mountain Red	112	0.5
Total	21616	

*Note: Does not include Unknown Wares or Pueblo IV Wares from the survey.

b. Ceramic Types.

WARE / TYPE	Count
Tusayan White	
Lino Black/gray	348
Kana-a Black/white	224
Black Mesa Black/white	289
Sosi Black/white	96
Dogoszhi Black/white	30
Flagstaff Blsck/white	74
Tusayan Gray	
Indeterminate TGW	7451
Lino Gray	216
Kana-a Gray	53
Tusayan Corrugated	3451
Moenkopi Corrugated	74
Little Colorado White	
Holbrook A Black/white	38
Holbrook B Black/white	112
Padre Black/white	21
Walnut Black/white	500
Leupp Black/white	4
Little Colorado Gray	
Little Colorado Corrugated	1236
Cibola White	
Kiathuthlanna Black/white	4
Puerco Black/white	26
Escavada Black/white	1
Snowflake Black/white	42
Reserve Black/white	46
Tularosa Black/white	26
Alameda Brown	
Sunset Brown	750
Winona Brown	3
Grapevine Brown	45
Kinnikinnick Brown	67
Chavez Pass Brown	526
Mogollon Brown	
Brown Plain	32
Brown Corrugated	490
Brown Polished	14
McDonald Painted Corrugated	6
Showlow Black/red	9

Table 5.3. Ceramic Wares from Loci in the Rock Art Ranch-Core Area.

Table 5.3. Ceramic Wares from Loci in the Rock Art Ranch-Core Area, cont'd.

ASZSITE (all "AZ P:")	Field Number	Jeddito Yellow	% JYW	Awatovi Yellow/ Homol'ovi Orange	% AYW/HOW	Alameda Brown	% ABW	White Mountain Red	% WMRW	Tusayan White	% TWW	Tusayan Gray	% TGW	Little Colorado White	% LCWW	Little Colorado Gray	% LCGW	Tsegi Orange	% TOW	Cibola White	% CWW	Roosevelt Red	% RRW	Mogollon Brown	% MBW	Ind. Plain	% Indet Plain	San Francisco Mtn Gray/ San Juan Red	% SFMGW/SJRW	Puerco Valley Utility	% PVUW	Puerco Valley-like Utility	% PV-like UW	Puerco Valley-like Decorated	% PV-like Dec	Totals	% Total
2:146J	RAR-98J																																	1	0
2:146R	RAR-99					3	33			1	33	2	67																					8	0
2:165A	RAR-101						13			1	4	17	71	1	4	3	12							2	4									24	0
2:165B	RAR-102									1	100																							1	0
3:213B	RAR-103B									4	160																							4	0
3:213C	RAR-103C			4	9					9	20	23	51	7	16									2	4									45	1
3:213D	RAR-103D									2	15	9	69											2	15									13	0
2:104E	RAR-104					2	9					4	18			2	9							14	64									22	0
2:167	RAR-107	1	100																															1	0
2:169	RAR-109	16	28									18	32	1	2					4	7			18	32									57	1
2:149	RAR-112									17	61	9	24	1	3					1														28	0
2:150A	RAR-113A																							1	100									1	0
2:150B	RAR-113B	25	35							5		45	63																					71	1
2:173	RAR-115									5	100																							5	0
2:174	RAR-116											3	60											2	40									5	0
2:175	RAR-117									1	100																							1	0
2:176E	RAR-119					5	6			22	25	35	40	2	2	2	2			4	7	1		21	24			1	1					88	1
3:232A	RAR-121A			1	100																													1	0
2:232B	RAR-121B											1	33											2	67									3	0
3:234	RAR-123					2	2			20	15	66	51	1	1	1	1							2	2					13	10			130	2
3:235A	RAR-124A			4				1	17			4	67	1	17																			6	0
3:235B	RAR-124B			12	100					2	11	3	17	6	33									7	39									18	0
2:178	RAR-125	1	8	5	42							1	8	2	17									3	25									12	0
2:179	RAR-126									3	10													26	90									29	0
2:180	RAR-127					2	0			4	1	132	33			2								3	1			260	65					402	7
3:237	RAR-129											1	100	11	100																			1	0
3:238	RAR-130																							2	100									11	0
2:162C	RAR-131																																	2	0
3:115	RAR-135			4	21	1	0			73	27	1	5	172	63	1								11	58			23	8					275	5
2:152	RAR-138	1	5	12	100					1				1	5	5																		19	0
2:152A	RAR-138A									1	100																							12	0
2:153	RAR-139									1	50			1	50																			2	0
2:155A	RAR-140											1	100							1	100													1	0
2:155C	RAR-141					8	10			22	28	2	3	7	9					12	15			27	35									78	1
2:156	RAR-143																			1	100													1	0
2:157	RAR-144											4	7	4	7									46	85									54	1
2:158	RAR-146			65	34					51	26													77	40									193	3
2:159	RAR-149																																		
Totals		101	2	100	2	239	4	8	0	862	14	1693	28	418	7	28	0	50	0	283	5	2	0	1789	30	14	0	16	0	295	5	85	1	3	0	6035

Table 5.4. Ceramic Wares Documented as Isolates in the Rock Art Ranch-Core Area.

Ware		Count	*Percent*
Alameda Brown		13	*1*
Cibola White		145	*8*
Little Colorado Gray & White		506	*27*
Mogollon Brown		251	*13*
Puerco Valley		4	*4*
Tusayan Gray & White		948	*51*
	Total	1867	*100*

5: Rock Art Ranch Area Surveys and Testing

148 Lange, Fladd, and E.C. Adams

Table 5.5. Ceramic Types from Loci in the Rock Art Ranch-Core Area, 1/8.

AZSITE (all: "AZ P:")	Field Number	Indet.--Tusayan WW	% Indet. TWW	Lino Black/gray	% Lino B/g	Kana-a Black/white	% Kana-a B/w	Black Mesa Black/white	% Black Mesa B/w	Sosi Black/white	% Sosi B/w	Dogoszhi Black/white	% Dogoszhi B/w	Flagstaff Black/white	% Flagstaff B/w	Shato Black/white	% Shato B/w	Indet.--Little Colorado WW	% Little Colorado WW	St Josephs Black/white	% St Josephs B/w	Holbrook A Black/white	% Holbrook A B/w	Holbrook B Black/white	% Holbrook B B/w	Padre Black/white	% Padre B/w	Walnut Black/white	% Walnut B/w	Leupp Black/white	% Leupp B/w	Chevelon Black/white	% Chevelon B/w	Totals	% Total
2:104A	RAR-4A	24	7	1		1	0	1	3									13	43															30	0
2:104B	RAR-4B	196	28	3	0	12	2	3	0			1	0					18	3															335	6
2:104C	RAR-4C							27	3			4	0											1	0									695	12
2:104D	RAR-4D	2	12					4	21																									19	0
3:124	RAR-12	1	0				6		1													10	59											17	0
3:125B	RAR-13B					1	2	1	1									2	2							1	0	1	1					106	2
3:125C	RAR-13C					2	2																											4	0
3:125D	RAR-13D	18	3	10	2	53	9	13	2									1	7			1	0											14	0
3:129	RAR-14																	7	1									16	3					583	10
3:130	RAR-15								6									6	3									9	100					9	0
3:132	RAR-17									1								5	11									12	6					211	3
3:133	RAR-18	2	3					3	6									3	5									4	9					47	0
3:136	RAR-21	31	5	6	1	24	4	1	2					1	2			9	2							3	1							66	1
3:137A	RAR-22A	20	4	6	1	14	3	5	1					1	0			5	1							1	0	10	2					567	9
3:137B	RAR-22B	2	8					1	0									1	4									1	0					445	7
3:140	RAR-22C																	1	3									5	17					25	0
3:141	RAR-23																	1	10									2	20					30	1
3:142	RAR-24																																	10	0
3:146A	RAR-25																																	24	0
3:152	RAR-29	91	24	5	1	8	2	6	2									1	0									2	0					3	0
3:153	RAR-35	43	20			1	2	2	0									17	5							7	2			1	0			376	6
3:146E	RAR-36	3	100																															336	6
3:171	RAR-43																																	1	0
3:172	RAR-54																																	6	0
3:173	RAR-55																	2	100															2	0
3:176A	RAR-56	2	20															3	1					1	10									210	4
2:105	RAR-60																																	45	1
3:229	RAR-79																																	3	0
3:230	RAR-86																																	5	0
2:162A	RAR-87																																	14	0
2:162B	RAR-88A																					6	60											26	0
2:231A	RAR-88B																																	10	0
2:231B	RAR-90A																																	2	0
3:212	RAR-90B	1	1			6	7	5	6									7	70									6	3					85	1
2:145	RAR-91	1	10																															10	0
2:146Q	RAR-92																																	2	0
2:146S	RAR-94																																	5	0
2:146T	RAR-95A																																	8	0
2:146U	RAR-95B																																	19	0
2:146D	RAR-95C	1	50																															2	0
2:146I	RAR-98D																																	1	0

SELECTED TYPES

Table 5.5. Ceramic Types from Loci in the Rock Art Ranch-Core Area, 2/8.

ASZITE (all: "AZ P:")	Field Number	Indet.–Tusayan WW	% Indet. TWW	Lino Black/gray	% Lino B/g	Kana-a Black/white	% Kana-a B/w	Black Mesa Black/white	% Black Mesa B/w	Sosi Black/white	% Sosi B/w	Dogoszhi Black/white	% Dogoszhi B/w	Flagstaff Black/white	% Flagstaff B/w	Shato Black/white	% Shato B/w	Indet.–Little Colorado WW	% Little Colorado WW	St Josephs Black/white	% St Josephs B/w	Holbrook A Black/white	% Holbrook A B/w	Holbrook B Black/white	% Holbrook B B/w	Padre Black/white	% Padre B/w	Walnut Black/white	% Walnut B/w	Leupp Black/white	% Leupp B/w	Chevelon Black/white	% Chevelon B/w	Totals	% Total
2:146J	RAR-98J																																	1	0
2:146R	RAR-99	1	12																									1	12					8	0
2:165A	RAR-101	1	4																															24	0
2:165B	RAR-102																																	1	0
3:213B	RAR-103B					1	100	4	100																									4	0
3:213C	RAR-103C	9	20															7	16															45	1
3:213D	RAR-103D	1	8							1	8																							13	0
2:104E	RAR-104																																	22	0
2:167	RAR-107																	1	2															1	0
2:169	RAR-109																																	57	1
2:149	RAR-112	16	57					1	4																									28	0
2:150A	RAR-113A																																	1	0
2:150B	RAR-113B			5	100																													71	1
2:173	RAR-115																																	5	0
2:174	RAR-116																																	5	0
2:175	RAR-117																																		
2:176E	RAR-119	19	22	3	2	1	1	1	4									1	1			1	1											88	1
3:232A	RAR-121A							3	3																									1	0
3:232B	RAR-121B																																	3	0
3:234	RAR-123	11	8			5	2											6	5															130	2
3:235A	RAR-124A																	1	17															6	0
3:235B	RAR-124B																	2	17									6	33					18	0
2:178	RAR-125							3	10																									12	0
2:179	RAR-126	4	1															9	82			1	0											29	0
2:180	RAR-127											1	50	1	100	1	100	166	60					1	0					2	18			402	7
3:237	RAR-129																																	1	0
2:238	RAR-130																	1	5															11	0
3:238	RAR-131																																	2	0
2:162C	RAR-135	37	24																									5	2					275	5
3:115	RAR-138																																	19	0
2:152	RAR-138A																	1	100															12	0
2:152A	RAR-139											1	100																					1	0
2:153	RAR-140																	1	100															2	0
2:155A	RAR-141																	5	6															1	0
2:155C	RAR-143	16	21					3	4													1	1			1	1					78	1
2:156	RAR-144																																	1	0
2:157	RAR-146																	4	7															54	1
2:158	RAR-149																																	193	3
Totals		553	9	39	1	129	2	86	1	2	0	7	0	3	0	2	0	307	5	0	0	21	0	4	0	13	0	81	1	3	0	0	0	6035	

5: Rock Art Ranch Area Surveys and Testing 149

Table 5.5. Ceramic Types from Loci in the Rock Art Ranch-Core Area, 3/8.

ASZSITE (all: "AZ P:")	Field Number	Indet.—Cibola WW	% Indet. CWW	Puerco Black/white	% Puerco B/w	Escavada Black/white	% Escavada B/w	Snowflake Black/white	% Snowflake B/w	Reserve Black/white	% Reserve B/w	Tularosa Black/white	% Tularosa B/w	Mogollon Brown Ware	Brown Plain	% Brown Plain	Brown Corrugated	% Brown Corrugated	Brown Polished	% Brown Polished	McDonald Painted Corrugated	% McDonald Ptd. Corrugated	Showlow Black/red	% Showlow B/r	Indet. White Mountain Red Ware	% White Mtn. RW	St Johns B/r-Poly	% St Johns B/r-Poly	Totals	% Total
2:104A	RAR-4A														4	13			5	17									30	0
2:104B	RAR-4B	1	0												85	25	21	6	20	6					1	0			335	6
2:104C	RAR-4C			1											186	27	38	5	10	1									695	12
2:104D	RAR-4D														2	11			6	32									19	0
3:124	RAR-12																1	6											17	0
3:125B	RAR-13B	5	5												33	31	12	11	2	2									106	2
3:125C	RAR-13C																2	50											4	0
3:125D	RAR-13D	4	0			2	0																						14	0
3:129	RAR-14														126	22	70	12	11	2									583	10
3:130	RAR-15	15	7	6	3			3									109	52											211	3
3:132	RAR-17			4	9				6	2	0						15	32											47	0
3:133	RAR-18			7	11	1	2	1	2						2	3	2	3											66	1
3:136	RAR-21	41	62					12		2	0	1	0		100	18	62	11	12	2									567	9
3:137A	RAR-22A	13	2					1	0						98	22	38	9	12	3									445	7
3:137B	RAR-22B	7	4					1	4						1	4	1	4											25	0
3:140	RAR-23	1	40	3	10												7	23											30	1
3:141	RAR-24														2	8	6	60											10	0
3:142	RAR-25																												24	0
3:146A	RAR-29																												3	0
3:152	RAR-35	7	2	2	0	8	2	1	0	7	2	2	0		88	23	16	4	10	3			2		2	0	3	0	376	6
3:153	RAR-36	62	18	11	3							2	100		13	4	109	32											336	6
3:146E	RAR-43									1																			1	0
3:171	RAR-54														1	17													6	0
3:172	RAR-55																												2	0
3:173	RAR-56														16	8	109	52											210	4
3:176A	RAR-60														4	9													45	1
2:105	RAR-79																												3	0
3:229	RAR-86																												5	0
3:230	RAR-87														12	86													14	0
2:162A	RAR-88A																2	20	26	100									26	0
2:162B	RAR-88B																												10	0
3:231A	RAR-90A																												2	0
3:231B	RAR-90B														8	9													85	1
3:212	RAR-91																												10	0
2:145	RAR-92																												2	0
2:146Q	RAR-94																												5	0
2:146S	RAR-95A																1	50											8	0
2:146T	RAR-95B																												19	0
2:146U	RAR-95C																												2	0
2:146D	RAR-98D																1	100											1	0
2:146I	RAR-98I																													

Table 5.5. Ceramic Types from Loci in the Rock Art Ranch-Core Area, 4/8.

AZSITE (all. "AZ P.")	Field Number	Indet.--Cibola WW	% Indet. CWW	Puerco Black/white	% Puerco B/w	Escavada Black/white	% Escavada B/w	Snowflake Black/white	% Snowflake B/w	Reserve Black/white	% Reserve B/w	Tularosa Black/white	% Tularosa B/w	Mogollon Brown Ware	Brown Plain	% Brown Plain	Brown Corrugated	% Brown Corrugated	Brown Polished	% Brown Polished	McDonald Painted Corrugated	% McDonald Ptd. Corrugated	Showlow Black/red	% Showlow B/r	Indet. White Mountain Red Ware	% White Mtn. RW	St Johns B/r-Poly	% St Johns B/r-Poly	Totals	% Total
2:146J	RAR-98J																												1	0
2:146R	RAR-99	1	12							3	38																		8	0
2:165A	RAR-101																													24	0
2:165B	RAR-102																													1	0
3:213B	RAR-103B																													4	0
3:213C	RAR-103C															10	45	2	4											45	1
3:213D	RAR-103D																	2	15	4	18									13	0
2:104E	RAR-104																													22	0
2:167	RAR-107															18	32													1	0
2:169	RAR-109	1	2			3	5																							57	1
2:149	RAR-112	1	4																											28	0
2:150A	RAR-113A	1	1																											1	0
2:150B	RAR-113B																													71	1
2:173	RAR-115																													5	0
2:174	RAR-116																			2	40									5	0
2:175	RAR-117															8	9	13	15											1	0
2:176E	RAR-119																	2	67											88	1
2:232A	RAR-121A	2	2													8	6			5	4									1	0
3:232B	RAR-121B																	6	33											3	0
3:234	RAR-123																	3	25											130	2
3:235A	RAR-124A															26	90	2	0					1	17	1	17			6	0
3:235B	RAR-124B															1	0													18	0
2:178	RAR-125																			2	100									12	0
2:179	RAR-126															11	58													29	0
2:180	RAR-127																													402	7
3:237	RAR-129																													1	0
3:238	RAR-130																													11	0
2:162C	RAR-131																													2	0
3:115	RAR-135			5	6	2	3	2	3	2	3																			275	5
2:152	RAR-138																													19	0
2:152A	RAR-138A																													12	0
2:153	RAR-139																													1	0
2:155A	RAR-140																													2	0
2:155C	RAR-141	1	1															26	33			1	1							78	1
2:156	RAR-143	1	100																											1	0
2:157	RAR-144																	44	81	2	4									54	1
2:158	RAR-146																	77	40											193	3
2:159	RAR-149																														
	Totals	178	3	39	1	16	0	21	0	16	0	4	0		863	14	799	13	129	2	1	0	3	0	4	0	3	0	6035	

Table 5.5. Ceramic Types from Loci in the Rock Art Ranch-Core Area, 5/8.

AZSITE (all: "AZ P:")	Field Number	Tusayan Gray Ware	% Tusayan GW	Kana-a Gray	% Kana-a Gray	Tusayan Corrugated	% Tusayan Corrugated	Moenkopi Corrugated	% Moenkopi Corrugated	Plain -- Puerco Valley Utility Ware	Plain PUW	% Plain PUW	Corrugated PUW	% Corrugated PUW	Plain -- PVUW-like	% Plain -- PVUW-like	Corrugated -- PVUW-like	% Corrugated -- PVUW-like	Sunset Brown	% Sunset Brown	Winona Brown	% Winona Brown	Grapevine Brown	% Grapevine Brown	Kinnikinnick Brown	% Kinnikinnick Brown	Chavez Pass Brown	% Chavez Pass Brown	Verde Brown	% Verde Brown	Totals	% Total
2:104A	RAR-4A	19	63																	4	1					1	3			30	0
2:104B	RAR-4B	81	24	1	0	15	4			2	0									7	1	9	1			53	16			335	6
2:104C	RAR-4C	41	6	11	2	6	0	4	0	2	0															93	13			695	12
2:104D	RAR-4D	5	26																							2	11			19	0
3:124	RAR-12	2	12																											17	0
3:125B	RAR-13B	41	39	2	2	2	2																							106	2
3:125C	RAR-13C	12	50																											4	0
3:125D	RAR-13D	12	86	2	2	2	2																							14	0
3:129	RAR-14	204	35	2	0											18	3			3				1	0			9	2	583	10
3:130	RAR-15													4	6					1										9	0
3:132	RAR-17	3	1											8	1	1	0			12	6	4	2							211	3
3:133	RAR-18	5	11			2								7	2					1	2									47	0
3:136	RAR-21			9	2	2								10	42					1	4	2		1	0					66	1
3:137A	RAR-22A	243	43	9	2																	1	0							567	9
3:137B	RAR-22B	224	50	6	1																									445	7
3:137C	RAR-22C	6	25	1	4																									25	0
3:140	RAR-23	2	7																											30	1
3:141	RAR-24																													10	0
3:142	RAR-25	22	92																											24	0
3:146A	RAR-29																													3	0
3:152	RAR-35	135	36	9	3	3	0									12	4			1	0	1	0			1	0			376	6
3:153	RAR-36	10	3		4	23	11																			3	7			336	6
3:146E	RAR-43																													1	0
3:171	RAR-54																													6	0
3:172	RAR-55	5	83																											2	0
3:173	RAR-56																													210	4
3:176A	RAR-60	10	5	2																											45	1
2:105	RAR-79	2	4																											3	0
3:229	RAR-86	5	100																											5	0
3:230	RAR-87																													14	0
2:162A	RAR-88A																													26	0
2:162B	RAR-88B																													10	0
3:231A	RAR-90A	2	100																											2	0
3:231B	RAR-90B	60	71																											85	1
3:212	RAR-91																													10	0
2:145	RAR-92																													2	0
2:146Q	RAR-94																													5	0
2:146S	RAR-95A																													8	0
2:146T	RAR-95B																													19	0
2:146U	RAR-95C																													2	0
2:146D	RAR-98D																													1	0
2:146I	RAR-98I																														

Table 5.5. Ceramic Types from Loci in the Rock Art Ranch-Core Area, 6/8.

AZSITE (all: "AZ P:")	Field Number	Tusayan Gray Ware	% Tusayan GW	Kana-a Corrugated	% Kana-a Corrugated	Tusayan Corrugated	% Tusayan Corrugated	Moenkopi Corrugated	% Moenkopi Corrugated	Plain -- Puerco Valley Utility Ware	% Plain PVUW	Corrugated PVUW	% Corrugated PVUW	Plain -- PVUW-like	% Plain -- PVUW-like	Corrugated -- PVUW-like	% Corrugated -- PVUW-like	Sunset Brown	% Sunset Brown	Winona Brown	% Winona Brown	Grapevine Brown	% Grapevine Brown	Kinnikinnick Brown	% Kinnikinnick Brown	Chavez Pass Brown	% Chavez Pass Brown	Verde Brown	% Verde Brown	Totals	% Total
2:146J	RAR-98J																													1	0
2:146R	RAR-99	2	25																											8	0
2:165A	RAR-101	17	71																											24	0
2:165B	RAR-102																													1	0
3:213B	RAR-103B																													4	0
3:213C	RAR-103C	23	51																	1	4									45	1
3:213D	RAR-103D	5	38	4	31																									13	0
2:104E	RAR-104	4	18																	2	9									22	0
2:167	RAR-107																													1	0
2:169	RAR-109	3	5			15	26																							57	1
2:149	RAR-112	7	25	2	7																									28	0
2:150A	RAR-113A																													1	0
2:150B	RAR-113B	34	48	1	1	10	14																							71	1
2:173	RAR-115																													5	0
2:174	RAR-116	3	60																											5	0
2:175	RAR-117																													1	0
2:176E	RAR-119	35	40																	4	5									88	1
3:232A	RAR-121A	1	33																											3	0
3:232B	RAR-121B	66	51																											130	2
3:234	RAR-123	4	67																											6	0
3:235A	RAR-124A	3	17																											18	0
3:235B	RAR-124B	1	8																											12	0
2:178	RAR-125																													29	0
2:179	RAR-126	41	10			91	23					260	65							1	0					1	0			402	7
2:180	RAR-127	1	100																											1	0
2:237	RAR-129																													11	0
3:238	RAR-130																													2	0
2:162C	RAR-131	6	2									2	0																	275	5
3:115	RAR-135	1	5																											19	0
2:152	RAR-138																													12	0
2:152A	RAR-138A																													1	0
2:153	RAR-139																													2	0
2:155A	RAR-140																													1	0
2:155C	RAR-141	1	1			1	1																							78	1
2:156	RAR-143																													1	0
2:157	RAR-144																													1	0
2:158	RAR-146	4	7																											54	1
2:159	RAR-149																													193	3
	Totals	1403	23	50	1	168	3	4	0	4	0	291	5	29	0	31	0	19	0	20	0	14	0	2	0	154	3	9	0	6035	

Table 5.5. Ceramic Types from Loci in the Rock Art Ranch-Core Area, 7/8.

AZSITE (all: "AZ P:")	Field Number	Kokop Black/orange	% Kokop B/o	Jeddito Yellow Ware	% JYW	Tsegi Orange Ware	% TOW	Tusayan Black/orange	% Tusayan B/o	Tusayan Polychrome	% Tusayan Polychrome	Jeddito Black/orange	% Jeddito B/o	Roosevelt Red Ware	% RRW	Totals	% Total
2:104A	RAR-4A															30	0
2:104B	RAR-4B															335	6
2:104C	RAR-4C							3	0							695	12
2:104D	RAR-4D															19	0
3:124	RAR-12															17	0
3:125B	RAR-13B															106	2
3:125C	RAR-13C															4	0
3:125D	RAR-13D															14	0
3:129	RAR-14					1	0	4	0							583	10
3:130	RAR-15															9	0
3:132	RAR-17							2	0							211	3
3:133	RAR-18															47	0
3:136	RAR-21															66	1
3:137A	RAR-22A															567	9
3:137A	RAR-22B															445	7
3:137B	RAR-22C															25	0
3:140	RAR-23															30	1
3:141	RAR-24															10	0
3:142	RAR-25															24	0
3:146A	RAR-29															3	0
3:152	RAR-35							1	0							376	6
3:153	RAR-36			1	0	16	4	11	3	1	0	5	1	1	0	336	6
3:146E	RAR-43															1	0
3:171	RAR-54															1	0
3:172	RAR-55															6	0
3:173	RAR-56															2	0
3:176A	RAR-60															210	4
2:105	RAR-79			24	53											45	1
3:229	RAR-86															3	0
3:230	RAR-87															5	0
2:162A	RAR-88A															14	0
2:162B	RAR-88B															26	0
3:231A	RAR-90A															10	0
3:231B	RAR-90B															2	0
3:212	RAR-91															85	1
2:145	RAR-92															10	0
2:146Q	RAR-94	1	20			1	20									2	0
2:146S	RAR-95A			2	40											5	0
2:146T	RAR-95B			7	88											8	0
2:146U	RAR-95C			19	100											19	0
2:146D	RAR-98D															2	0
2:146I	RAR-98I															1	0

Table 5.5. Ceramic Types from Loci in the Rock Art Ranch-Core Area, 8/8.

AZSITE (all: "AZ P:")	Field Number	Kokop Black/orange	% Kokop B/o	Jeddito Yellow Ware	% JYW	Tsegi Orange Ware	% TOW	Tusayan Black/orange	% Tusayan B/o	Tusayan Polychrome	% Tusayan Polychrome	Jeddito Black/orange	% Jeddito B/o	Roosevelt Red Ware	% RRW	Totals	% Total
2:146J	RAR-98J															1	0
2:146R	RAR-99															8	0
2:165A	RAR-101															24	0
2:165B	RAR-102															1	0
3:213B	RAR-103B															4	0
3:213C	RAR-103C															45	1
3:213D	RAR-103D															13	0
2:104E	RAR-104															22	0
2:167	RAR-107			1	100											1	0
2:169	RAR-109			16	28											57	1
2:149	RAR-112															28	0
2:150A	RAR-113A															1	0
2:150B	RAR-113B			25	35											71	1
2:173	RAR-115															5	0
2:174	RAR-116															5	0
2:175	RAR-117															1	0
2:176E	RAR-119															88	1
3:232A	RAR-121A															1	0
3:232B	RAR-121B															3	0
3:234	RAR-123															130	2
3:235A	RAR-124A															6	0
3:235B	RAR-124B															18	0
2:178	RAR-125			1	8											12	0
2:179	RAR-126															29	0
2:180	RAR-127															402	7
3:237	RAR-129															1	0
3:238	RAR-130															11	0
2:162C	RAR-131															2	0
3:115	RAR-135															275	5
2:152	RAR-138			1	5											19	0
2:152A	RAR-138A															12	0
2:153	RAR-139															1	0
2:155A	RAR-140															2	0
2:155C	RAR-141															1	0
2:156	RAR-143															78	1
2:157	RAR-144															1	0
2:158	RAR-146															54	1
2:159	RAR-149															193	3
	Totals	1	0	97	2	18	0	21	0	1	0	5	0	1	0	6035	

Table 5.6. Comparison of Ceramic Wares from Homolovi State Park and Rock Art Ranch Project Areas.

WARE	Homolovi State Park	% HSP	RAR-Core	% RAR-Core	AZLAC-Adjacent	% AZLAC-Adjacent	AZLAC-Far North	% AZLAC-Far North	RAR-South	% RAR-South	RAR-Southeast	% RAR-Southeast	Multi-Kiva Site	% Multi-Kiva Site
Alameda Brown	2485	12	239	4	123	2	211	18	156	3	8	2	51	2
Tusayan White	2745	13	862	15	841	13	150	13	960	18	45	12	479	16
Tusayan Gray	11305	53	1693	30	2066	32	263	22	397	8	7	2	243	8
Little Colorado White	2514	12	418	7	768	12	116	10	1223	23	128	33	848	28
Little Colorado Gray	1238	6	28	0.5	64	1	19	2	164	3	4	1	68	2
Cibola White	453	2	283	5	241	4	9	0.8	360	7	12	3	167	5
Mogollon Brown	413	2	1789	31	2234	35	377	32	1568	30	141	36	948	31
Puerco Valley Utility			380	7	135	2	39	3	378	7	42	11	264	9
Totals	21153		5692		6472		1184		5206		387		3068	

*Note: Totals and percentages are based on the counts represented by the wares in this table, not the complete ceramic assemblages.

Table 5.7. Comparison of Ceramic Wares and Types from Homolovi State Park and Rock Art Ranch Project Areas.

WARE / TYPE	Homolovi State Park	% HSP	RAR-Core	% RAR-Core	AZLAC-Adjacent	% AZLAC-Adjacent	AZLAC-Far North	% AZLAC-Far North	RAR-South	% RAR-South	RAR-Southeast	% RAR-Southeast	Multi-Kiva Site	% Multi-Kiva Site
Tusayan White	1734	8	553	10	501	7	90	8	352	10	16	4	286	9
Lino Black/gray	348	2	39	0.7	13	0.2	13	1	7	0.2			4	0.1
Kana-a Black/white	224	1	129	2	140	2	1	0.08	39	1			30	1
Black Mesa Black/white	289	1	86	2	191	3	21	2	167	5	15	4	111	4
Sosi Black/white	96	0.4	2	0.04	26	0.4	3	0.3	82	2	12	3	16	0.5
Dogoszhi Black/white	30	0.1	7	0.1	25	0.4	15	1	13	0.4	2	0.5	8	0.3
Flagstaff Black/white	74	0.3	3	0.05	5	0.07	5	0.4	11	0.3			9	0.3
Tusayan Gray														
Indeterminate TGW	7511	35	1403	26	1113	16			146	4			117	4
Lino Gray	216	1			529	8	41	3						
Kana-a Gray	53	0.2			9	0.1	3	0.3	12	0.3	5	1	6	0.2
Tusayan Corrugated	3451	16	168	3	347	5	219	19	134	4	2	0.5	121	4
Moenkopi Corrugated	74	0.3	4	0.07					3	0.08			3	0.1
Little Colorado White	1839	9	307	6	566	8	75	19	595	16	47	12	510	16
Holbrook A Black/white	38	0.2	21	0.4	47	0.7	1	0.08	59	2	10	3	38	1
Holbrook B Black/white	112	0.5	4	0.07	29	0.4	6	0.5	41	1			33	1
Padre Black/white	21	0.1	13	0.2	14	0.2	5	0.4	33	0.9	3	0.8	27	0.9
Walnut Black/white	500	2	81	1	170	2	28	2	244	7	76	19	236	8
Leupp Black/white	4	0.02	3	0.05	1	0.01								
Little Colorado Gray														
Little Colorado Corrugated	1236	6			60	0.9	19	2	92	2	4	1	68	2
Cibola White	308	1	178	3	75	1	5	0.4	153	4	4	1	124	4
Kiathuthlanna Black/white	4	0.02			4	0.06			4	0.1	1	0.3	1	0.03
Puerco Black/white	26	0.1	39	0.7	84	1	1	0.08	26	0.7			18	0.6
Escavada Black/white	1	0.005	16	0.3	22	0.3			3	0.8				
Snowflake Black/white	42	0.2	21	0.3	46	0.7			23	0.6	1	0.3	20	0.6
Reserve Black/white	46	0.2	16	0.3	28	0.4	6	0.5	136	4	2	0.5	132	4
Tularosa Black/white	26	0.1	4	0.07	1	0.01								
Alameda Brown	1094	5			34	0.5	35	3	14	0.4	2	0.5	12	0.4
Sunset Brown	750	4	19	0.3					8	0.2			8	0.3
Winona Brown	3	0.01	12	0.2	9	0.1	57	5	6	0.2			3	0.1
Grapevine Brown	45	0.2	14	0.3	3	0.04	96	8	4	0.1			4	0.1
Kinnikinnick Brown	67	0.3	2	0.04			1	0.08	7	0.2			7	0.2
Chavez Pass Brown	526	2	154	3	75	1	22	2	30	0.8	5	1	11	0.4
Mogollon Brown														
Brown Plain	32	0.1	863	16	512	8	17	1	244	7	9	2	213	7
Brown Corrugated	490	2	799	15	1868	27	342	29	630	17	108	28	580	19
Brown Polished	14	0.07	129	2	99	1	1	0.08	145	4	1	0.3	134	4
McDonald Painted Corrugated	6	0.03	1	0.02	9	0.1	4	0.3	9	0.2	12	3	9	0.3
Showlow Black/red	9	0.04	3	0.05	21	0.3	10	0.8	10	0.3	11	3	10	0.3
Puerco Valley Utility			380	7	135	2	39	3	199	5	42	11	199	6
*Totals	21339		5473		6811		1181		3681		390		3108	

*Note: Totals and percentages are based on the counts represented by the types in this table, not the complete ceramic assemblages.

Table 5.8. Comparisons of Ceramic Wares and Types for Rock Art Ranch Loci and Habitation Types.

WARE	TYPE	RAR-Core–Hpi*	% RAR-Core–Hpi	AZLAC-Adjacent–Hpi	% AZLAC-Adjacent–Hpi	AZLAC-Adjacent–Hpu	% AZLAC-Adjacent–Hpu	AZLAC-Far North-Hpu	% AZLAC-Far North-Hpu	RAR-Southeast-Hpu	% RAR-Southeast-Hpu	Multi-Kiva Site-RAR-S-Hpu	% Multi-Kiva Site-RAR-S-Hpu
Tusayan White		299	10	217	7	33	7	90	8	16	4	286	9
	Lino Black/gray	22	0.7	10	0.3			13	1			4	0.1
	Kana-a Black/white	90	3	111	4	1	0.2	1	0.08			30	1
	Black Mesa Black/white	53	2	87	3	20	4	21	2	15	4	111	4
	Sosi Black/white			18	0.6			3	0.3	12	3	16	0.5
	Dogoszhi Black/white	5	0.2	6	0.2			15	1	2	0.5	8	0.3
	Flagstaff Black/white	1	0.03	3	0.1			5	0.4			9	0.3
Tusayan Gray													
	Indeterminate TGW	907	31	1069	35	33	7					117	4
	Lino Gray			292	9	5	1	41	3				
	Kana-a Gray	38	1	1	0.03			3	0.3	5	1	6	0.2
	Tusayan Corrugated	26	0.9	134	4	20	4	219	19	2	0.5	121	4
	Moenkopi Corrugated	4	0.1									3	0.1
Little Colorado White		64	2	127	4	37	8	75	19	47	12	510	16
	Holbrook A Black/white	3	0.1	3	0.1			1	0.08	10	3	38	1
	Holbrook B Black/white	2	0.07	6	0.2			6	0.5			33	1
	Padre Black/white	11	0.4			7	1	5	0.4	3	0.8	27	0.9
	Walnut Black/white	40	1	28	9	54	11	28	2	76	19	236	8
	Leupp Black/white	1	0.03										
Little Colorado Gray													
	Little Colorado Corrugated			11	0.4	1	0.2	19	2	4	1	68	2
Cibola White		97	3	23	0.7	9	2	5	0.4	4	1	124	4
	Kiathuthlanna Black/white					3	0.6			1	0.3	1	0.03
	Puerco Black/white	17	0.6	8	0.3	9	2	1	0.08			18	0.6
	Escavada Black/white	10	0.3			1	0.2						
	Snowflake Black/white	13	0.4	3	0.1	3	0.6			1	0.3	20	0.6
	Reserve Black/white	11	0.4	2	0.03	6	1	6	0.5	2	0.5	132	4
	Tularosa Black/white	3	0.1										
Alameda Brown				17	0.5	2	0.4	35	3	2	0.5	12	0.4
	Sunset Brown	14	0.5									8	0.3
	Winona Brown	12	0.4	4	0.1	1	0.2	57	5			3	0.1
	Grapevine Brown	14	0.5					96	8			4	0.1
	Kinnikinnick Brown	2	0.07					1	0.08			7	0.2
	Chavez Pass Brown	146	5	25	0.8	8	2	22	2	5	1	11	0.4
Mogollon Brown													
	Brown Plain	518	18	282	9	24	5	17	1	9	2	213	7
	Brown Corrugated	422	14	485	16	196	41	342	29	108	28	580	19
	Brown Polished	58	2	97	3			1	0.08	1	0.3	134	4
	McDonald Painted Corrugated							4	0.3	12	3	9	0.3
	Showlow Black/red							10	0.8	11	3	10	0.3
Puerco Valley Utility		50	2	25	0.8	8	2	39	3	42	11	199	6
	*Totals	2953		3094		481		1181		390		3108	

*Note: Hpi = Habitation--pithouse(s); Hpu--Habitation--pueblo or surface room(s).
**Note: Totals and percentages are based on the counts represented by the types in this table, not the complete ceramic assemblages.

5: Rock Art Ranch Area Surveys and Testing 159

Table 5.9. Comparisons of White Ware Types from Homolovi State Park and Rock Art Ranch Project Areas by Time Period.

WARE	TYPE	Date Range*	Homolovi State Park	% HSP	RAR-Core	% RAR-Core	AZLAC-Adjacent	% AZLAC-Adjacent	AZLAC-Far North	% AZLAC-Far North	RAR-South	% RAR-South	RAR-Southeast	% RAR-Southeast	Multi-Kiva Site	% Multi-Kiva Site
TWW	Lino Black/gray	625-825	348	19	39	8	13	2	13	12	7	0.8			4	0.6
TWW	Kana-a Black/white	825-1025	224	12	129	27	140	17	1	1	39	4			30	4
CWW	Kiatuthlanna Black/white	850-950	4	0.2			4	0.5			4	0.5	1	0.8	1	0.1
TWW	Black Mesa Black/white	1000-1125	289	15	86	18	191	23	21	2	167	19	15	12	111	16
LCWW	Holbrook A Black/white	1050-1150	38	2	21	4	47	6	1	1	59	7	10	8	38	6
CWW	Escavada Black/white	1050-1200	1	0.05	16	3	22	3			3	0.3				
TWW	Sosi Black/white	1050-1200	96	5	2	0.4	26	3	3	3	82	9	12	10	16	2
TWW	Dogoszhi Black/white	1050-1200	30	2	7	1	25	3	15	14	13	1	2	2	8	1
CWW	Puerco Black/white	1050-1225	26	1	39	8	84	10	1	1	26	3			18	3
LCWW	Holbrook B Black/white	1075-1175	112	6	4	0.8	29	3	6	6	41	5			33	5
LCWW	Padre Black/white	1075-1175	21	1	13	3	14	2	5	5	33	4	3	2	27	4
CWW	Reserve Black/white	1100-1250	46	2	16	3	28	3	6	6	136	15	2	2	132	20
CWW	Snowflake Black/white	1100-1275	42	2	21	4	46	5			23	3	1	0.8	20	3
TWW	Flagstaff Black/white	1130-1230	74	4	3	0.6	5	0.6	5	5	11	1			9	1
LCWW	Walnut Black/white	1130-1230	500	27	81	17	170	20	28	27	244	27	76	62	236	35
CWW	Tularosa Black/white	1200-1325	26	1	4	0.8	1	0.1								
LCWW	Leupp Black/white	1225-1275	4	0.2	3	0.6	1	0.1								
	**Totals		1881		484		846		105		888		122		683	

*Note: Date ranges are based on compilations of date ranges done by E. C. Adams and B. M. Estes for the Rock Art Ranch full report.
**Note: Totals and percentages are based on the counts represented by the types in this table, not the complete ceramic assemblages.

160 Lange, Fladd, and E.C. Adams

Table 5.10. Comparisons of White Ware Types for Rock Art Ranch Loci and Habitation Types by Time Period.

WARE	TYPE	Date Range (CE)*	RAR-Core--Hpi**	% RAR-Core--Hpi	RAR-Core--Hpu	% RAR-Core--Hpu	AZLAC-Adjacent-Hpi	% AZLAC-Adjacent-Hpi	AZLAC-Adjacent-Hpu	AZLAC-Adjacent-Hpu	AZLAC-Far North	% AZLAC-Far North	RAR-Southeast	% RAR-Southeast	Multi-Kiva Site	% Multi-Kiva Site
TWW	Lino Black/gray	625-825	22	8	0	0	10	4			13	12			4	0.6
TWW	Kana-a Black/white	825-1025	90	32	0	0	111	39	1	1	1	1			30	4
CWW	Kiatuthlanna Black/white	850-950			4	0.6			3	3			1	0.8	1	0.1
TWW	Black Mesa Black/white	1000-1125	53	19	1	0	87	31	20	19	21	2	15	12	111	16
LCWW	Holbrook A Black/white	1050-1150	3	1	2	0	3	1			1	1	10	8	38	6
CWW	Escavada Black/white	1050-1200	10	4	68	11			1	1						
TWW	Sosi Black/white	1050-1200	5	2	0	0	18	6			3	3	12	10	16	2
TWW	Dogoszhi Black/white	1050-1200	17	6	203	32	6	2			15	14	2	2	8	1
CWW	Puerco Black/white	1050-1225	2	0.7	3	0.5	8	3	9	9	1	1			18	3
LCWW	Holbrook B Black/white	1075-1175					6	2			6	6			33	5
LCWW	Padre Black/white	1075-1175	11	4	34	5			7	7	5	5	3	2	27	4
CWW	Reserve Black/white	1100-1250	11	4	25	4	2	0.7	6	6	6	6	2	2	132	20
CWW	Snowflake Black/white	1100-1275	13	5	125	20	3	1	3	3			1	0.8	20	3
TWW	Flagstaff Black/white	1130-1230	1	0.4	2	0	3	1			5	5			9	1
LCWW	Walnut Black/white	1130-1230	40	14	170	27	28	10	52	52	28	27	76	62	236	35
CWW	Tularosa Black/white	1200-1325	3	1	2	0										
LCWW	Leupp Black/white	1225-1275	1	0.4												
	***Totals		282		641		285		104		105		122		683	

*Note: Date ranges are based on compilations of date ranges done by E. C. Adams and B. M. Estes for the Rock Art Ranch full report.
**Note: Hpi-Habitation--pithouse(s); Hpu-Habitation-pueblo or surface room(s).
***Note: Totals and percentages are based on the counts represented by the types in this table, not the complete ceramic assemblages.

Table 5.11. Comparisons of Ceramic Type Ratios for Homolovi State Park and Rock Art Ranch Project Areas.

Project Areas	Lino Black/gray	Kana-a Black/white	BMIII/PI Ratio	Black Mesa Black/white	Walnut Black/white	PII/PIII Ratio
Homol'ovi Survey	348	224	1.55	289	500	0.58
RAR-Core	39	129	0.30	86	81	1.06
AZLAC-Adjacent	13	140	0.09	191	170	1.12
AZLAC-Far North	13	1	13.00	21	28	0.75
RAR-South	7	39	0.18	182	320	0.57

Table 5.12. Comparisons of Raw Material Types for Flaked Stone from Loci from RAR-Core Area and HSP and Various Quarries.

Material*	RAR Count (Isolates)**	RAR Percent	HSP Count	HSP Percent	HSP Quarries	HSP Quarry %	RAR-139A	RAR-139A %	RAR-57-1	RAR-57-1 %	RAR-57-2	RAR-57-2 %
Basalt	227	4										
Chalcedony	110	2										
Chert	1420	73	17780	74	1138	51	3	9	5	19	97	33
Igneous	49	1					5	15	5	19	23	8
Jasper	3	0										
Obsidian	14	0										
Petrified Wood	767	13	2107	9	2	0.09	2	6				
Quartzite	479	8	4262	18	1099	49	24	71	17	63	177	60
Rhyolite	5	0										
Total	6074	100	24149	100	2239	100	34	100	27	100	297	100

*Note: sources for data in this table are Lange (1998:68) and Soza (2018:81-83).
**Note: RAR Count is for flaked stone from all loci in the RAR Core area, HSP Count is for flaked stone at all loci in the Homolovi State Park area, HSP Quarries is the raw materials present at the quarry/cobble exposures sampled; RAR-139A and RAR-57 are quarries/lag gravel concentrations in the RAR Core area; 57-1 is the first collection from RAR-57, 57-2 is a second collection from the quarry; RAR-139 is AZ P:2:153(ASM); RAR-57 is AZ P:2:161(ASM).

Table 5.13. Raw Material Types for Flaked Stone Cores from Rock Art Ranch-Core Area.

Material	Count	Percent
Basalt	21	8
Chert	159	58
Igneous	9	3
Petrified Wood	16	6
Quartzite	68	25
Total	273	100

Table 5.14. Projectile Points from the Rock Art Ranch-Core Area.

Time Period	Type	Total	Percent of Total	Total by Time Period	Percent by Time Period	Local Chert	Percent Local Chert	Non Local Chert	Percent Non-local Chert	Chalcedony	Percent Chalcedony	Quartzite	Percent Quartzite	Igneous	Percent Igneous	Petrified Wood	Percent Petrified Wood	Obsidian	Percent Obsidian	Rhyolite	Percent Rhyolite	Unknown	Percent Unknown
Indeterminate	Indeterminate	63	26	63	26	10	4	23	9	1	0.4	1	0.4	1	0.4	19	8					8	3
Indeterminate Paleo	Indeterminate Paleo*	7	3			2	1	2	1							3	1						
Early Paleoindian	Clovis	3	1	31	13	1	0.4									2	1						
Middle Paleoindian	Lanceolete Plano**	11	4			1	0.4	7	3							2	1	1	0.4				
Late Paleoindian	Scottsbluff***	6	2			2	1	2	1							2	1						
Paleoarchaic	Lake Mojave	4	2			2	1									2	1						
Early/Middle Archaic	Bajada	16	6	80	33	6	2	5	2			1	0.4			4	2						
Middle Archaic	Pinto	19	8			3	1	12	5					2	1	2	1						
Middle/Late Archaic	San Jose	17	7			5	2	5	2			1	0.4	2	1.0	4	2						
	Northern Side Notched	4	2			2	1									2	1						
	Ventana Side Notched	4	2					3	1					1	0.4								
Late Archaic	San Rafael Side Notched	3	1					2	1							1	0.4						
	Datil	10	4					6	2	1	0.4			2	1	1	0.4						
	Maljamar	1	0.4							1	0.4												
	Cortaro	1	0.4											1	0.4								
	Gypsum	3	1			2	1							1	0.4								
	Durango	2	1					1	0.4							1	0.4						
Basketmaker II	Black Mesa	8	3	34	14	2	1	2	1							4	2						
	San Pedro	21	9			2	1	12	5							6	2			1	0.4		
Basketmaker III/PI	Cienega	4	2					3	1							1	0.4						
	Livermore	1	0.4													1	0.4						
Pueblo I	Dolores	3	1	38	15	2	1	1	0.4														
Pueblo I/II	Chaco	2	1			1	0.4	1	0.4														
Pueblo II/III	Western Triangular	5	2			1	0	3	1							1	0.4						
Pueblo III/IV	Pueblo Side Notched	27	11			2	1	13	5	1	0.4					5	2					6	2
	Indeterminate Pueblo	1	0.4																			1	0.4
	Totals	246	100	246	100	46	19	103	42	4	2	3	1	10	4	63	26	1	0.4	1	0.4	15	7

*Note: Paleo points were typed based on the presence of blade grinding, collateral, horizontal transverse, oblique transverse, or chevron flaking patterns (Van Buren 1974), the observations of C. Vance Haynes, or the observations of Vance T. Holliday.
**Note: Lanceolate Plano contains the following number of subtypes: 2 Plainview, 2 Midland, 3 Agate Basin, 2 Hell Gap, and 1 Milnesand.
***Note: Scottsbluff contains the following numbers of subtypes: 3 Eden and 3 Cody knives.

Table 5.15. Comparisons of Ground Stone Artifacts from the RAR-Core Area, HSP Loci, and HSC Pueblos.

a. Ground Stone Artifact Types from Loci in the Rock Art Ranch Core Area (Pitroff 2014).

Artifact Type	Artifact Subtype	Count	Percent	Percent of Total
Metate	Flat	82	48	
	Basin	66	39	
	Trough	3	2	
	Indeterminate	19	11	
	Subtotal	170	100	70
Mano	One-Hand	31	44	
	Two-Hand	34	48	
	Indeterminate	6	8	
	Subtotal	71	100	30
	TOTAL	241		100

b. Ground Stone Artifact and Material Types from Homolovi State Park loci (Lange 1998:202-203).

Artifact Type		Shinarump	Moenkopi	Coconino	Total	Percents
Manos	flat	78	5	1	84	35
	trough	12	1		13	5
	indeterminate	43	2		45	19
	basin	1		7	8	3
	blank	4	4		8	3
	Subtotal	138	12	8	158	66
Metates	flat	39	2		41	17
	trough	14	2		16	7
	indeterminate	9	1		10	4
	shallow basin	4	3	4	11	5
	deep basin			1	1	0.4
	indet. Basin	3			3	1
	Subtotal	69	8	5	82	34
	TOTALS	207	20	13	240	
	Percents	86	8	5	100	

c. Ground Stone Artifact and Material Types from Homol'ovi Settlement Cluster Pueblos.*

Site	Material Type	Manos	Metates	Total	Percents
Homol'ovi I	Shinarump	751	73	824	87
AZ J:14:3(ASM)	Moenkopi	109	12	121	13
	Subtotal	860	85	945	
Homol'ovi II	Shinarump	145	24	169	60
AZ J:14:15(ASM)	Moenkopi	106	9	115	40
	Subtotal	251	33	284	
Homol'ovi III	Shinarump	276	44	320	95
AZ J:14:14(ASM)	Moenkopi	12	3	15	5
	Subtotal	288	47	335	
Homol'ovi IV	Shinarump	18	4	22	59
AZ J:14:13(ASM)	Moenkopi	12	3	15	41
	Subtotal	30	7	37	
Chevelon	Shinarump	84	12	96	96
AZ P:2:11(ASM)	Moenkopi	4	0	4	4
	Subtotal	88	12	100	
All HSC Pueblos	Shinarump	1274	157	1431	84
	Moenkopi	243	27	270	16
	TOTALS	1517	184	1701	
	Percents	89	11	100	

*Note: Data derived from projecct data sets and publications: Adams (2001), Adams (2004), Adams (ed. 2016), and Lange (2020).

Table 5.16. Radiocarbon Results from NSF-Arizona AMS Laboratory for Testing at Rock Art Ranch-Core Loci.

AA#	Sample ID	Material	D13C	F	14C age BP	CalBP	68% range BP	Age in years
95987	RAR12/2/2	Charcoal	-21.9	0.8212±.0038	1582±37	1473±45	1427-1518	AD 477±23
95988	RAR22C/10/2	Charcoal	-21.8	0.7750±.0037	2047±38	2018±57	1961-2075	BC 68±28
105873	RAR13D/2/2	Charcoal	-23.1	0.7831±.0026	1687±27	1928±64	1865-1991	AD 22±32
104306	RAR33/6/2	Charcoal	-21.5	0.8000±.0035	2587±33	2656±116	2540-2772	BC 706±58
104874	RAR88B/3/2	Charcoal	-22.1	0.7910±.0025	1883±25	1851±156	1695-2006	AD 155±78
104875	RR98E/5/2	Charcoal	-23.0	0.8868±.0050	965±46	872±86	783-961	AD 1090±43
104872	RAR100/6/2	Charcoal	-21.2	0.8106±.0028	1687±29	1581±48	1533-1629	AD 369±24

Calibration of raw ^{14}C dates done by CalPal 2007 HULU created by the Cologne Radiocarbon Calibration using Quicken 2007 version 1.5. Baseline for calculations for BP is AD1950.

Table 5.17. Ceramic Wares from Loci on Aztec Land and Cattle Properties.

Site/Locus Type*	Location**	AZSITE	Field#	Jeddito Yellow	Winslow Orange	Alameda Brown	White Mountain Red	Tusayan White	Tusayan Gray	Little Colorado White	Little Colorado Gray	Tsegi Orange	Cibola White	Roosevelt Red	Mogollon Brown	San Francisco Mtn Gray	San Juan Red	Puerco Valley Utility	Count
Hpi	A	AZ P:3:119A (ASM)	FN-007	1		10		128	688	25	10	31	17		252				1162
Hpi	A	AZ P:3:119B (ASM)	FN-008			1		38	246	15	1	12	15		86				414
Hpi	A	AZ P:3:121A (ASM)	FN-009					54	332	7		2			89				484
Hpi	A	AZ P:3:176B (ASM)	FN-160			20		156	213	29	4	3	6		140			20	591
Hpi	A	AZ P:3:223 (ASM)	FN-164			15		15	97	13			1		22			5	168
Hpu	A	AZ P:3:121B (ASM)	FN-010			2		30	49	29		5			133				248
Hpu	A	AZ P:3:227A (ASM)	FN-169A	1		9	2	24	9	69	1	7	31	1	94		1	8	257
Sc	A	AZ P:3:118 (ASM)	FN-006					103	272	277	19	5			835				1511
Sc	A	AZ P:3:119C (ASM)	FN-147					22		6			3		1				32
Sc	A	AZ P:3:121C (ASM)	FN-148			3		1	24	1					2				31
Sc	A	AZ P:3:176C (ASM)	FN-161A			5		104	39	58	1	1	25		72			2	307
Sc	A	AZ P:3:176D (ASM)	FN-162					1	2				4		6			2	15
Sc	A	AZ P:3:214 (ASM)	FN-145			1		9	5	49			47		113	21		11	256
Sc	A	AZ P:3:217A (ASM)	FN-155A			4		19	3	28	6	3	10		29			4	106
Sc	A	AZ P:3:217B (ASM)	FN-155B			6	3	10	1	14		11	23		75			10	153
Sc	A	AZ P:3:217C (ASM)	FN-155C					2	1	10		3	5		5			4	30
Sc	A	AZ P:3:218 (ASM)	FN-156			2		4	5	6		1	1		8			6	33
Sc	A	AZ P:3:219 (ASM)	FN-157			8		38	11	19	15		3		63			28	185
Sc	A	AZ P:3:220 (ASM)	FN-158			11		11	6	1					7			4	40
Sc	A	AZ P:3:221 (ASM)	FN-159			4				11			20		16			5	56
Sc	A	AZ P:3:222 (ASM)	FN-163					18	1	6			23		36				84
Sc	A	AZ P:3:224 (ASM)	FN-165					23	7	14		4			31			4	83
Sc	A	AZ P:3:225A (ASM)	FN-166A			7		1	2	41	5				37			12	105
Sc	A	AZ P:3:225B (ASM)	FN-166B			1				13					2				16
Sc	A	AZ P:3:226A (ASM)	FN-167			8		19	44	5		2	2		59		1	6	146
Sc	A	AZ P:3:226B (ASM)	FN-168			3		4	4	9	1				7			1	29
Sc	A	AZ P:3:227B (ASM)	FN-169B			3		7	5	13	1		5		14			3	51
		Adjacent Subtotals		2	0	123	5	841	2066	768	64	90	241	1	2234	21	2	135	6593
		Adjacent %'s		0.03	0	2	0.08	13	31	12	1	1	4	0.02	34	0.3	0.03	2	100
Hpu	FN	AZ P:3:215A (ASM)	FN-151A			4		12	21	11	4	12			16			4	84
Hpu	FN	AZ P:3:215B (ASM)	FN-151B		1	77		22	42	37	6	9	1		83			26	304
Hpu	FN	AZ P:3:215C (ASM)	FN-151C			42		39	47	13		26	4		43				214
Hpu	FN	AZ P:3:215D (ASM)	FN-151D	1		76	3	26	86	29	1	11	1		103			1	338
Hpu	FN	AZ P:3:216A (ASM)	FN-152A			9	4	30	18	11	6		3		73			4	158
Hpu	FN	AZ P:3:216B (ASM)	FN-152B			3		21	49	15	2	6			59			4	159
		Far North Subtotals		1	1	211	7	150	263	116	19	64	9		377			39	1257
		Far North %'s		0.08	0.08	17	0.6	12	21	9	2	5	0.7		30			3	100
Hpu	SE	AZ P:3:240 (ASM)	FN-154			5		27	7	66	3	2	7		91			24	232
Sc	S	AZ P:3:164 (ASM)	FN-047					5					3						8
		TOTALS		3	1	339	12	1023	2336	950	86	159	257	1	2702	21	2	198	8090

*Note: Hpi = Habitation-pithouses; Hpu = Habitation-pueblo; Sc = Artifact scatter.
**Note: A = AZLAC land adjacent to RAR, north of ranch; FN = far north, east of Chevelon Canyon at the LCR; SE = Southeast of RAR; S = South of RAR.

Table 5.18. Comparison of Ceramic Wares at Pithouses vs. Pueblos from Aztec Land and Cattle Properties.

Habitation Site Type	AZSITE	Location*	Tusayan White	Tusayan Gray	Little Colorado White	Little Colorado Gray	Cibola White	Tsegi Orange	Mogollon Brown	Alameda Brown	Puerco Valley Utility	Counts
Pithouses	AZ P:3:119A (ASM)	A	11	59	2	0.9	1	3	22	0.9		1162
	AZ P:3:121A (ASM)	A	11	69	1			0.4	18			484
	AZ P:3:174 (ASM)	A	3	12	23		2	2	58			261
	AZ P:3:175 (ASM)	A	18	31	6			0.7	44			281
	AZ P:3:176B (ASM)	A	26	36	5	0.7	1	0.5	24	3	3	591
	AZ P:3:223 (ASM)	A	9	58	8		0.6		13	9	3	168
	Average % for pithouses		*13*	*44*	*8*	*0.3*	*0.8*	*1*	*30*	*2*	*1*	*100*
Pueblos	AZ P:3:121B (ASM)	A	12	20	12			2	54	0.8		248
	AZ P:3:227A (ASM)	A	9	4	27	0.4	12	3	37	4	3	257
	Average % for adjacent		*12*	*36*	*10*	*0.2*	*2*	*1*	*34*	*2*	*1*	*100*
	AZ P:3:240 (ASM)	SE	12	3	28	1	3	0.9	39	2	10	232
	AZ P:3:215A (ASM)	FN	14	25	13	5		14	19	5	5	84
	AZ P:3:215B (ASM)	FN	7	14	12	2	0.3	3	27	25	9	304
	AZ P:3:215C (ASM)	FN	18	22	6		2	12	20	20		214
	AZ P:3:215D (ASM)	FN	8	25	9	0.3	0.3	3	30	22	0.3	338
	AZ P:3:216A (ASM)	FN	19	11	7	4	2		46	6	3	158
	AZ P:3:216B (ASM)	FN	13	31	9	1		4	37	2	3	159
	Average % for far north		*13*	*21*	*9*	*2*	*0.8*	*6*	*30*	*13*	*3*	*100*
	Average % for pueblos		*12*	*17*	*14*	*2*	*2*	*5*	*34*	*10*	*4*	*100*

*Note: A = AZLAC land adjacent to RAR, north of ranch; SE = Southeast of RAR; FN = far north, east of Chevelon Canyon at the LCR.

Table 5.19. Selected Decorated Ceramic Types by Locus for Aztec Land and Cattle Properties.

Site/Locus Type*	Location**	AZSITE	Idt. TWW***	Lino B/g	Kana-a B/w	Black Mesa B/w	Sosi B/w	Dogoszhi B/w	Flagstaff B/w	Tusayan B/w	Shato B/w	Indet. LCWW	Holbrook A B/w	Holbrook B B/w	Padre B/w	Walnut B/w	Leupp B/w	Chevelon B/w	Indet. CWW	Kiatuthlanna B/w	Red Mesa B/w	Puerco B/w	Escavada B/w	Snowflake B/w	Reserve B/w	Tularosa B/w
Hpi	A	AZ P:3:119A (ASM)	94	4	23	6		1				25							17							
Hpi	A	AZ P:3:119B (ASM)	28		10							15							4		9	2				
Hpi	A	AZ P:3:121A (ASM)	19		4	31						2				5										
Hpi	A	AZ P:3:174 (ASM)	50			8						59										6				
Hpi	A	AZ P:3:175 (ASM)	24	1	69	40	17	5	3		1	16	2	6		13			1					3		
Hpi	A	AZ P:3:176B (ASM)	2	5	5	2	1	1				8	1			10			1						2	
Hpi	A	AZ P:3:223 (ASM)	19		1	10						2				15			1							
Hpi	A	AZ P:3:121B (ASM)	14			10		14				14			7	39			9	3		9	1	3	6	
Hpi	A	AZ P:3:227A (ASM)	103									23														
Sc	A	AZ P:3:118 (ASM)	6		7	6			1		1	277		1		4			1			1	1	1	1	
Sc	A	AZ P:3:119C (ASM)										1														
Sc	A	AZ P:3:121C (ASM)	54		2	27	3	14				41		3	1	13			16			6	1	3	2	
Sc	A	AZ P:3:176C (ASM)			1		1					1							1							
Sc	A	AZ P:3:176D (ASM)	9					1	1			18	8		2	31	1		11			38	13	6		
Sc	A	AZ P:3:214 (ASM)	1		6	5	4			2		10				7	1					1	2	1		
Sc	A	AZ P:3:217A (ASM)	8			1		1				1	5	2		11			8			9		3	5	
Sc	A	AZ P:3:217B (ASM)	2									4		1	1	1				1		1		1	5	1
Sc	A	AZ P:3:217C (ASM)	18	2		2		2				2	3	7	1	2			1			1		2		
Sc	A	AZ P:3:218 (ASM)	5		6	20						8	1											1		
Sc	A	AZ P:3:219 (ASM)	14			5						1			1	10			2			1	4	13	3	
Sc	A	AZ P:3:220 (ASM)	15		4	7	1							1		4			1			6		13		
Sc	A	AZ P:3:221 (ASM)	1									15	26	8												
Sc	A	AZ P:3:222 (ASM)	11	1		5		5	1		1	5				12			4			1				
Sc	A	AZ P:3:224 (ASM)	20			9		3				5	2	1		6									1	
Sc	A	AZ P:3:225A (ASM)	13			7		3	2			4		2	1	5									2	
Sc	A	AZ P:3:225B (ASM)	4						4			8														
Sc	A	AZ P:3:226A (ASM)				6		1							1	5			5			2			3	1
Adjacent Subtotals			501	13	140	191	26	25	5	3	4	566	47	29	14	170	1	1	75	4	9	84	22	46	28	1
Hpu	FN	AZ P:3:215A (ASM)	9		1		2					10	1		1											
Hpu	FN	AZ P:3:215B (ASM)	6	12				3	1			30	3	3	2	2			4						3	
Hpu	FN	AZ P:3:215C (ASM)	29			5		4				9				3			1						1	
Hpu	FN	AZ P:3:215D (ASM)	13			9		3		1		16		1		12						1			2	
Hpu	FN	AZ P:3:216A (ASM)	20			7		3				3		1		6										
Hpu	FN	AZ P:3:216B (ASM)	13	1				2	4			7		2	1	5			5							
Far North Subtotals			90	13	1	21	3	15	5	2		75	1	6	5	28			5			1		1	6	
Hpu	SE	AZ P:3:240 (ASM)	15				10	2				25	2			39			4	1				1	1	
Sc	S	AZ P:3:164 (ASM)			5																						
Totals			606	26	146	212	39	42	10	3	4	666	50	35	19	237	1	1	84	5	9	85	22	47	35	1

*Note: Hpi = Habitation - pithouses; Hpu = Habitation - pueblo; Sc = Artifact scatter.

**Note: A = AZLAC land adjacent to RAR, north of ranch; FN = far north, east of Chevelon Canyon at the LCR; SE = Southeast of RAR; S = South of RAR.

***Note: TWW = Tusayan White Ware; B/g = Black-on-gray; B/w = Black-on-white; LCWW = Little Colorado White Ware; CWW = Cibola White Ware.

Table 5.19. Selected Decorated Ceramic Types by Locus for Aztec Land and Cattle Properties, cont'd.

Site/Locus Type*	Location**	AZSITE	Idt. TOW***	Tsegi B/o	Tsegi Poly	Jeddito B/o	Tusayan B/r	Tusayan Poly A	Dogoszhi Poly	Jeddito Plain	Idt. Jeddito YW	Jeddito B/y	Homolovi Poly	Idt. White Mtn	St. Johns Poly	Cedar Creek Poly	Idt. Roosevelt Red	McDonald Ptd Corr	Showlow B/r	Deadman's B/r	Totals
Hpi	A	AZ P:3:119A (ASM)	29									1									202
Hpi	A	AZ P:3:119B (ASM)	11				2														80
Hpi	A	AZ P:3:121A (ASM)	2				1														63
Hpi	A	AZ P:3:174 (ASM)		4																	78
Hpi	A	AZ P:3:175 (ASM)	1											1							67
Hpi	A	AZ P:3:176B (ASM)	3																1		199
Hpi	A	AZ P:3:223 (ASM)																			30
Hpu	A	AZ P:3:121B (ASM)	3				2			1											64
Hpu	A	AZ P:3:227A (ASM)	7											2			1	1	6	1	143
Sc	A	AZ P:3:118 (ASM)	5																		385
Sc	A	AZ P:3:119C (ASM)																			31
Sc	A	AZ P:3:121C (ASM)																	1		2
Sc	A	AZ P:3:176C (ASM)	1																		186
Sc	A	AZ P:3:176D (ASM)																			5
Sc	A	AZ P:3:214 (ASM)																4	3		134
Sc	A	AZ P:3:217A (ASM)	3						3						3			2	2		62
Sc	A	AZ P:3:217B (ASM)	8						3									2	5		69
Sc	A	AZ P:2:217C (ASM)																1			21
Sc	A	AZ P:3:218 (ASM)	1																1		13
Sc	A	AZ P:3:219 (ASM)																			60
Sc	A	AZ P:3:220 (ASM)																			12
Sc	A	AZ P:3:221 (ASM)																			31
Sc	A	AZ P:3:222 (ASM)																			48
Sc	A	AZ P:3:224 (ASM)	4																		31
Sc	A	AZ P:3:225A (ASM)																			42
Sc	A	AZ P:3:225B (ASM)						1			1										13
Sc	A	AZ P:3:226A (ASM)	2																2		30
Sc	A	AZ P:3:226B (ASM)																1			12
Sc	A	AZ P:3:227B (ASM)																			25
		Adjacent Subtotals	80	4			5	1	6	1		1	1	3	3			9	21	1	2138
Hpu	FN	AZ P:3:215A (ASM)	11		1														1		36
Hpu	FN	AZ P:3:215B (ASM)	9																3		76
Hpu	FN	AZ P:3:215C (ASM)	14			11	2							3				4			86
Hpu	FN	AZ P:3:215D (ASM)	7		2						1								3		74
Hpu	FN	AZ P:3:216A (ASM)												4		1					48
Hpu	FN	AZ P:3:216B (ASM)	5		1								1	7	1				3		45
		Far North Subtotals	46		4	11	2				1		1	7	1			4	10		365
Hpu	SE	AZ P:3:240 (ASM)				2												4	9		115
Sc	S	AZ P:3:164 (ASM)	3																		8
		Totals	129	4	4	13	7	1	6	1	1	1	2	10	3	1	1	17	40	1	2626

*Note: Hpi = Habitation - pithouses; Hpu = Habitation - pueblo; Sc = Artifact scatter.
**Note: A = AZLAC land adjacent to RAR, north of ranch; FN = far north, east of Chevelon Canyon at the LCR; SE = Southeast of RAR; S = South of RAR.
***Note: TOW = Tsegi Orange Ware; B/o = Black-on-orange; B/r = Black-on-red; B/y = Black-on-yellow; Poly = Polychrome.

5: Rock Art Ranch Area Surveys and Testing 169

Table 5.20. Selected Utility Ceramic Types by Locus from Aztec Land and Cattle Properties.

Site/Locus Type*	Location**	AZSITE	Idt. Tusayan Gray W	Lino Gray	Kana-a Gray	Honani Tooled	Tusayan Corrugated	O'leary Tooled	Little Colorado Corr	Idt. Alameda Bm W	Winona	Grapevine	Kinnikinnick	Chavez Pass	Winona Corr	Idt. Decorated ABW	Brown Plain	Brown Corrugated	Brown Polished	Puerco V UW–Plain	Puerco V UW–Corr	Totals
Hpi	A	AZ P:3:119A (ASM)	636				52		10	10							124	121	7			960
Hpi	A	AZ P:3:119B (ASM)	201				45		1					1			43	43				334
Hpi	A	AZ P:3:121A (ASM)	128				4										52	37				221
Hpi	A	AZ P:3:174 (ASM)	22				10										21	130				183
Hpi	A	AZ P:3:175 (ASM)	82				6										27	98				214
Hpi	A	AZ P:3:176B (ASM)		195	1		17			6	4			9			12	41	87		20	392
Hpi	A	AZ P:3:223 (ASM)		97						1				14			3	15	3		5	138
Hpu	A	AZ P:3:121B (ASM)	33				16			2							16	117				184
Hpu	A	AZ P:3:227A (ASM)		5			4		1					8			8	79			8	114
Sc	A	AZ P:3:118 (ASM)	11	135			126		19								129	704	2			1126
Sc	A	AZ P:3:119C (ASM)															1					1
Sc	A	AZ P:3:121C (ASM)		24										3			1	2			2	29
Sc	A	AZ P:3:176C (ASM)		16	4	1	21		1	1				3			11	60			2	121
Sc	A	AZ P:3:176D (ASM)					2										1	5				10
Sc	A	AZ P:3:214 (ASM)		4						1							1	105			11	122
Sc	A	AZ P:3:217A (ASM)		3			1		6	2	1							27			4	44
Sc	A	AZ P:3:217B (ASM)					1			4				1		2		67			10	84
Sc	A	AZ P:2:217C (ASM)					1											4			4	9
Sc	A	AZ P:3:218 (ASM)		3			2			2							2	5			6	20
Sc	A	AZ P:3:219 (ASM)		6			5		15					7			1	62			28	125
Sc	A	AZ P:3:220 (ASM)		4			2					3		8			5	2			4	28
Sc	A	AZ P:3:221 (ASM)							5					4				16			5	25
Sc	A	AZ P:3:222 (ASM)																36				36
Sc	A	AZ P:3:224 (ASM)		2			17							7			13	18			4	52
Sc	A	AZ P:3:225A (ASM)																37			12	63
Sc	A	AZ P:3:225B (ASM)								1								2				3
Sc	A	AZ P:3:226A (ASM)		31	2		11		1	11				8			39	18			6	116
Sc	A	AZ P:3:226B (ASM)		2	2		2		1	1	2			1			2	4			1	17
Sc	A	AZ P:3:227B (ASM)		7	1		3		1	3							1	13			3	26
Adjacent Subtotals			1113	529	9	1	347	1	60	34	9	3	1	75	1	2	512	1868	99		135	4797
Hpu	FN	AZ P:3:215A (ASM)		6	1		14		4	4							1	14			4	48
Hpu	FN	AZ P:3:215B (ASM)		6			36		6	22	36			18			7	70			26	228
Hpu	FN	AZ P:3:215C (ASM)			1		46			16	26							39				128
Hpu	FN	AZ P:3:215D (ASM)		22			64		1	11	60			4			9	91			1	264
Hpu	FN	AZ P:3:216A (ASM)		7			11		6	1								73			4	110
Hpu	FN	AZ P:3:216B (ASM)			1		48		2	3	8				1			55	1	2	2	114
Far North Subtotals				41	3		219		19	35	57	96	1	22	1		17	342	1	2	37	892
Hpu	SE	AZ P:3:240 (ASM)		4	1		2		3					4			9	68	1		24	117
Sc	S	AZ P:3:164 (ASM)																				
Totals			1113	574	13	1	568	1	82	69	66	99	1	101	1	2	538	2278	101	2	196	5806

*Note: Hpi = Habitation - pithouses; Hpu = Habitation - pueblo; Sc = Artifact scatter.
**Note: A = AZLAC land adjacent to RAR, north of ranch; FN = far north, east of Chevelon Canyon at the LCR; SE = Southeast of RAR; S = South of RAR.
***Note: W = Ware; Corr = Corrugated; VUW = Valley Utility Ware.

170 Lange, Fladd, and E.C. Adams

Table 5.21. Percentages of Selected Ceramic Types for Pithouses and Pueblos on Aztec Land and Cattle Properties.

Habitation Site Type	AZSITE	Location*	Lino Black/gray	Kana-a Black/white	Black Mesa Black/white	Sosi Black/white	Dogoszhi Black/white	Holbrook A Black/white	Holbrook B Black/white	Walnut Black/white	Counts
Pithouses	AZ P:3:119A (ASM)	A	2	11	3		0.5				202
	AZ P:3:121A (ASM)	A		6	49					8	63
	AZ P:3:176B (ASM)	A	0.5	35	20	9	3	1	3	7	199
	AZ P:3:223 (ASM)	A	17	17	7		3	3		33	30
Pueblos	AZ P:3:121B (ASM)	A		2	16					23	64
	AZ P:3:227A (ASM)	A			7					27	143
	AZ P:3:240 (ASM)	SE				9	2	2		34	115
	AZ P:3:215A (ASM)	FN	16	3		6	4				36
	AZ P:3:215B (ASM)	FN			6		5		4	3	76
	AZ P:3:215C (ASM)	FN			12		4	1		3	86
	AZ P:3:215D (ASM)	FN			15		6		2	16	74
	AZ P:3:216A (ASM)	FN								12	48
	AZ P:3:216B (ASM)	FN	2			2	4		4	11	45

(Row Percents)

*Note: A = AZLAC land adjacent to RAR, north of ranch; SE = Southeast of RAR; FN = far north, east of Chevelon Canyon at the LCR.

5: Rock Art Ranch Area Surveys and Testing 171

Table 5.22. Ceramic Types for AZLAC Habitation Loci.

a. Decorated Ceramic Types.

Site/Locus Type*	Location**	AZSITE	Idt. TWW***	Lino B/g	Kana-a B/w	Black Mesa B/w	Sosi B/w	Dogoszhi B/w	Flagstaff B/w	Tusayan B/w	Shato B/w	Indet. LCWW	Holbrook A B/w	Holbrook B B/w	Padre B/w	Walnut B/w	Leupp B/w	Chevelon B/w	Indet. CWW	Kiatuthlanna B/w	Red Mesa B/w	Puerco B/w	Escavada B/w	Snowflake B/w	Reserve B/w	Tularosa B/w
Hpi	A	AZ P:3:119A (ASM)	94	4	23	6		1				25							17								
Hpi	A	AZ P:3:119B (ASM)	28		10							15							4		9	2					
Hpi	A	AZ P:3:121A (ASM)	19		4	31						2				5											
Hpi	A	AZ P:3:174 (ASM)	50			8						59										6					
Hpi	A	AZ P:3:175 (ASM)	24	1	69	40	17	5	3			16	2	6		13		1	1						3	2	
Hpi	A	AZ P:3:176B (ASM)	2	5	5	2	1				1	8	1			10			1								
Hpi	A	AZ P:3:223 (ASM)										2															
		A-Hpi	217	10	111	87	18	6	3		1	127	3	6		28		1	23		9	8	1	3	2	
Hpu	A	AZ P:3:121B (ASM)	19		1	10						14				15											
Hpu	A	AZ P:3:227A (ASM)	14			10						23			7	39			9	3		9	1	3	6	
		A-Hpu	33		1	20						37			7	54			9	3		9	1	3	6	
Hpu	FN	AZ P:3:215A (ASM)	9				2					10			1				4							
Hpu	FN	AZ P:3:215B (ASM)	6	12				3	1			30	2	3	2	2									3	
Hpu	FN	AZ P:3:215C (ASM)	29			5		4		1		9	1		1	3			1						1	
Hpu	FN	AZ P:3:215D (ASM)	13			9		3		1		16		1		12										
Hpu	FN	AZ P:3:216A (ASM)	20			7		3				3			2	6						1			2	
Hpu	FN	AZ P:3:216B (ASM)	13	1			1	2	4			7			1	5										
		Far North Subtotals	90	13	1	21	3	15	5	2		75	1	6	5	28			5			1			6	
Hpu	SE	AZ P:3:240 (ASM)	15				10	2				25	2	12		39		1	4	1				1	1	
		Totals	355	23	113	128	31	23	8	2	1	264	6	12	12	149		1	41	4	9	18	1	7	15	

*Note: Hpi = Habitation - pithouses; Hpu = Habitation - pueblo; Sc = Artifact scatter.
**Note: A = AZLAC land adjacent to RAR, north of ranch; FN = far north, east of Chevelon Canyon at the LCR; SE = Southeast of RAR; S = South of RAR.
***Note: TWW = Tusayan White Ware; B/g = Black-on-gray; B/w = Black-on-white; LCWW = Little Colorado White Ware; CWW = Cibola White Ware.

172 Lange, Fladd, and E.C. Adams

Table 5.22. Ceramic Types for AZLAC Habitation Loci, cont'd.

b. Utility Ceramic Types.

Site/Locus Type*	Location**	AZSITE	Idt. Tusayan Gray W	Lino Gray	Kana-a Gray	Honani Tooled	Tusayan Corrugated	O'Leary Tooled	Little Colorado Corr	Idt. Alameda Brn W	Winona	Grapevine	Kinnikinnick	Chavez Pass	Winona Corr	Idt. Decorated ABW	Brown Plain	Brown Corrugated	Brown Polished	Puerco V UW--Plain	Puerco V UW--Corr	Totals
Hpi	A	AZ P:3:119A (ASM)	636				52		10	10							124	121	7			960
Hpi	A	AZ P:3:119B (ASM)	201				45		1					1			43	43				334
Hpi	A	AZ P:3:121A (ASM)	128				4										52	37				221
Hpi	A	AZ P:3:174 (ASM)	22				10										21	130				183
Hpi	A	AZ P:3:175 (ASM)	82				6			6	4			1			27	98				214
Hpi	A	AZ P:3:176B (ASM)		195	1		17			1				9			12	41	87		20	392
Hpi	A	AZ P:3:223 (ASM)		97										14			3	15	3		5	138
		A-Hpi	1069	292	1		134		11	17	4			25			282	485	97		25	2442
Hpu	A	AZ P:3:121B (ASM)	33				16		1	2							16	117				184
Hpu	A	AZ P:3:227A (ASM)		5			4		1		1			8			8	79			8	114
		A-Hpu	33	5			20		1	2	1			8			24	196			8	298
Hpu	FN	AZ P:3:215A (ASM)		6	1		14		4	4							1	14			4	48
Hpu	FN	AZ P:3:215B (ASM)		6			36		6		22	36		18			7	70			26	228
Hpu	FN	AZ P:3:215C (ASM)			1		46		1	16	26		1					39				128
Hpu	FN	AZ P:3:215D (ASM)		22			64		1	11	1	60		4			9	91			1	264
Hpu	FN	AZ P:3:216A (ASM)		7			11		6	1	8		1					73	4		4	110
Hpu	FN	AZ P:3:216B (ASM)			1		48		2	3								55	1	2	2	114
		Far North Subtotals		41	3		219		19	35	57	96	1	22			17	342	1	2	37	892
Hpu	SE	AZ P:3:240 (ASM)		4	1		2		3			96	1	4	1		9	68	1		24	117
		Totals	1102	342	5		375		34	54	62	96	1	59	1		332	1091	99	2	94	3749

*Note: Hpi = Habitation - pithouses; Hpu = Habitation - pueblo; Sc = Artifact scatter.
**Note: A = AZLAC land adjacent to RAR, north of ranch; FN = far north, east of Chevelon Canyon at the LCR; SE = Southeast of RAR; S = South of RAR.
***Note: W = Ware; Corr = Corrugated; VUW = Valley Utility Ware.

Table 5.23. Flaked Stone Counts for Loci on Aztec Land and Cattle Properties.

Site/Locus Type*	Location**	AZSITE	Field	Total
		Isolates		3
Hpi	A	AZ P:3:176B (ASM)	160	142
Hpi	A	AZ P:3:223 (ASM)	164	58
Hpi	A	AZ P:3:227A (ASM)	169A	92
Sc	A	AZ P:3:121C (ASM)	148	16
Sc	A	AZ P:3:176C (ASM)	161A	160
Sc	A	AZ P:3:214 (ASM)	145	122
Sc	A	AZ P:3:217A (ASM)	155A	4
Sc	A	AZ P:3:217B (ASM)	155B	43
Sc	A	AZ P:3:217C (ASM)	155C	8
Sc	A	AZ P:3:218 (ASM)	156	11
Sc	A	AZ P:3:219 (ASM)	157	74
Sc	A	AZ P:3:220 (ASM)	158	50
Sc	A	AZ P:3:221 (ASM)	159	55
Sc	A	AZ P:3:222 (ASM)	163	3
Sc	A	AZ P:3:225A (ASM)	166A	79
Sc	A	AZ P:3:225B (ASM)	166B	5
Sc	A	AZ P:3:226A (ASM)	167	135
Sc	A	AZ P:3:226B (ASM)	168	5
Sc	A	AZ P:3:227B (ASM)	169B	13
Sc	S	AZ P:3:164 (ASM)	47	12
Hpu	FN	AZ P:3:215A (ASM)	151A	3
Hpu	FN	AZ P:3:215B (ASM)	151B	141
Hpu	FN	AZ P:3:215C (ASM)	151C	89
Hpu	FN	AZ P:3:215D (ASM)	151D	132
Hpu	FN	AZ P:3:216A (ASM)	152A	124
Hpu	FN	AZ P:3:216B (ASM)	152B	101
		Total		1680

*Note: Hpi = Habitation - pithouses; Hpu = Habitation - pueblo;
  Sc = Artifact scatter.

**Note: A = AZLAC land adjacent to RAR, north of ranch;
  FN = far north, east of Chevelon Canyon at the LCR;
  S = south of RAR.

Table 5.24. Flaked Stone Material Types for Loci on Aztec Land and Cattle Properties.

Site/Locus Type*	Location**	AZSITE	Field	Chert	Chalcedony	Quartzite	Igneous	Petrified Wood	Obsidian	Other	Total
		Isolates		2					1		3
Hpi	A	AZ P:3:176B (ASM)	160	95	1	24		22			142
Hpi	A	AZ P:3:223 (ASM)	164	32	3	9		14			58
Hpi	A	AZ P:3:227A (ASM)	169A	46	2	14		29	1		92
Sc	A	AZ P:3:121C (ASM)	148	9		4		3			16
Sc	A	AZ P:3:176C (ASM)	161A	113	1	13		33			160
Sc	A	AZ P:3:214 (ASM)	145	77		33		12			122
Sc	A	AZ P:3:217A (ASM)	155A	2	2						4
Sc	A	AZ P:3:217B (ASM)	155B	30		5		8			43
Sc	A	AZ P:3:217C (ASM)	155C	7		1					8
Sc	A	AZ P:3:218 (ASM)	156	8		1		2			11
Sc	A	AZ P:3:219 (ASM)	157	54		8		12			74
Sc	A	AZ P:3:220 (ASM)	158	20	7	7		16			50
Sc	A	AZ P:3:221 (ASM)	159	9	6	8		31	1		55
Sc	A	AZ P:3:222 (ASM)	163	4				1			5
Sc	A	AZ P:3:225A (ASM)	166A	60		9		10			79
Sc	A	AZ P:3:225B (ASM)	166B	2		3					5
Sc	A	AZ P:3:226A (ASM)	167	77	5	21		32			135
Sc	A	AZ P:3:226B (ASM)	168	3		2					5
Sc	A	AZ P:3:227B (ASM)	169B	7	1	2		3			13
		Totals Adjacent		657	28	164		228	3		1080
		Percents Adjacent		*61*	*3*	*15*		*21*	*0.3*		*100*
Sc	S	AZ P:3:164(ASM)	47	3	1	2		6			12
		Percents South		*25*	*8*	*17*		*50*			*100*
Hpu	FN	AZ P:3:215A (ASM)	151A	1		2					3
Hpu	FN	AZ P:3:215B (ASM)	151B	84		21		36			141
Hpu	FN	AZ P:3:215C (ASM)	151C	51		12		26			89
Hpu	FN	AZ P:3:215D (ASM)	151D	81		25		26			132
Hpu	FN	AZ P:3:216A (ASM)	152A	80		23		21			124
Hpu	FN	AZ P:3:216B (ASM)	152B	61	1	13		26			101
		Totals Far North		358	1	96		135			590
		Percents Far North		*61*	*0.2*	*16*		*23*			*100*
		Totals		1018	30	262		369	3		1682
		Percents		*61*	*2*	*16*		*22*	*0.2*		*100*

*Note: Hpi = Habitation - pithouses; Hpu = Habitation - pueblo; Sc = Artifact scatter.

**Note: A = AZLAC land adjacent to RAR, north of ranch; FN = far north, east of Chevelon Canyon at the LCR; S = south of RAR.

Table 5.25. Flaked Stone Artifact Types for Loci on Aztec Land and Cattle Properties.

Site/Locus Type*	Location**	AZSITE	Field	Complete Flake	Broken Flake	Split Flake	Flake Fragment	Debris	Peckingstone	Hammerstone	Hammerstone Spall	Core	Core/Retouched Piece	Other/Tested Piece	Chopper	Scraper	Edge-damaged Piece	Retouched Piece	Biface	Drill	Wedge	Projectile Point	Total
		Isolates	PD 0																				3
Hpi	A	AZ P:3:176B (ASM)	160	29	23	1	10	56		4	6	3					7	2	1				142
Hpi	A	AZ P:3:223 (ASM)	164	8	10			32		1	3	3					4	3					58
Hpi	A	AZ P:3:227A (ASM)	169A	23	12	1	3	29	1		11					1	5	3					92
Sc	A	AZ P:3:121C (ASM)	148	3	1			10									1	1					16
Sc	A	AZ P:3:176A (ASM)	161A	21	27	1	7	84			6	4					9	1					160
Sc	A	AZ P:3:214 (ASM)	145	24	9	2	8	65			4	1					6	3					122
Sc	A	AZ P:3:217A (ASM)	155A		1			3															4
Sc	A	AZ P:3:217B (ASM)	155B	11	2		1	26			1						1		2				43
Sc	A	AZ P:3:217C (ASM)	155C	2	2	1	1	1									1						8
Sc	A	AZ P:3:218 (ASM)	156	2	2		1	3			2												11
Sc	A	AZ P:3:219 (ASM)	157	26	5	2	2	34	1			1		1			1	1					74
Sc	A	AZ P:3:220 (ASM)	158	15	6	2	2	18			2	1					4						50
Sc	A	AZ P:3:221 (ASM)	159	17			4	26			2							2	1			3	55
Sc	A	AZ P:3:222 (ASM)	163	1				3									1						5
Sc	A	AZ P:3:225A (ASM)	166A	3	13	1	3	48			9	1					1	1					79
Sc	A	AZ P:3:225B (ASM)	166B	2				2							1								5
Sc	A	AZ P:3:226A (ASM)	167	23	26	2	3	58	1		19						2	1					135
Sc	A	AZ P:3:226B (ASM)	168	2				1				2											5
Sc	A	AZ P:3:227B (ASM)	169B	1	3		1	2	1		2						3						13
		Totals Adjacent		213	142	13	46	501	4	5	67	16		1	1	1	46	17	4			3	1080
		Percents Adjacent		20	13	1	4	46	0.4	0.5	6	1		0.09	0.09	0.09	4	2	0.4			0.3	100
Sc	S	AZ P:3:164(ASM)	47	6				4									1	1					12
		Percents South		50				33									8	8					100
Hpu	FN	AZ P:3:215A (ASM)	151A	1				2															3
Hpu	FN	AZ P:3:215B (ASM)	151B	31	8	2	1	86		2	6	2	1				2	2					141
Hpu	FN	AZ P:3:215C (ASM)	151C	24	4	4	6	36		2	4	1			1		4	2				1	89
Hpu	FN	AZ P:3:215D (ASM)	151D	34	9	2	13	53		1	6	7	1				5	1					132
Hpu	FN	AZ P:3:216A (ASM)	152A	47	13	1	4	47		1	3	6						1	1				124
Hpu	FN	AZ P:3:216B (ASM)	152B	36	8	1	5	39		1	2	2		3			3	1					101
		Totals Far North		173	42	10	29	263		5	21	18	2	3	1		14	7	1			1	590
		Percents Far North		29	7	2	5	45		0.8	4	3	0.3	0.5	0.2		2	1	0.2			0.2	100
		Totals		392	184	23	75	768	4	10	88	34	2	4	2	1	61	25	5			4	1682
		Percents		23	11	1	4	46	0.2	0.6	5	2	0.1	0.2	0.1	0.06	4	1	0.3			0.2	100

*Note: Hpi = Habitation - pithouses; Hpu = Habitation - pueblo; Sc = Artifact scatter.
**Note: A = AZLAC land adjacent to RAR, north of ranch; FN = far north, east of Chevelon Canyon at the LCR; S = south of RAR.

Table 5.26. Flaked Stone Artifact Type by Material Type for Loci on Aztec Land and Cattle Properties.

Material	Complete Flake	Broken Flake	Split Flake	Flake Fragment	Debris	Peckingstone	Hammerstone	Hammerstone Spall	Core	Core/Retouched Piece	Other/Tested Piece	Chopper	Scraper	Edge-damaged Piece	Retouched Piece	Biface	Drill	Wedge	Projectile Point	Totals	Percents
Chert	134	71	14	37	163	2	4	35			3		1	33	18				4	519	53
Chalcedony	1	2			12				1					2						18	2
Quartzite	45	27	4	9	79	2	4	32	2	1		2		2	2					209	21
Petrified Wood	55	38	5	16	82		1	7	7		1			20	2	1				235	24
Obsidian					1										2					3	0.3
Totals	235	138	23	62	337	4	9	74	10	1	4	2	1	57	22	1			4	984	100
Percents	24	14	2	6	34	0.4	0.9	8	1	0.1	0.4	0.2	0.1	6	2	0.1			0.4	100	

Table 5.27. Flaked Stone Material by Size for Loci on Aztec Land and Cattle Properties.

	Size*	Chert	Chalcedony	Quartzite	Petrified Wood	Obsidian	Totals	Percents
	≤1	45	5	12	20	1	83	8
	≤4	192	7	72	114	1	386	38
	≤9	186	5	68	72	1	332	33
	≤16	93	1	33	21		148	15
	≤25	24		15	7		46	5
	≤36	3		5	1		9	0.9
	≤49							
	≤64	1		3			4	0.4
	≤81			1			1	0.1
Totals		544	18	209	235	3	1009	100
Percents		54	2	21	23	0.3	100	

*Note: Size is given in square centimeters.

Table 5.28. Flaked Stone Artifact Types by Amount of Cortex for Loci on Aztec Land and Cattle Properties.

Percent Cortex	Complete Flake	Broken Flake	Split Flake	Flake Fragment	Debris	Peckingstone	Hammerstone	Hammerstone Spall	Core	Core/Retouched Piece	Other/Tested Piece	Chopper	Scraper	Edge-damaged Piece	Retouched Piece	Biface	Drill	Wedge	Projectile Point	Totals	Percents
not recorded		3			10			3	2					4	4	1			1	24	2
100	43	14	4	8	42	1	2	8	5		1			4	2					134	13
present	111	66	9	21	122	3	6	38	19	1	2	2	1	22	11					434	43
absent	81	55	10	33	163		1	25	5		1			31	5	4			3	417	41
Totals	235	138	23	62	337	4	9	74	31	1	4	2	1	57	22	5			4	1009	100
Percents	23	14	2	6	33	0.4	0.9	7	3	0.1	0.4	0.2	0.1	6	2	0.5			0.4		100

Table 5.29. Flaked Stone Material by Amount of Cortex for Loci on Aztec Land and Cattle Properties.

Percent Cortex	Chert	Chalcedony	Quartzite	Petrified Wood	Obsidian	Totals	Percents
not recorded	14	1	4	4	1	24	2
100	77	1	45	12		134	13
present	245	16	95	93		434	43
absent	208		65	126	2	417	41
Totals	544	18	209	235	3	1009	100
Percents	54	2	21	23	0.3	100	

Table 5.30. Flaked Stone Size by Locus for loci on Aztec Land and Cattle Properties.

Site/Locus Type*	Location**	AZSITE	Field	≤1	≤4	≤9	≤16	≤25	≤36	≤49	≤64	≤81	≤100	Total
		Isolates	PD 0		1	1	1							3
Hpi	A	AZ P:3:176B (ASM)	160	14	58	44	13	8	3		2			142
Hpi	A	AZ P:3:223 (ASM)	164	5	32	16	4	1	1					58
Hpi	A	AZ P:3:227A (ASM)	169A	3	41	31	11	3	2		1			92
Sc	A	AZ P:3:121C (ASM)	148	6	4	6								16
Sc	A	AZ P:3:176C (ASM)	161A	17	80	37	17	7						160
Sc	A	AZ P:3:214 (ASM)	145	9	57	37	16	3	2					122
Sc	A	AZ P:3:217A (ASM)	155A	2		1	1							4
Sc	A	AZ P:3:217B (ASM)	155B	8	30	4	1							43
Sc	A	AZ P:3:217C (ASM)	155C		3	4	1							8
Sc	A	AZ P:3:218 (ASM)	156		4	6	1							11
Sc	A	AZ P:3:219 (ASM)	157	6	41	18	6	3						74
Sc	A	AZ P:3:220 (ASM)	158	1	19	24	5	1						50
Sc	A	AZ P:3:221 (ASM)	159	15	23	10	6	1						55
Sc	A	AZ P:3:222 (ASM)	163	1	2	2								5
Sc	A	AZ P:3:225A (ASM)	166A	3	44	26	4	2						79
Sc	A	AZ P:3:225B (ASM)	166B		1	1	1	1						5
Sc	A	AZ P:3:226A (ASM)	167	13	74	34	12	2				1		135
Sc	A	AZ P:3:226B (ASM)	168			1	1	3						5
Sc	A	AZ P:3:227B (ASM)	169B		2	7	3	1						13
		Totals Adjacent		103	516	310	104	35	8		3	1		1080
		Percents Adjacent		10	48	29	10	3	0.7		0.3	0.09		100
Sc	S	AZ P:3:164(ASM)	47		5	5	2							12
		Percents South			42	42	17							100
Hpu	FN	AZ P:3:215A (ASM)	151A		1	2								3
Hpu	FN	AZ P:3:215B (ASM)	151B	16	84	27	10	3	1					141
Hpu	FN	AZ P:3:215C (ASM)	151C	9	49	26	2	2			1			89
Hpu	FN	AZ P:3:215D (ASM)	151D	7	40	62	21	2						132
Hpu	FN	AZ P:3:216A (ASM)	152A	4	49	44	22	4	1					124
Hpu	FN	AZ P:3:216B (ASM)	152B	8	51	29	11	2						101
		Totals Far North		44	274	190	66	13	2		1			590
		Percents Far North		7	46	32	11	2	0.3		0.2			100
		Totals		147	795	505	172	48	10		4	1		1682
		Percents		9	47	30	10	3	0.6		0.2	0.06		100

*Note: Hpi = Habitation - pithouses; Hpu = Habitation - pueblo; Sc = Artifact scatter.
**Note: A = AZLAC land adjacent to RAR, north of ranch; FN = far north, east of Chevelon Canyon at the LCR; S = south of RAR.
***Note: The size dimensions are in square centimeters.

Table 5.31. Flaked Stone Size by Material Type for Loci on Aztec Land and Cattle Properties.

Material	SIZE*								Totals	Percents
	≤1	≤4	≤9	≤16	≤25	≤36	≤49	≤64	≤81	≤100		
Chert	84	481	307	113	25	4		1			1015	61
Chalcedony	7	14	7	1							29	2
Quartzite	15	97	88	35	16	5		3	1		260	16
Igneous												
Petrified Wood	40	197	97	21	7	1					363	22
Obsidian	1	1	1								3	0.2
Other												
Totals	147	790	500	170	48	10		4	1		1670	100
Percents	9	47	30	10	3	0.6		0.2	0.06		100	

*Note: The size dimensions are in square centimeters.

Table 5.32. Periods of Occupation for Loci West of Chevelon Canyon.

Site	AZSITE	MAJOR PERIOD		Periods of Occupation					
		Archaic	Ceramic	Middle-Late Archaic	Late Archaic	Basketmaker II/III	Basketmaker III	Basketmaker III/ Pueblo I	Pueblo I	Pueblo II/III	Pueblo III
BLH-1	P:2:106	X	X								
BLH-2	P:2:107	X		X							
BLH-3	P:2:108	X		X	X						
BLH-4	P:2:109		X			X					
BLH-5	P:2:110		X			X					
BLH-6	P:2:111		X				X				
BLH-7	P:2:112								X		
BLH-8	P:2:113	X									
BLH-9	P:2:114	X	X			X					
BLH-16-1	P:2:184							X			
BLH-16-2	P:2:185A	X	X	X							
BLH-16-3	P:2:185B	X									
BLH-16-4	P:2:186A	X		X							
BLH-16-5	P:2:186B	X									X
BLH-16-6	P:2:186C	X	X								
BLH-17-7	P:2:187A	X		X						X	
BLH-16-8	P:2:187B	X		X							
Isolates					X						

Table 5.33. Ceramic Wares Present at AZ P:2:56(ASM) — 1989 HRP Collections.

Provenience	Jeddito Yellow Ware	Homolovi Orange Ware	Alameda Brown Ware	Tusayan White Ware	Tusayan Gray Ware	Little Colorado White Ware	Unknown Plain Ware	Total
Surface Isolates	4	8	7	2	8	3	5	37
Collection Unit #4		10	2	1	1			14
Totals	4	18	9	3	9	3	5	51
Percents	8	35	18	6	18	6	10	100

Table 5.34. Ceramic Types Present at AZ P:2:56(ASM) — 1989 HRP Collections.

Provenience	Awatovi/Jeddito Yellow Ware	Indeterminate Jeddito Yellow Ware	Indeterminate Little Colorado White Ware	Indeterminate Tusayan White Ware	Homolovi Plain	Homolovi Plain Corrugated	Indeterminate Tusayan Gray Ware	Angell Brown	Verde Brown	Indeterminate Alameda Brown Ware	Unknown Burned Corrugated	Brown Corrugated	Brown Indented Corrugated	Total
Surface Isolates	1	3	3	2	8		8	1	1	6	1	3	1	37
Collection Unit #4				1		10	1		1					14
Totals	1	3	3	3	8	10	9	1	2	6	1	3	1	51
Percents	2	6	6	6	16	20	18	2	4	12	2	6	2	100

Table 5.35. Flaked Stone Material Type by Provenience at AZ P:2:56(ASM).

Provenience (PD)	Collection Year*	Chert	Chalcedony	Quartzite	Igneous	Petrified Wood	Obsidian	Other	Total
Surface Collections									
0	1989	7		6			1		14
1	1989	3		3				1	7
2	1989	142	8	52		22		1	225
3	1989	22	2			8			32
4	1989	18	2	4		5			29
5	1989	3		12				2	17
Subtotals		195	12	77		35	1	4	324
Percents		*60*	*4*	*24*		*11*	*0.3*	*1*	*100*
Testing									
90	1999	2			1				3
91	1999	5		2	2	1			10
92	1999	9							9
93	1999	8							8
94	1999	6							6
95	1999	89	3	7	16	25			140
98	1999	1							1
99	1999	2			3				5
100	1999	3							3
101	1999	15				1			16
102	1999	1							1
103	1999	45	3	2	9	14			73
104	1999	2		1	1				4
105	1999	4							4
106	1999	40	1	2	5				48
110	1999	1							1
111	1999	14	1	1	5	2			23
Subtotals		247	8	15	42	43			355
Percents Testing		*70*	*2*	*4*	*12*	*12*			*100*
Totals		442	20	92	42	78	1	4	679
Percents		*442*	*20*	*92*	*42*	*78*	*1*	*4*	*100*

*Note: 1989 = original survey surface collection, analyzed by Karen Harry in 1989;
1999 = Huckell work in 1999, analyzed by Rich Lange in 2021.

Table 5.36. Flaked Stone Artifact Type by Provenience at AZ P:2:56(ASM).

Provenience (PD)	Collection Year*	Complete Flake	Broken Flake	Split Flake	Flake Fragment	Debris	Core	Edge-damaged Piece	Retouched Piece	Biface	Total
Surface Collections											
0	1989	1	1	1			4		1	2	10
1	1989						3		1	2	6
2	1989	69	51	25	70	3	2		1	1	222
3	1989	10	4	1	16	1					32
4	1989	7	3	6	11	1			1		29
5	1989	6	1	2			3		1		13
Subtotals		93	60	35	97	5	12		5	5	312
Percents		*30*	*19*	*11*	*31*	*2*	*4*		*2*	*2*	*100*
Testing											
90	1999		1			1		1			3
91	1999					10					10
92	1999	1	1			5		2			9
93	1999	2	2			4					8
94	1999	1				3		2			6
95	1999	1				137	1		1		140
98	1999					1					1
99	1999				1	4					5
100	1999					1		2			3
101	1999					15		1			16
102	1999							1			1
103	1999	1	1	1	2	67		1			73
104	1999	1				2	1				4
105	1999	1			2			1			4
106	1999	1				46	1				48
110	1999					1					1
111	1999	2				21					23
Subtotals		11	5	1	5	318	3	11	1		355
Percents Testing		*3*	*1*	*0.3*	*1*	*90*	*0.8*	*3*	*0.3*		*100*
Totals		104	65	36	102	323	15	11	6	5	667
Percents		*16*	*10*	*5*	*15*	*48*	*2*	*2*	*0.9*	*0.7*	*100*

*Note: 1989 = original survey surface collection, analyzed by Karen Harry in 1989; 1999 = Huckell work in 1999 analyzed by Rich Lange in 2021.

Table 5.37. Flaked Stone Material Type by Artifact Type at AZ P:2:56(ASM).

Artifact Type	Chert	Chalcedony	Quartzite	Igneous	Petrified Wood	Obsidian	Other	Total
Surface Collections -- 1989*								
Complete Flake	49	1	27		16			93
Broken Flake	40	1	11		7		1	60
Split Flake	21	1	11		1	1		35
Flake Fragment	65	9	13		10			97
Debris	5							5
Core	5		5				2	12
Edge-damaged Piece								
Retouched Piece	3		1				1	5
Biface	4				1			5
Drill	1							1
Other	1		2					3
Subtotals	194	12	70		35	1	4	316
Percents	*61*	*4*	*22*		*11*	*0.3*	*1*	*100*
Testing -- 1999*								
Complete Flake	7	1	2	1				11
Broken Flake	4		1					5
Split Flake	1							1
Flake Fragment	5							5
Debris	217	9	8	41	43			318
Edge-damaged Piece	11							11
Retouched Piece	1							1
Subtotals	246	10	11	42	43			352
Percents Testing	*70*	*3*	*3*	*12*	*12*			*100*
Totals	440	22	81	42	78	1	4	668
Percents	*66*	*3*	*12*	*6*	*12*	*0.1*	*0.6*	*100*

*Note: 1989 = original survey surface collection, analyzed by Karen Harry in 1989;
1999 = Huckell work in 1999 analyzed by Rich Lange in 2021.

Table 5.38. Size of Flaked Stone Artifacts by Provenience at AZ P:2:56(ASM).

Provenience (PD)	≤1 sq cm	≤4 sq cm	≤9 sq cm	≤16 sq cm	≤25 sq cm	≤36 sq cm	≤49 sq cm	≤64 sq cm	Total
90		3							3
91	1	7	2						10
92	4	4		1					9
93	2	3	3						8
94	1	2	3						6
95	108	25	4	3					140
98	1								1
99		4	1						5
100	1		1	1					3
101	9	6	1						16
102		1							1
103	51	15	4	1	2				73
104		1	1	1				1	4
105		4							4
106	40	7					1		48
110	1								1
111	18	1	1	1	1	1			23
Totals	237	83	21	8	3	1	1	1	355

Table 5.39. Size of Flaked Stone Artifacts by Material Type at AZ P:2:56(ASM).

Material	≤1 sq cm	≤4 sq cm	≤9 sq cm	≤16 sq cm	≤25 sq cm	≤36 sq cm	≤49 sq cm	≤64 sq cm	Total
Chert	171	58	14	4					247
Chalcedony	6	4							10
Quartzite		6	1	2	2		1	1	13
Igneous	24	8	6	2	1	1			42
Petrified Wood	36	7							43
Totals	237	83	21	8	3	1	1	1	355

5: Rock Art Ranch Area Surveys and Testing 185

Table 5.40. Projectile Points from Sites and Isolates from West of Chevelon Canyon (Figure 5.28).

Figure	Site	AZSITE	Point Type	Period
a	near BLH-3	AZ P:2:108(ASM)	Elko	Middle-Late Archaic
b	east of BLH-4	AZ P:2:109(ASM)	San Jose	Middle-Late Archaic
c	near BLH-5a	AZ P:2:110(ASM)	Cortaro	Late Archaic
d	BLH-1-1	AZ P:2:106(ASM)	Western Triangular - Cottonwood Var.	Pueblo II/III
e	BLH-1-2	AZ P:2:106(ASM)	indeterminate	
f	BLH-1-3	AZ P:2:106(ASM)	indeterminate	
g	BLH-1-4	AZ P:2:106(ASM)	San Pedro	Basketmaker II/III
h	BLH-2-1	AZ P:2:107(ASM)	Northern Side Notched - Sudden Valley Var.	Middle-Late Archaic
i	BLH-2-2	AZ P:2:107(ASM)	Northern Side Notched - Elko	Middle-Late Archaic
j	BLH-2-4	AZ P:2:107(ASM)	San Jose	Middle-Late Archaic
k	BLH-3-1	AZ P:2:108(ASM)	San Pedro	Basketmaker II/III
l	BLH-3-2	AZ P:2:108(ASM)	Datil	Late Archaic
m	BLH-3-3	AZ P:2:108(ASM)	Northern Side Notched - Elko	Middle-Late Archaic
n	BLH-3-4	AZ P:2:108(ASM)	San Pedro	Basketmaker II/III
o	BLH-3-5	AZ P:2:108(ASM)	San Jose	Middle-Late Archaic
p	BLH-9-1	AZ P:2:114(ASM)	Northern Side Notched - Elko	Middle-Late Archaic
q	BLH-9-2	AZ P:2:114(ASM)	indeterminate -- San Jose?	
r	BLH-9-3	AZ P:2:114(ASM)	Cienega - Tularosa Basal Notched	Basketmaker II/Pueblo I

Table 5.41. Projectile Points from Surveys West of Chevelon Canyon after 1989 (Figure 5.29).

Figure	Site	AZSITE	Artifact Type	Material	PD	FS
a	HP-349	AZ P:2:56(ASM)	San Jose point	petrified wood	1	
b	HP-349	AZ P:2:56(ASM)	Pueblo Side-Notched point	petrified wood	95	13
c	HP-349	AZ P:2:56(ASM)	biface	chert	101	15
d	HP-349	AZ P:2:56(ASM)	indeterminate point	chert	95	14
e	HP-349	AZ P:2:56(ASM)	San Rafael point	black chert cf. basalt	0	14
f	HP-349	AZ P:2:56(ASM)	San Pedro point	chert	0	15
g	HP-349	AZ P:2:56(ASM)	Datil point	petrified wood	0	13
h	BLH-1-5	AZ P:2:106(ASM)	indeterminate point	black chert cf. basalt		
i	BLH-5b-1	AZ P:2:110(ASM)	Scraper	chert		

Table 5.42. Mano and Metate Types from AZ P:2:56(ASM)—1989.

| | Artifact Type | | | | | |
Artifact	Basin	Flat	Trough	Indeterminate	Total	*Percents*
Mano	15	2			17	*65*
Metate	7			2	9	*35*
TOTALS	22	2		2	26	*100*
Percents	*85*	*8*		*8*	*100*	

Table 5.43. Loci on State Land and Aztec Land and Cattle Properties South and West of the Rock Art Ranch-Core Area.

Jurisdiction and Location	Loci	Mapped and Collected*	No Map or Collections
Aztec Land & Cattle Company			
RAR-South-a	1	1	
RAR-Southeast	1	1	
RAR-South-b	3		3
State of Arizona Trust Land			
RAR-South-a	28	28	
RAR-Southeast	1	1	
RAR-South-b	1		1
RAR-West	9	1	8

*Note: "Mapped and Collected" or "No Map or Collections" means there was or was not formal mapping done by instrument or collections were or were not made by formal collection units.

Table 5.44. Locus Type by Time Period South of the Rock Art Ranch-Core Area.

Time Period*	Date Ranges	Pueblos/Pithouses	Fieldhouses	Non-Habitation	Total	*Percent*
Archaic/ Basketmaker II	pre-600 CE			9	9	*21*
Ceramic Period	post-600 CE			2	2	*5*
Basketmaker III/ Pueblo I	600-1025 CE			4	4	*9*
Pueblo II/Pueblo III	1100-1255 CE	6	3	19	28	*65*
TOTALS		6	3	34	43	*100*
PERCENTS		*14*	*7*	*79*	*100*	

*Note: temporally multi-component loci are counted in each relevant time period.

Table 5.45. Ceramic Wares from Loci on State Land West and South of the Rock Art Ranch-Core Area.

Field Locus	AZSITE	Loction 1*	Location 2*	Locus Type**	Awatovi/Jeddito Yellow	Homolovi Orange	Alameda Brown	Tusayan White	Tusayan Gray	Little Colorado White	Little Colorado Gray	Tsegi Orange	Cibola White	White Mountain Red	Mogollon Brown	Unknown Plain	Cibola Gray	Puerco Valley-like Utility	Puerco Valley-like Decorated	Totals
HP-349	AZ P:2:56 (ASM)	W	NW	Hpi	4	18	9	3	9	3						5				51
	Percents West				8	35	18	6	18	6						10				100
FN 81	AZ P:3:155B (ASM)	S	in	Hpi			51	147	28	47	29	16	46		92	2		16	4	478
FN 83	AZ P:3:198B (ASM)	S	in	Hpi			23	66	16	10		16	45		63			1		240
FN 52	AZ P:3:156B (ASM)	S	in	Hpu				4	2	23	3		7		44			1		84
FN 53	AZ P:3:156C (ASM)	S	in	Hpu						11	4		2							17
FN 48	AZ P:3:165 (ASM)	S	in	Hpu			4	21	2	176	24		43		209			35	21	531
FN 84	AZ P:3:200 (ASM)	S	in	Hpu				10	12	6					16			4		52
FN-37	AZ P:3:112 (ASM)	S	in	Hpu			51	479	243	848	68	40	167		948	3		264		3111
FN 38	AZ P:3:155A (ASM)	S	in	Sc				129	44	31	32	7	34		145		1	52	1	476
FN 39	AZ P:3:156A (ASM)	S	in	Sc				5		1	1				4			2	1	13
FN 46	AZ P:3:163A (ASM)	S	in	Sc						1										1
FN 51	AZ P:3:163B (ASM)	S	in	Sc				8	1	19	1		3		8			3	1	44
FN 47	AZ P:3:164 (ASM)	S	N	Sc				5				3								8
FN 69	AZ P:3:185 (ASM)	S	in	Sc			1	6	3	7	1		2							20
FN 70	AZ P:3:186 (ASM)	S	in	Sc				2	2		1		2		2					9
FN 71	AZ P:3:187 (ASM)	S	in	Sc			1	5	1						3			1		11
FN 72	AZ P:3:188 (ASM)	S	in	Sc			3	18	10	4			1		1					36
FN 73	AZ P:3:189 (ASM)	S	in	Sc				2	17	5			2		2					27
FN 74	AZ P:3:190 (ASM)	S	in	Sc			12	12	9	13					22	1		2	2	73
FN 75	AZ P:3:191A (ASM)	S	in	Sc						1										1
FN 76	AZ P:3:191B (ASM)	S	in	Sc				12		8										20
FN 77	AZ P:3:193 (ASM)	S	in	Sc			8	16	3	12					9	1			1	50
FN 80	AZ P:3:196 (ASM)	S	in	Sc	2		2	5	4	1										13
FN 82	AZ P:3:198A (ASM)	S	in	Sc				8					6							14
	Subtotal				2		156	960	397	1223	164	82	360		1568	7	1	378	31	5329
	Percents South				0.04		3	18	7	23	3	2	7		29	0.1	0.02	7	0.6	100
FN 153	AZ P:3:239 (ASM)	SE	E/NE	Hpu			3	18	18	62	1		5	8	50			18		165
FN 154	AZ P:3:240 (ASM)	SE	E/NE	Hpu			5	27	7	66	3	2	7		91			24		232
	Subtotal						8	45	7	128	4	2	12	8	141			42		397
	Percents Southeast						2	11	2	32	1	0.5	3	2	36			11		100
	Totals				2		164	1005	404	1351	168	84	372	8	1709	7	1	420	31	5726
	Percents				0.03		3	18	7	24	3	1	6	0.1	30	0.1	0.02	7	0.5	100

*Note Location 1 is relative to the RAR core area: S = south of Rock Art Ranch; W = west of Chevelon Canyon and Rock Art Ranch; SE = southeast of Rock Art Ranch; also, shaded cells are on AZLAC property, unshaded are on State Land.

*Note: Location 2 is relative to the State Land section in RAR-South: in = in State Land section; NW = northwest of section; S = south of section; N = north of section; E/NE = northeast of section.

**Note Locus Type: Hpi = Habitation - pithouses; Hpu = Habitation - pueblo; Sc = Artifact scatter, may have feature(s).

Table 5.46. Decorated Ceramic Types from State Land and Other Loci West and South of the Rock Art Ranch-Core Area.

Field Locus**	AZ SITE	Awatovi/Jeddito YW	Indet. TWW	Lino B/g	Kana-a B/w	Black Mesa B/w	Sosi B/w	Dogoszhi B/w	Flagstaff B/w	Shato B/w	Indet. LCWW	Holbrook A B/w	Holbrook B B/w	Padre B/w	Walnut B/w	Chevelon B/w	St. Joseph B/w	Indet. CWW	Kiatuthlanna B/w	Red Mesa B/w	Puerco B/w	Escavada B/w	Snowflake B/w	Reserve B/w	Indet. TOW	Tsegi Orange	Tsegi B/o	Tsegi Poly	Jeddito B/o	Tusayan B/r	Kiet Siel Poly	McDonald P/d Corr	Showlow B/r	Unknown Decorated	Totals
HP-349	AZ P:2:56 (ASM)	4	3								3																								10
	Percents West	40	30								30																								100
FN 81	AZ P:3:155B (ASM)		23		1	17	2	2	1		16	5		1	1			8		1			2	1	6	2	24		2			1			92
FN 83	AZ P:3:198B (ASM)		7			5	2	1			4	1			1			2		1			1	1	3	1	5								29
FN 52	AZ P:3:156B (ASM)		2								3	3						1			1	2													12
FN 53	AZ P:3:156C (ASM)										1																								3
FN 48	AZ P:3:165 (ASM)		4	1		2					35	6	3	1	1			9			2	1													67
FN 84	AZ P:3:200 (ASM)					6							4																						10
FN-37	AZ P:3:112 (ASM)		286	4	30	111	16	8	9	4	510	38	33	27	236	3	1	124		3	18		20	132	5	1	24	1		4	1	9	10	2	1675
FN 38	AZ P:3:155A (ASM)		10			20	1	1		1	7	2		2				6	1	1					2		5								59
FN 39	AZ P:3:156A (ASM)		2																																2
FN 46	AZ P:3:163A (ASM)														1																				1
FN 51	AZ P:3:163B (ASM)		2			2	1			1	9	2						1			1			1											20
FN 47	AZ P:3:164 (ASM)				5									2											3										8
FN 69	AZ P:3:185 (ASM)		1	1							1				2	1		1	1																3
FN 70	AZ P:3:186 (ASM)		2			3														1															3
FN 71	AZ P:3:187 (ASM)										1	1											1												7
FN 72	AZ P:3:188 (ASM)		4						1																										4
FN 73	AZ P:3:189 (ASM)		1		1			1															1												4
FN 74	AZ P:3:190 (ASM)		2	1					1	1	3	1			1			1			1														12
FN 75	AZ P:3:191A (ASM)										1																								1
FN 76	AZ P:3:191B (ASM)		1								1																								2
FN 77	AZ P:3:193 (ASM)		1		2	2	1				2																								8
FN 80	AZ P:3:196 (ASM)		1								1																								2
FN 82	AZ P:3:198A (ASM)		2																		2														4
	Subtotals		352	7	39	167	22	13	11	9	595	59	41	33	244	3	1	153	4	6	26	3	23	136	19	8	29	1	2	4	1	9	10	2	2032
	Percents South		17	0.3	2	8	1	0.6	0.5	0.4	29	3	2	2	12	0.1	0.1	8	0.2	0.3	1	0.1	1	7	1	0.4	1	0.1	0.1	0.2	0.1	0.4	0.5	0.1	100
FN 153	AZ P:3:239 (ASM)		1			15	2				22	8		3	37									1								8	2		99
FN 154	AZ P:3:240 (ASM)		15				10	2			25	2			2			4	1				1	1	1					2		4	9		115
	Subtotals		16			15	12	2			47	10		3	76			4	1				1	2	1					2		12	11		214
	Percents Southeast		7			7	6	0.9			22	5		1	36			2	0.5				0.5	1	0.5					1		6	5		100
	Totals	4	371	7	39	182	34	15	11	9	645	69	41	36	320	3	1	157	5	6	26	3	24	138	19	8	29	1	2	4	1	21	21	2	2256
	Percents	0.2	16	0.3	2	8	2	0.7	0.5	0.4	29	3	2	2	14	0.1	0.0	7	0.2	0.3	1	0.1	1	6	0.8	0.4	1	0.0	0.1	0.2	0.0	0.9	0.9	0.1	100

*Note: YW = yellow ware; WW = white ware; TWW = Tusayan WW; LC = Little Colorado; CWW = Cibola WW; B/g = Black-on-gray; B/w = Black-on-white; B/r = Black-on-red; TOW = Tsegi Orange Ware; B/o = Black-on-orange; Poly = polychrome.
**Note: shaded loci are on AZLAC property; unshaded loci are on State Land.

Table 5.47 Utility Ceramic Types from State Land and Other Loci West and South of the Rock Art Ranch-Core Area.

Field Locus	AZSITE	Location**	Locus Type***	Indet. TGW	Kana-a Gray	Honani Tooled	Tusayan Corrugated	Moenkopi Corrugated	Little Colorado Corr	Indet. ABW	Sunset	Winona	Grapevine	Kinnikinnick	Chavez Pass	Winona Corr	Indet. Decorated ABW	Jeddito Corrugated	Jeddito Tooled	Indet. MBW	Brown Plain	Brown Corrugated	Brown Polished	Puerco V UW–Plain	Puerco V UW–Corr	Unknown – Brown Plain	Unknown – Orange Plain	Unknown – Gray Plain	Unknown – Gray Corr	Cibola Gray Corr	RAR – Utility Ware	Totals
HP-349	AZ P:2:56 (ASM)	W	Hpi	9						9												5										23
	Percents West			39						39												22										100
FN 81	AZ P:3:155B (ASM)	S	Hpi	8			3		7	2		3			5	4			1		8	9							2		2	54
FN 83	AZ P:3:198B (ASM)	S	Hpi	6				1	1						4	1					3	5										19
FN 52	AZ P:3:156B (ASM)	S	Hpu	1			1		1												5	4	3									15
FN 53	AZ P:3:156C (ASM)	S	Hpu																				1									1
FN 48	AZ P:3:165 (ASM)	S	Hpu	1	2		2		5											1	2	11	3									4	27
FN 84	AZ P:3:200 (ASM)	S	Hpu		2										2						2												8
FN 37	AZ P:3:112 (ASM)	S	Hpu	117	6	9	121	3	68	12	8	3	4	7	11	5				2	213	580	134	4	195			1		1		65	1569
FN 38	AZ P:3:155A (ASM)	S	Sc	3	2		2		6												6	9	5								1	1	35
FN 39	AZ P:3:156A (ASM)	S	Sc						1													1										1	3
FN 46	AZ P:3:163A (ASM)	S	Sc																														
FN 51	AZ P:3:163B (ASM)	S	Sc				1		1													3											5
FN 47	AZ P:3:164 (ASM)	S	Sc		1				1						1																		4
FN 69	AZ P:3:185 (ASM)	S	Sc				1								1							2											4
FN 70	AZ P:3:186 (ASM)	S	Sc	1											1							1	1									1	4
FN 71	AZ P:3:187 (ASM)	S	Sc	2																		1											4
FN 72	AZ P:3:188 (ASM)	S	Sc	2																		1											3
FN 73	AZ P:3:189 (ASM)	S	Sc	3	1										2							3	3				1					1	14
FN 74	AZ P:3:190 (ASM)	S	Sc																														
FN 75	AZ P:3:191A (ASM)	S	Sc															1															1
FN 76	AZ P:3:191B (ASM)	S	Sc				1			1					1						1	1											6
FN 77	AZ P:3:193 (ASM)	S	Sc	1			1			2					2						1												5
FN 80	AZ P:3:196 (ASM)	S	Sc																							1							
FN 82	AZ P:3:198A (ASM)	S	Sc																														
	Subtotals			146	12	9	134	3	92	14	8	6	4	7	30	10			1	3	244	630	145	4	195	1	1	1	1	3	1	75	1780
	Percents South			8	0.7	0.5	8	0.2	5	0.8	0.4	0.3	0.2	0.4	2	0.6			0.1	0.2	14	35	8	0.2	11	0.1	0.1	0.1	0.1	0.2	0.1	4	100
FN 153	AZ P:3:239 (ASM)	SE	Hpu						1	2												40	18										62
FN 154	AZ P:3:240 (ASM)	SE	Hpu	5			2		3						4	1					9	68	1		24								117
	Subtotals			5			2		4	2					5	1					9	108	1		42								179
	Percents Southeast			3			1		2	1					3	0.6					5	60	0.6		23								100
	TOTALS			155	17	9	136	3	96	25	8	6	4	7	35	11		1	1	3	253	743	146	4	237	1	1	1	1	3	1	75	1982
	PERCENTS			8	0.9	0.5	7	0.2	5	1.0	0.4	0.3	0.2	0.4	2	0.6		0.1	0.1	0.2	13	37	7	0.2	12	0.1	0.1	0.1	0.1	0.2	0.1	4	100

*Note: TGW = Tuasyan Gray Ware; Corr = Corrugated; ABW = Alamadea Brown Ware; MBW = Mogollon Brown Ware; VUW = Valley Utility Ware.
**Note: S = South of Rock Art Ranch; E = East of Rock Art Ranch.
***Note: Hpi = Habitation - pithouses; Hpu = Habitation - pueblo; Sc = Artifact Scatter (may have features); also, shaded loci are on AZLAC property, unshaded loci are on State Land.

Table 5.48. Worked Sherds from Loci and Isolates from RAR-South (Figures 5.33 and 5.34).

Figure	Letter	Provenience	PD	FS	Type	Ware
33	a	Isolate	0	126	indeterminate	Tusayan Gray
	b	Isolate	0	122	indeterminate	Little Colorado White
	c	Isolate	0	116	Puerco Black-on-white	Cibola White
	d	Isolate	0	117	indeterminate	Tusayan White
	e	Isolate	1	70	Walnut Black-on-white	Little Colorado White
34	a	AZ P:3:112B	189	14	Walnut Black-on-white	Little Colorado White
	b	AZ P:3:155A	5	14	indeterminate	Tsegi Orange Ware
	c	AZ P:3:163B	1	13	Walnut Black-on-white	Little Colorado White
	d	AZ P:3:163B	1	14	indeterminate	Tusayan White
	e	AZ P:3:155B	3	13	Black Mesa Black-on-white	Tusayan White
	f	AZ P:3:155B	4	14	Black Mesa Black-on-white	Tusayan White
	g	AZ P:3:155B	4	13	Black Mesa Black-on-white	Tusayan White
	h	AZ P:3:198A	1	13	Sosi Black-on-white	Tusayan White
	i	AZ P:3:198B	3	13	Holbrook-B Black-on-white	Little Colorado White

Table 5.49. Worked Sherds from Multi-Kiva Site (AZ P:3:112[ASM]) Surface Collections in RAR-South (Figure 5.35).

Letter	PD	FS	Type	Ware
a	0	1	Holbrook-A/B Black-on-white	Little Colorado White
b	0	1	Holbrook-A/B Black-on-white	Little Colorado White
c	0	1	Indeterminate	Little Colorado White
d	0	1	Indeterminate	Little Colorado White
e	0	1	Indeterminate	Alameda Brown
f	5	13	Indeterminate	Tusayan White

Table 5.50. Flaked Stone Material Types for Isolates in RAR-South.

Material Type	Count	Percent
Chalcedony	15	10
Chert	52	36
Obisidan	9	6
Petrified Wood	31	22
Quartzite	7	5
TOTAL	144	100

Table 5.51. Flaked Stone Material Types for Loci in RAR-South.

Site	Field Number	Chert	Chalcedony	Quartzite	Igneous	Petrified Wood	Obsidian	Other	Total
a. Pithouses									
AZ P:3:112B(ASM)	37B	14	5	5	2	21			47
AZ P:3:155B(ASM)	81	1							1
AZ P:3:198B(ASM)	83					1			1
Subtotal		15	5	5	2	22			49
Percents Pithouses		*31*	*10*	*10*	*4*	*45*			*100*
b. Pueblos									
AZ P:3:112A(ASM)	37	2114	161	398	14	1528	11	19	4245
AZ P:3:165(ASM)	48	70	3	11		45		2	131
Subtotal		2184	164	409	14	1573	11	21	4376
Percents Pueblos		*50*	*4*	*9*	*0.3*	*36*	*0.3*	*0.5*	*100*
c. Scatters									
AZ P:3:112C(ASM)	37C	11	2	11		21		6	51
AZ P:3:155A(ASM)	38	65	4	8		67	1	4	149
AZ P:3:156A(ASM)	39	4	2	1		1			8
AZ P:3:164(ASM)*	47	3	1	2		6			12
AZ P:3:163B(ASM)	51	10	1	2		14		1	28
AZ P:3:156B(ASM)	52	15	1	6		26		1	49
AZ P:3:156C(ASM)	53					6		1	7
AZ P:3:194(ASM)	78	3							3
AZ P:3:198A(ASM)	82	1							1
Subtotal		112	11	30		141	1	13	308
Percents Scatters		*36*	*4*	*10*		*46*	*0.3*	*4*	*100*
TOTALS		2311	180	444	16	1736	12	34	4733
PERCENTS		*49*	*4*	*9*	*0.3*	*37*	*0.3*	*0.7*	*100*

*Note: AZ P:3:164(ASM) is on AZLAC property, all other sites are on State Trust land.

Table 5.52. Flaked Stone Artifact Types by Provenience for Loci in RAR-South.

Site	Field Number	Complete Flake	Broken Flake	Split Flake	Flake Fragment	General Flake	Debris	Peckingstone	Hammerstone	Hammerstone Spall	Core	Other/Tested Piece	Chopper	Scraper	Edge-damaged Piece	Retouched Piece	Biface	Drill	Wedge	Projectile Point	Total
a. Pithouses																					
AZ P:3:112B(ASM)	37B					10	20			5	2				2	1					40
AZ P:3:155B(ASM)	81															1					1
AZ P:3:198B(ASM)	83															1					1
Subtotals						10	20			5	2				2	3					42
Percents Pithouses						24	48			12	5				5	7					100
b. Pueblos																					
AZ P:3:112A(ASM)	37	91	40	2	7	765	2590	4	28	255	55	8		7	304	56	7	2	10	13	4245
AZ P:3:165(ASM)	48					10	101			10	1		1		4	5					131
Subtotals		91	40	2	7	775	2691	4	28	265	56	8	1	7	308	61	7	2	10	13	4376
Percents Pueblos		2	0.9	0.05	0.2	18	61	0.09	0.6	6	1	0.2	0.02	0.2	7	1	0.2	0.05	0.2	0.3	100
c. Scatters																					
AZ P:3:112C(ASM)	37C	1				7	34		2	5	4	1		1	2						51
AZ P:3:155A(ASM)	38	1				15	113			3		1			11	2	1			1	149
AZ P:3:156A(ASM)	39					2	1								1						4
AZ P:3:164(ASM)*	47					6	4							1	1	1					12
AZ P:3:163B(ASM)	51					2	19			1	3				1	1				1	28
AZ P:3:156B(ASM)	52					3	34			2					9	1					49
AZ P:3:156C(ASM)	53						7														7
AZ P:3:194(ASM)	78																3				3
AZ P:3:198A(ASM)	82															1					1
Subtotals		2				35	212		2	11	4	1		1	24	6	4			2	304
Percents Scatters		0.7				12	70		0.7	4	1	0.3		0.3	8	2	1			0.7	100
TOTALS		93	40	2	7	820	2923	4	30	281	62	9	1	8	334	70	11	2	10	15	4722
PERCENTS		2	0.8	0.04	0.1	17	62	0.08	0.6	6	1	0.2	0.02	0.2	7	1	0.2	0.04	0.2	0.3	100

Note: All sites are south of RAR core; FN-47 is on AZLAC land, all others are on State Trust Land.

*Note: All sites are south of RAR core; FN-47 is on AZLAC land, all others are on State Trust Land.

Table 5.53. Flaked Stone Artifact Types by Material Type for Loci in RAR-South.

Material	Complete Flake	Broken Flake	Split Flake	Flake Fragment	General Flake	Debris	Peckingstone	Hammerstone	Hammerstone Spall	Core	Core/Retouched Piece	Other/Tested Piece	Chopper	Scraper	Edge-damaged Piece	Retouched Piece	Biface	Drill	Wedge	Projectile Point	Total	Percent
Chert	55	18	1	4	464	1351	1	10	100	40	1	8	1	5	183	43	7		7	10	2309	49
Chalcedony	1				21	129			3	2					17	1					174	4
Quartzite	17	3			46	261	3	12	95	3		1			2						443	9
Igneous	1				2	7		1	2	1											14	0.3
Petrified Wood	18	19	1	3	284	1145		6	77	16	1			3	130	24	3		3	3	1736	37
Obsidian						5			1						2	2				2	12	0.3
Other	1				3	25		1	3						2		1				34	0.7
Totals	93	40	2	7	820	2923	4	30	281	62	2	9	1	8	334	70	11		10	15	4722	100
Percents	2	0.8	0.04	0.1	17	62	0.08	0.6	6	1	0.04	0.2	0.02	0.2	7	1	0.2	0.8	0.2	0.3	100	

Table 5.54. Flaked Stone Material by Size for Loci in RAR-South.

Size*	Chert	Chalcedony	Quartzite	Igneous	Petrified Wood	Obsidian	Other	Total	Percent
≤ 1	193	47	25		198	2		465	10
≤ 4	1349	99	187		993	9	13	2650	56
≤ 9	526	22	124	2	408	1	9	1092	23
≤ 16	186	6	65	10	107		7	381	8
≤ 25	37		27	1	22		4	91	2
≤ 36	13		10	1	6		1	31	0.7
≤ 49	2		3		1			6	0.1
≤ 64	2		1		1			4	0.08
≤ 81			1					1	0.02
≤ 100	1							1	0.02
Totals	2309	174	443	14	1736	12	34	4722	100
Percents	49	4	9	0.3	37	0.3	0.7	100	

*Note: Size is given in square centimeters.

5: Rock Art Ranch Area Surveys and Testing 195

Table 5.55. Flaked Stone Artifact Type by Amount of Cortex for Loci in RAR-South.

Percent Cortex	Complete Flake	Broken Flake	Split Flake	Flake Fragment	General Flake	Debris	Peckingstone	Hammerstone	Hammerstone Spall	Core	Core/Retouched Piece	Other/Tested Piece	Chopper	Scraper	Edge-damaged Piece	Retouched Piece	Biface	Drill	Wedge	Projectile Point	Total	Percent
100	21	5		1	52	90	4	19	44	9		5	1		22	5			2		278	6
present	35	6	1	3	247	442		10	107	39		2		5	80	14	1		8	15	994	21
absent	37	29	1	3	521	2391		1	130	14	2	2		3	232	51	10				3450	73
Totals	93	40	2	7	820	2923	4	30	281	62	2	9	1	8	334	70	11		10	15	4722	100
Percents	2	0.8	0.04	0.1	17	62	0.08	0.6	6	1	0.04	0.2	0.02	0.2	7	1	0.2		0.2	0.2	100	

Table 5.56. Flaked Stone Material Type by Amount of Cortex for Loci in RAR-South.

Percent Cortex	Chert	Chalcedony	Quartzite	Igneous	Petrified Wood	Obsidian	Other	Total	Percent
100	134	2	98	4	36		4	278	6
present	603	7	127	7	235	1	14	994	21
absent	1572	165	218	3	1465	11	16	3450	73
Totals	2309	174	443	14	1736	12	34	4722	100
Percents	49	4	9	0.3	27	0.3	0.7	100	

Table 5.57. Flaked Stone Size by Provenience for Loci in RAR-South.

Site	Field Number	≤1	≤4	≤9	≤16	≤25	≤36	≤49	≤64	≤81	≤100	Total
a. Pithouses												
AZ P:3:112B(ASM)	37B	5	19	10	4	1			1			40
AZ P:3:155B(ASM)	81			1								1
AZ P:3:198B(ASM)	83		1									1
Subtotals		5	20	11	4	1		1	2			42
Percents Pithouses		12	48	26	10	2						100
b. Pueblos												
AZ P:3:112A(ASM)	37	423	2399	967	334	83	29	6	2	1		4245
AZ P:3:165(ASM)	48	8	83	31	8	1						131
Subtotals		431	2482	998	342	84	29	6	2	1	1	4376
Percents Pueblos		10	57	23	8	2	0.7	0.1	0.05	0.02	0.02	100
c. Scatters												
AZ P:3:112C(ASM)	37C	4	24	19	2				1			51
AZ P:3:155A(ASM)	38	23	92	20	13		2	1				149
AZ P:3:156A(ASM)	39		1	1	2							4
AZ P:3:164(ASM)**	47		5	5	2							12
AZ P:3:163B(ASM)	51		6	15	6	1						28
AZ P:3:156B(ASM)	52	2	18	19	8	2						49
AZ P:3:156C(ASM)	53		2	3	1	1						7
AZ P:3:194(ASM)	78			1	1	1						3
AZ P:3:198A(ASM)	82											1
Subtotals		29	148	83	35	6	2		1			304
Percents Scatters		10	49	27	12	2	0.7		0.3			100
TOTALS		465	2650	1092	381	91	31	6	4	1	1	4722
PERCENTS		10	56	23	8	2	0.7	0.1	0.08	0.02	0.02	100

*Note: The size dimensions are in square centimeters.
**Note: All sites are south of RAR-Core; AZ P:3:164(ASM)–FN-47 is on AZLAC land, all others are on State Trust Land.

Table 5.58. Flaked Stone Size by Material Type for Loci in RAR-South.

Material	≤1	≤4	≤9	≤16	≤25	≤36	≤49	≤64	≤81	≤100	Total	Percent
Chert	193	1349	526	186	37	13	2	2		1	2309	49
Chalcedony	47	99	22	6							174	4
Quartzite	25	187	124	65	27	10	3	1	1		443	9
Igneous			2	10	1	1					14	0.3
Petrified Wood	198	993	408	107	22	6	1	1			1736	37
Obsidian	2	9	1								12	0.3
Other		13	9	7	4	1					34	0.7
Totals	465	2650	1092	381	91	31	6	4	1	1	4722	100
Percents	10	56	23	8	2	0.7	0.1	0.08	0.02	0.02	100	

*Note: The size dimensions are in square centimeters.

Table 5.59. Material Type by Time Period for Projectile Points from Loci in RAR-South.

	Material Type						
Time Period	Chalcedony	Chert	Igneous	Obsidian	Petrified Wood	Total	Percent
South of RAR Core							
Paleoindian/Early Archaic		1			1	2	11
Middle Archaic		2	3			5	26
Late Archaic/Early Agriculture		2			1	3	16
PI - PIII		2				2	11
Unknown		4	1		2	7	37
Subtotals		11	4		4	19	100
Percents South		58	21		21	100	
Multi-Kiva Site (AZ P:3:112[ASM])							
Paleoindian/Early Archaic		2				2	15
Middle Archaic		1			2	3	23
Late Archaic/Early Agriculture				1		1	
PI - PIII		3			1	6	46
Unknown	1	2				2	15
Subtotals	1	8		1	3	13	100
Percents M-K Site	8	62		8	23	100	
TOTALS	1	19	4	1	7	32	100
PERCENTS	3	59	12	3	22	100	

Table 5.60. Source Directions for Projectile Points on Loci in RAR-South.

Projectile Point Type/Style	North/ Northwest	East/ Northeast	South/ Southeast	West/ Southwest	Unknown/ Other	Total
State Land South of RAR-Core						
Bajada		2				2
Chaco		1				1
Datil		1				1
Gypsum	1					1
Northern Side Notched	2					2
Pinto				2		2
Pueblo Side Notched					1	1
San Jose		1				1
San Pedro			1			1
Unknown					7	7
Subtotals	3	5	1	2	8	19
Column Percents	*16*	*26*	*5*	*11*	*42*	*100*
Multi-Kiva Site (AZ P:3:112[ASM])						
Bajada		1				1
Lanceolate Plano		1				1
Northern Side Notched	1					1
Pinto				1		1
Pueblo Side Notched					4	4
San Jose		1				1
Western Triangular					1	1
Unknown					3	3
Subtotals	1	3		1	8	13
Column Percents	*8*	*23*		*8*	*62*	*100*
TOTALS	4	8	1	3	16	32
Column Percents	*12*	*25*	*3*	*9*	*50*	*100*

Direction from RAR Core Area

Table 61. Isolated Projectile Points from RAR-South (Figure 5.36).

Letter	PD	FS	Type	Material	Period
a	0	44	San Pedro	chert	Basketmaker II/III
b	0	74	Indeterminate	chert	
c	0	69	Bajada	petrified wood	Early-Middle Archaic
d	0	76	San Pedro	chert	Basketmaker II/III
e	0	97	Pinto	basalt	Early-Middle Archaic
f	0	98	Pinto or Northern Side-Notched	chert	Early-Late Archaic
g	0	106	Indeterminate--mid & tip	chert	
h	0	107	Northern Side-Notched--Ventana var.	basalt	Middle-Late Archaic
i	0	114	Bajada	chert	Early-Middle Archaic
j	0	118	Northern Side-Notched - concave base	chert	Middle-Late Archaic

Table 5.62. Projectile Points from Loci in RAR-South (Figure 5.37).

Letter	Site*	Field Number	PD	FS	Type	Material	Period
a	AZ P:3:155A(ASM)	38	2	12	Western Triangular	chert	Pueblo II/III and later
b	AZ P:3:165(ASM)	48	0	13	Indeterminate - serrated flake	petrified wood	
c	AZ P:3:165(ASM)	48	1	16	Datil	petrified wood	Late Archaic
d	AZ P:3:165(ASM)	48	1	17	drill	chert	
e	AZ P:3:165(ASM)	48	5	13	Gypsum	petrified wood	Late Archaic
f	AZ P:3:163B(ASM)	51	0	12	Indeterminate--mid-section	chert	
g	AZ P:3:191A(ASM)	75	1	17	San Jose	chert	Middle-Late Archaic
h	AZ P:3:193(ASM)	77	1	13	Chaco--Bonito Notched	chert	Pueblo I/II
i	AZ P:3:198B(ASM)	83	1	13	Indeterminate	petrified wood	
j	AZ P:3:198A(ASM)	81	1	13	Indeterminate	chert	

*Note: FN-48 points are from a pueblo; FN-81 and -83 are from pithouse sites; the other sites are artifact scatters.

Table 5.63. Other Flaked Stone Artifacts from Loci in RAR-South (Figure 5.38).

Letter	Site*	Field Number	PD	FS	Type	Material
a	AZ P:3:198A(ASM)	82	1	14	scraper	chert
b	AZ P:3:198B(ASM)	83	1	17	burin	petrified wood

*Note: FN-83 is a pithouse village, FN-82 is an artifact scatter.

Table 5.64. Flaked Stone "Serrated" Tools from Loci in RAR-South (Figure 5.39).

Letter	Site*	Field Number	PD	FS	Material
a	AZ P:3:164(ASM)**	47	0	12	petrified wood
b	AZ P:3:165(ASM)	48	3	12	petrified wood
c	AZ P:3:165(ASM)	48	6	12	petrified wood
d	AZ P:3:165(ASM)	48	6	12	chert
e	AZ P:3:163B(ASM)	51	0	12	petrified wood

*Note: AZ P:3:165(ASM) is a pueblo site, the others are artifact scatters.
**AZ P:3:164(ASM) is on AZLAC land, the others are on State Trust Land.

Table 5.65. Ground Stone Artifact Types from Loci in RAR-South.

Artifact	Basin	Flat	Trough	Indeterminate	Total	Percent
Mano	2	5	2		9	60
Metate		4	1	1	6	40
TOTALS	2	9	3	1	15	100
PERCENTS	13	60	20	7	100	

Table 5.66. Flaked Stone Artifact Types from Loci in the Rock Art Ranch-Core Area.

Artifact Type	Chert	Percent Chert	Chalcedony	Percent Chalcedony	Quartzite	Percent Quartzite	Igneous	Percent Igneous	Petrified Wood	Percent Petrified Wood	Total	Percent of Total
Edge-damaged	135	66	3	1	3	1	4	2	60	29	205	25
Scraper	6	100									6	1
Retouched	8	100									8	1
Flake Core	13	81							3	19	16	2
Core	3	75							1	25	4	1
Drill									1	100	1	0
Complete Flake	64	72	3	6	5	6	3	3	14	16	89	11
Broken Flake	147	77			8	4	4	2	33	17	192	24
Split Flake	6	38	1	6	3	19	2	12	4	25	16	2
Flake Fragment	69	76			3	3	3	3	16	18	91	11
Other	2	100									2	0
Pecking Stone							1	100			1	0
Hammerstone					1	100					1	0
Debris	126	72	2	1	8	5	7	4	33	19	176	22
Fire-cracked Rock							1	100			1	0
Totals	579	71.6	9	1.1	31	3.8	25	3.1	165	20.4	809	100